Maritime Command Pacific

Studies in Canadian Military History

Series editor: Andrew Burtch, Canadian War Museum

The Canadian War Museum, Canada's national museum of military history, has a threefold mandate: to remember, to preserve, and to educate. Studies in Canadian Military History, published by UBC Press in association with the Museum, extends this mandate by presenting the best of contemporary scholarship to provide new insights into all aspects of Canadian military history, from earliest times to recent events. The work of a new generation of scholars is especially encouraged, and the books employ a variety of approaches – cultural, social, intellectual, economic, political, and comparative – to investigate gaps in the existing historiography. The books in the series feed immediately into future exhibitions, programs, and outreach efforts by the Canadian War Museum. A list of the titles in the series appears at the end of the book.

CANADIAN WAR MUSEUM
MUSÉE CANADIEN DE LA GUERRE

Maritime Command Pacific

The Royal Canadian Navy's West Coast Fleet in the Early Cold War

By David Zimmerman

UBCPress · Vancouver · Toronto

23 22 21 20 19 18 17 16 15   5 4 3 2 1

Printed in Canada on FSC-certified ancient-forest-free paper (100% post-consumer recycled) that is processed chlorine- and acid-free.

Library and Archives Canada Cataloguing in Publication

Zimmerman, David, author

Maritime Command Pacific : the Royal Canadian Navy's West Coast fleet in the early Cold War / David Zimmerman.

(Studies in Canadian military history)
Includes bibliographical references and index.
Issued in print and electronic formats.
ISBN 978-0-7748-3034-8 (bound). – ISBN 978-0-7748-3035-5 (pbk.)
ISBN 978-0-7748-3036-2 (pdf). – ISBN 978-0-7748-3037-9 (epub)

1. Canada. Canadian Armed Forces. Maritime Command – History – 20th century. 2. Sea-power – Canada – History – 20th century. 3. Canada – History, Naval – 20th century. 4. Pacific Area – History, Naval – 20th century. 5. Cold War. I. Title. II. Series: Studies in Canadian military history

VA400.Z54 2015   359′.03097109045   C2015-905082-0
C2015-905083-9

Canadä

UBC Press gratefully acknowledges the financial support for our publishing program of the Government of Canada (through the Canada Book Fund), the Canada Council for the Arts, and the British Columbia Arts Council.

Publication of this book has been financially supported by the Canadian War Museum.

UBC Press
The University of British Columbia
2029 West Mall
Vancouver, BC V6T 1Z2
www.ubcpress.ca

To Wendy, love of my life and my best friend

Contents

Illustrations

Acknowledgments

THIS WORK WAS originally commissioned as part of the initial research for the forthcoming third volume of the Official History of the Royal Canadian Navy, *The Restless Wave: The Official History of the RCN, 1945–68. Maritime Command Pacific*'s publication reflects the Directorate of History and Heritage and the RCN's long-standing support and encouragement of research into Canadian naval history. The author particularly wishes to acknowledge the contribution and support of Dr. Steve Harris, Acting Director and Chief Historian, and Michael Whitby, Senior Naval Historian.

I worked closely with the late Dr. Shawn Cafferky in conducting the research for this project. Shawn and I shared our research findings as I worked on this study and he completed several other projects on the history of the navy in the early Cold War. He provided much guidance and many useful comments during the completion of this groundbreaking study.

I also want to thank the staff of Library and Archives Canada for assisting in the research and declassification of the large number of documents that inexplicably remained secret despite the passage of almost fifty years. Photographs were provided by the CFB Esquimalt Naval and Military Museum and the Department of National Defence.

My warmest appreciation to Emily Andrew for shepherding this work through the often tortuous process of turning this manuscript into a book. The Canadian War Museum provided crucial support to make this book a reality. I would like to thank Dr. Andrew Burtch for including this book in the museum's publication series.

Finally, this work would not have been possible without the love and support of Wendy Muscat-Tyler.

Abbreviations

ABCD	Atomic-Bacteriological-Chemical Defence
AEW	airborne early warning
AOC NWAC	Air Officer in Command, North West Air Command
ASW	antisubmarine warfare
CANAVHED	Canadian Naval Headquarters
CANCON	Control of Merchant Shipping in Canadian Coastal Waters
CANCOMCORTRON	Canadian Commanding Escort Squadron
CANCOMPARPAC	Canadian Maritime Commander Pacific
CANCORTRON TWO	2nd Escort Squadron
CANFLAGPAC	Canadian Flag Officer Pacific
CANLEX	Canadian Landing Exercise
CANMINRON TWO	2nd Minesweeping Squadron
CINCPACFLT	Commander-in-Chief Pacific Fleet
CNS	Chief of Naval Staff
COMALSEAFRON	Commander Alaskan Sea Frontier
COMBRAX	Commander of *Naden*
COMDESDIV	Commander Destroyer Division
COMNASDEFFORPAC	Commander A/S Force Pacific
COMNAVDEFEASTPAC	Naval Defence Forces Eastern Pacific
COMWESTSEAFRON	Commander Western Sea Frontier
CONTRON	Canadian Squadron
COPC	Commanding Officer Pacific Coast
CORTRON 2	2nd Escort Squadron
CORTRON 4	4th Escort Squadron
CSC	Chiefs of Staff Committee
CUSRPG	Canada–US Regional Planning Group
DDH	helicopter-carrying destroyer
DE	destroyer escort
DND	Department of National Defence
ECM	electronic counter-measures
EDPEX	emergency defence preparation exercise
FOPC	Flag Officer Pacific Coast

GOC WC	General Officer in Command of Western Command
HMS	His or Her Majesty's Ship
HMCS	His or Her Majesty's Canadian Ship
HUK	hunter-killer
IFF	identify friend or foe
ICBM	intercontinental ballistic missile
JET	Joint Exercise and Training
JMDF	Japanese Maritime Defence Force
JMWS	Joint Maritime Warfare School
JPC	Joint Planning Committee
JSCP	Joint Service Committee, Pacific
LOFAR	low-frequency analysis and recording
MAD	magnetic anomaly detection
MARCOMPAC	Maritime Commander Pacific
MAROPEDPAC	Operational Emergency Defence Plan Pacific – 1958
MARPAC	Maritime Command Pacific
MCC	Military Cooperation Committee
MINRON	2nd Minesweeper Squadron
MNLO	Merchant Navy Liaison Officer
MTB	Motor Torpedo Boat
NATO	North Atlantic Treaty Organization
NORAD	North American Air Defence Command
NRC	National Research Council
NSHQ	Naval Service Headquarters
OPORDER	Emergency Defence Operational Order
OTC	Officer in Tactical Command
PACTRAEX	Pacific Training Excercise
PPCLI	Princess Patricia's Canadian Light Infantry
RCAF	Royal Canadian Air Force
RCN	Royal Canadian Navy
RCNR	Royal Canadian Navy Reserve
RCNVR	Royal Canadian Navy Volunteer Reserve
REGSUBEX	Regular Submarine Excercise
RFA	Royal Fleet Auxiliary
ROTP	Regular Officer Training Plan
SACLANT	Supreme Allied Commander Atlantic
SAGE	Semi-Automatic Ground Environment
SAU	surface attack unit

SIGINT	signals intelligence
SOSUS	sound surveillance system
SQS	type of sonar
SUPYARD	Superintendent of the Dockyard
TAS	Torpedo and Antisubmarine School
TD	torpedo detector
UNTD	University Naval Training Division
USN	United States Navy
VDS	variable depth sonar

Maritime Command Pacific

Introduction

"Yacht Club" was a derogatory term used by Royal Canadian Navy sailors on the Atlantic coast to refer to their counterparts on the Pacific coast. It amounted to a criticism of the comparatively easy lives supposedly enjoyed by West Coast sailors. "Yacht Club" appears to have originated during the Second World War, reflecting the derision felt by sailors operating out of Halifax for those who sailed out of Esquimalt, Canada's West Coast naval base – derision rooted in the unwarranted belief that the waters of the North Pacific were placid and pleasant compared to the tumult of the North Atlantic. The term also came to refer to the far less strenuous operational environment faced by the wartime navy on the West Coast.

In the postwar period, East Coast–based sailors still believed not only that the weather was far rougher in the Atlantic but also that the Pacific Fleet was rarely involved in the intensive operational environment they experienced. In 1948, in the first issue of *The Crowsnest*, the RCN's official magazine, an article titled "Come West Young Men!" tried to persuade personnel from Halifax to volunteer for transfer to Esquimalt. That article began by trying to dispel the myth that life in the Pacific Fleet was uneventful.

> While serving on the East Coast of Canada, I shared the belief that the West Coast navy remained in a state of complete placidity, whereas we in the east lived in a fever of activity. On returning to British Columbia, I found this to be far from true. Admittedly, the climate is unsurpassed – sunshine in February and summer days in November (well, usually).[1]

After a lengthy summary of the exciting activities of the Pacific Fleet witnessed by the unnamed author, the article concluded: "Yes, the West Coast is a great place, it is no more placid than the East Coast and activities here can be just as lively as anywhere else."[2]

Yet the myth persisted; indeed, it grew. In the early 1950s the RCN in the Atlantic became integrated with other Allied navies through the North Atlantic Treaty Organization (NATO). The RCN's direct commitments to provide forces to the Supreme Allied Commander Atlantic (SACLANT) appeared to have no equivalent for ships operating in the Pacific.

As with many derisive terms, the perceptions in which the term "Yacht Club" was rooted were the result of ignorance. True, Atlantic operations dominated the wartime navy; but for most of the postwar period until unification in 1968, the RCN's Pacific-based squadrons were every bit as active as their Atlantic-based cousins. Halifax-based ships were incorporated into SACLANT and engaged in regular exercises with NATO navies; meanwhile, Esquimalt-based ships had an equally close working relationship with the US Navy's Pacific Fleet. Defence relationships on the West Coast were never as formally structured as those governed by NATO on the East Coast, but the RCN had important responsibilities when it came to guaranteeing the security of the West Coast and the waters immediately adjacent to it. As well, the West Coast was a crucial area for training officers and men for the entire navy. The West Coast fleet was never as big as its Atlantic counterpart, but this imbalance was in large part caused by the basing of the RCN's sole aircraft carrier at Halifax. However, manning the carrier placed a heavy burden on the navy, and frequently there were more ships ready for sea on the West Coast. This was the situation at the start of the Korean War, when the only ships ready for immediate deployment to Asia were three West Coast–based destroyers.

Only a few works have examined the history of the postwar navy, and most of this literature has focused on naval policy as developed at Naval Service Headquarters in Ottawa, on the few occasions that warships were sent into a war zone (such as in Korea or during the Cuban Missile Crisis), or on the unification crisis. Very little has been written about normal day-to-day fleet operations, and no one has specifically examined the role of the Pacific Fleet from 1945 to 1965. Marc Milner's *Canada's Navy* is the best of a group of rather unsatisfactory accounts of postwar Canadian naval policy. Remarkably, Milner, while claiming to have written a history of the entire navy, fails to make any reference to the Pacific after 1945, except for a few minor mentions of training facilities at Esquimalt. He certainly provides no insight into how the naval staff in Ottawa allocated resources, something that this book addresses with regard to the Pacific.

It is understandable that the focus of scholarship in the postwar period has been on naval policy, combat operations, and some aspects of international defence agreements. However, this focus has resulted in a huge gap in our understanding of the navy from 1945 to 1965. Only a few studies, none of them published, even mention the West Coast.[3] Tyrone Pile has examined immediate postwar planning and policy development and discussed tangentially the importance the RCN placed on the Pacific in this period.[4] Wilfred Lund has examined the seemingly endless personnel issues that bedeviled the navy from the end of the Second World War to unification in 1968. Naval Service Headquarters is portrayed as generally unable to come to grips with issues such as naval training and education, manpower management, adaptation to new technologies, and the need to align strategic requirements with the resources likely to be available. Lund argues that the RCN suffered from a chronic overcommitment to NATO: "Over-commitment, trying to man too many ships with too few personnel, immediately became the major factor affecting personnel policy. This demand created an environment of instability in ships' companies that eventually became chronic. Instability worked like dry rot against fleet operational effectiveness."[5] Yet after the rash of mutinies in the late 1940s, there is little evidence that this "dry rot" was so invasive as to lead to a breakdown in fleet operations. The problem with this "top down" approach is that the perceptions of the Chief of Naval Staff and the Naval Board in Ottawa might not have reflected what was taking place in the two major operational commands. The one aspect of the history of the postwar Pacific Fleet that has been considered in any detail is the involvement of three West Coast–based ships – HMCS *Ontario*, *Athabaskan*, and *Crescent* – in a series of work stoppages or mutinies in 1947 and 1949.[6]

Other aspects of Canada's defence relations with its allies since 1945 have been examined extensively, especially in the context of NATO, the North American Air Defence Command (NORAD), and the UN.[7] Invariably in all of these studies, the bilateral naval defence arrangements between Canada and the United States are ignored. For example, James Fergusson in his recent examination of US–Canadian defence relations writes that "North American defence was almost exclusively air force and neither the army nor navy faced the same specific functional requirements for close cooperation with its American counterpart in North America."[8] This is manifestly incorrect.

The failure to consider the RCN's Pacific Command's unique relations with the US Navy's Pacific Fleet is a major gap in our understanding of postwar defence policy. This is a surprising omission, since the Canadian Maritime Pacific area of operations are among the most important continental defence responsibilities of the Canadian Armed Forces. The area extends some 1,700 kilometres to the west of Vancouver Island and north to the Alaskan coastline. The Aleutian Islands, Alaska, and its panhandle describe that area's northwestern, northern, and (most of its) eastern boundaries. In the south, the boundary is an imaginary line due west of the Strait of Juan de Fuca. This area encompasses major routes for sea and air trade between North America and Asia, as well as for North American domestic trade – for example, 25 percent of all oil imported into the lower forty-eight United States comes from Alaska through the port of Valdez from there along Canada's West Coast. Yet there is no understanding of how this defence responsibility has evolved since 1945. Recent studies in diplomatic history have shown the central importance of the Asia–Pacific to Canadian foreign policy.[9] The navy's role in fostering connections with countries

FIGURE 1 HMC Dockyard at Esquimalt on Navy Days, August 17, 1955. In the left foreground is the visiting HMS *Superb*. Various RCN destroyer escorts, frigates, and minesweepers are lying alongside various jetties. Victoria Harbour can be seen in the distance at the top of the picture. (Courtesy DND)

throughout the region will be a continuing theme of this study. In the background will be some of the crucial events that shaped the Asia–Pacific world in the early Cold War, such as the Chinese Revolution and the Korean War. However, the principal threat to North American security came from the growing might of the Soviet Pacific Fleet, particularly its submarines.

This work also breaks new ground regarding the work of navies during the Cold War. Far too often, naval history has focused on battle and ignored the mundane but important task of maintaining a navy in peacetime. The Cold War was a unique time, for the RCN had to remain ready in a dynamic peacetime environment where war was potentially just around the corner. The key role played by training and exercises in sustaining the Pacific Fleet's high state of readiness is a central theme of this book.

Part of the ongoing struggle with creating an effective defence was dealing with rapid changes in technology that dramatically altered the nature of antisubmarine warfare in the quarter-century after the Second World War. The evolution of defence planning in the Pacific will be set against the emergence of new threats posed by submarines capable of high underwater speeds and carrying long-range nuclear-tipped missiles.

The Pacific Fleet had to contend with the vagaries of political and defence policy decisions of the sort that have shaped the service ever since its formation in 1910. Immediately after the Second World War, the RCN in the Pacific was reduced to a mere shadow of its wartime strength. The increased tensions of the Cold War resulted in the largest peacetime increase in the size of the navy in history. By the late 1950s, Maritime Command Pacific (MARPAC) had established a defensive scheme based on the Canadian-designed St. Laurent-class destroyer escorts. Within a few years, as this study ends, however, the looming threat of atomic-powered submarines and cuts in the defence budget resulted in an unravelling of these carefully laid plans. The waxing and waning of the RCN's Pacific Fleet in the early Cold War is told here for the first time.

This work is a fundamental building block that will eventually be used to write a new history of Cold War defence and naval policy; however, it is only one of several such detailed studies required before an overall revision can be undertaken. At the moment, we can only use the extant secondary sources to link my study to other aspects of Canadian military history in the Cold War.

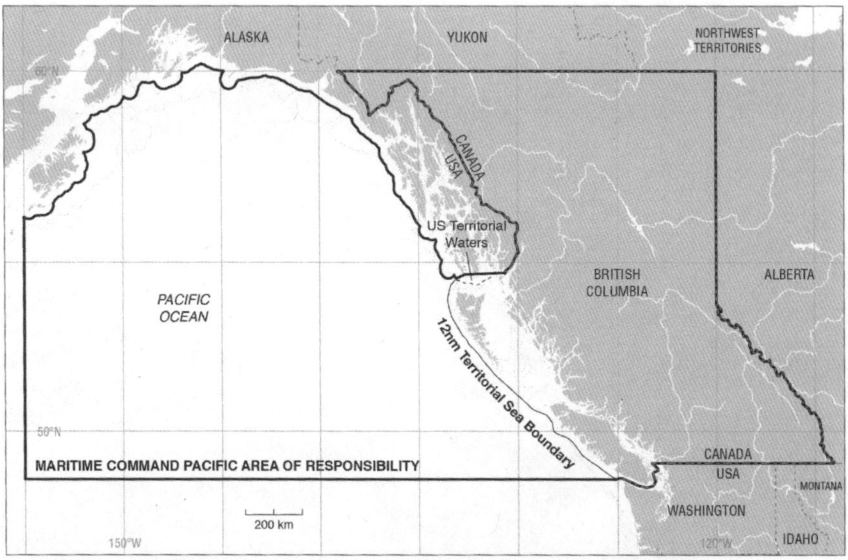

Figure 2 MARPAC area of responsibility. (Map by Eric Leinberger).

It is expected that the forthcoming third volume of the official history of the RCN, covering the period from 1945 to 1965, will provide a long overdue overview of Cold War naval policy. After the publication of this work, however, it will no longer be possible to ignore the Pacific dimension of Canadian defence policy during the Cold War.

1
The Legacy of War and Demobilization

THE TRANSITION FROM war to peace was difficult for the entire Canadian armed forces. During the Second World War, the RCN was determined to make the best of its phenomenal wartime growth – by war's end, it would be the world's third biggest navy – by establishing a large postwar balanced fleet that could defend Canada's coasts. But wartime planning failed to account for the political and economic realities of postwar Canada. As a result, the navy's vision for a balanced force on both coasts never materialized.

At Esquimalt, the Commanding Officer Pacific Coast had to contend with the very difficult challenges posed by demobilization with increasingly limited resources. The need to provide for a large number of sailors who wanted to return rapidly to civilian life, the arrival of large numbers of Canadian and Commonwealth prisoners of war from Japan, and the appearance of drifting mines carried by the Japanese Current to the West Coast strained the resources of Pacific Command close to the breaking point.

Prewar and Wartime Antecedents

The harbour of Esquimalt was first surveyed as a potential anchorage for the Royal Navy's Pacific Squadron in 1842. Located on the southern tip of Vancouver Island, Esquimalt is adjacent to Victoria Harbour, was which chosen by the Hudson's Bay Company to be the capital of what would eventually become the colony of British Columbia. For most of the next sixty-three years, Esquimalt remained a sleepy backwater as one of the most isolated of all Imperial naval bases. The completion of the Canadian Pacific Railway in 1885 linked the Pacific coast with the rest of the new Dominion of Canada. With the opening of the first graving dock at the centre of the small naval dockyard in 1887, Esquimalt become the first ship repair facility in British Columbia. That same year, the Canadian Pacific Steamship line began sailing between Vancouver/Victoria and Hong Kong, linking Canada to the wider Asia–Pacific world.

When, in 1906, the Royal Navy abandoned its Canadian Imperial naval bases at Esquimalt and at Halifax on the East Coast, the Dominion took over the facilities as an interim measure. Four years later, the Royal Canadian Navy was formed by an act of Parliament. Two obsolete Royal Navy cruisers were purchased to allow for the training of personnel; the smaller of the two, HMCS

Rainbow, was based at Esquimalt. With one exception, until just before the Second World War, Canada's West Coast naval base remained small and isolated, with few ships or personnel.

The one exception occurred in the first desperate days of the First World War, when Maximilian von Spee's German East Asia Squadron roamed the Pacific. The heroic but fortunately unsuccessful cruise of the *Rainbow*, under the command of Captain Walter Hose, to locate a German cruiser is the stuff of RCN legend. For a few months, panic gripped British Columbia. The provincial government took the desperate step of secretly purchasing two submarines being built in the United States for Chile. After the arrival of powerful Japanese and British warships off Canada's West Coast and the destruction of Graf Spee's ships at the Battle of the Falkland Islands on December 8, 1914, Esquimalt again sank back into relative obscurity.

After the First World War, Canada's small navy of four destroyers was evenly divided between the two coasts. In the late 1930s, faced with growing international tension, the government of William Lyon Mackenzie King authorized modest growth for the RCN, increasing the force to seven relatively modern destroyers. The Canadian government viewed the most immediate security threat as coming from Japan (which at the time was strongly committed to a war of conquest in China) and determined that the majority of the RCN's destroyers should be based on the West Coast. All of these ships, however, were immediately transferred to the Atlantic upon the commencement of the war in Europe in September 1939.

When the war with Japan began in December 1941, the RCN was fully committed to the Battle of Atlantic. Despite massive expansion, the navy had few resources available to protect Canada's Pacific coast. Despite having a limited number of ships, the Commanding Officer Pacific Coast acquired extensive responsibilities for the defence of Canada and North America. Ships operating out of Esquimalt and secondary bases, most notably Prince Rupert, were required to conduct a seaward defence of British Columbia. This "posed a considerable challenge as its rugged coastline extends more than 5,550 miles, including the offshore islands. Complete surveillance was out of the question, even with the assistance of the RCAF (Royal Canadian Air Force), given the limited naval strength available to the Commanding Officer Pacific Coast."[1] There was no real security threat to the coast until the Japanese attack on Pearl Harbor on December 7, 1941. At that point, ABC-22, the joint American-Canadian Continental Defence Plan, was implemented on the West Coast. These expanded responsibilities included the following:

> Under ABC-22, the Canadian-American hemispheric defence plan, Canada's air and naval forces were responsible for defending the seaward approaches to Esquimalt–Victoria, Vancouver and Prince Rupert, controlling shipping in

Canadian waters and patrolling the inshore waters of British Columbia. The RCN was also called upon to help defend Alaska by assisting in the movement, by sea, of American forces to the northern state. For its part, the USN was given responsibility for offshore surface and air patrols in the approaches off south-eastern Alaska, British Columbia and the American north-west, protection of shipping in the Gulf of Alaska and control of shipping in all areas they patrolled.[2]

Canadian warships operating on the West Coast regularly worked closely with USN vessels and eventually participated in amphibious operations to retake the Aleutian Islands that the Japanese had seized in June 1942. This tactical integration with the USN was something that East Coast vessels rarely did, one exception being the mixed US Coast Guard–RCN A3 mid-ocean escort group.

The Commanding Officer Pacific Coast (COPC) rarely had more than the three Prince-class armed merchant cruisers, a handful of corvettes, Bangor-class minesweepers, and smaller patrol vessels, supplemented by the fisherman's reserve, to perform the tasks at hand. Still, given the limited direct threat posed by the Imperial Japanese Navy to the coast, the force was sufficient.

The naval base at Esquimalt, HMCS *Naden*, which by 1939 had barely changed since it was acquired from the RN prior to the First World War, was greatly expanded in physical size by the expropriation of much of the old village site

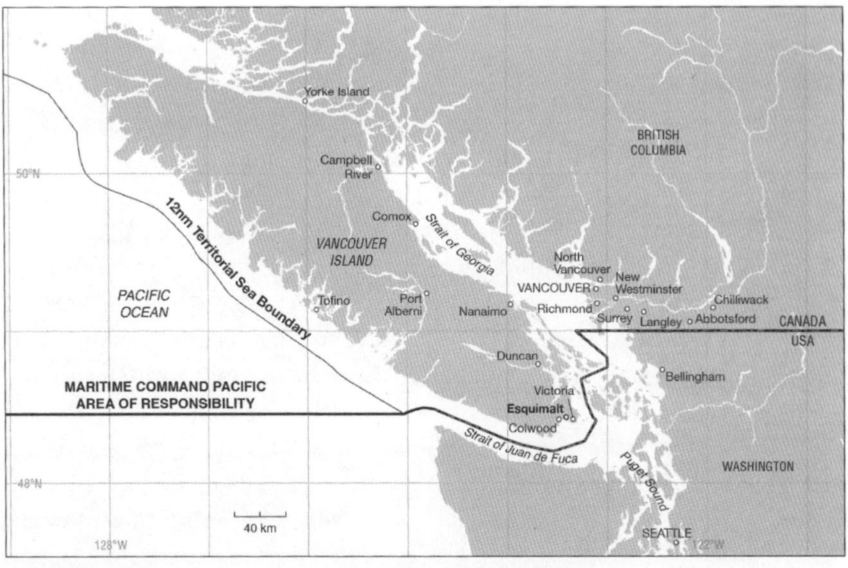

FIGURE 3 Esquimalt and environs. (Map by Eric Leinberger).

of Esquimalt. The late-nineteenth-century dry dock, which had been buried after the commissioning of the huge Dominion government graving dock at Skinner's Cove in 1927, was brought back into service. While some buildings were erected, the base saw no dramatic construction activity of the sort carried out in Halifax during the war. Commissioned during the conflict was a new naval officers' training college, HMCS *Royal Roads*, located close to *Naden* on the great estate of the famous Dunsmuir family.[3] A smaller naval base was added at the northern post of Prince Rupert, expanded naval facilities were acquired in Vancouver, a number of wireless stations were manned along the coast, and a naval magazine was established in the BC interior at Kamloops.

The Pacific and Planning the Postwar Navy

Planning for the postwar navy was under way by late 1943. The RCN was caught between its own desire for an extremely expensive "balanced fleet" of aircraft carriers, cruisers, destroyers, and frigates, and the uncertainty of sufficient funding from the Mackenzie King government. The prime minister desired a quick and painless transition to the peacetime world, in which social spending would take absolute precedence over needless military expenditures.[4] Naval planners struggled to justify the cost of the "balanced fleet" by finding some sort of strategic requirement for it. Coastal security, including along the Pacific coast, was an important component in the planning and policy papers of the period because it was one task Mackenzie King supported.[5]

In April 1944, Lieutenant-Commander G.F. Todd submitted to the Post Hostilities Problems Committee his appreciation of the issues Canada faced in defending itself in the postwar world. Todd argued that the armed forces should be prepared to provide Canada with "absolute strategic security under all circumstance." This would require a much wider security zone than existed prior to 1939. In the Pacific, this would include a zone stretching at least 300 miles off the coast, but Todd also listed the defence of Hawaii and the Aleutians as being vital to Canada. Todd wrote that "the holding or occupying of any or all of these islands would constitute a threat to Canada security." A powerful two-ocean navy would be required to guarantee Canadian interests. While the RCN would have to provide some of these forces, Canadian security could only be assured by maintaining close continental defence arrangements with the United States as well as military cooperation with Great Britain.[6]

On July 31, 1945, at the request of the naval minister and on behalf of the Chief of Naval Staff, Commodore H.G. DeWolf wrote a briefing paper for Cabinet. In that paper he outlined the navy's requirements for sending a fleet to fight against Japan in the last phase of the war, as well as proposals for the composition of the postwar navy. DeWolf stated that "proposals for a Post-War Navy are based on maintaining in commission on *both coasts*, a number of ships, which, when concentrated, will form a Naval Force capable of making an effective contribution to Canadian security and a modest but reasonable contribution to world security."[7]

DeWolf envisioned one navy divided between the two coasts, which would constitute a workable fleet only when joined together. Halifax and Esquimalt, along with an auxiliary base at Sydney, Nova Scotia, would provide most of the training schools and facilities for the entire RCN. The exception to this would be the Signal School, to be maintained at St-Hyacinthe, Quebec.

DeWolf's planning paper seems to have been based on a more extensive late war report titled "The Continuing Royal Canadian Navy." This report emphasized the navy's need to maintain a strong presence on both coasts. It argued that

> a further governing factor arises from Canada's geographic position. Canada flanks two oceans, both of which have been involved in both the War of 1914–18 and the present war. Therefore the Navy should in peacetime be trained to fight in both oceans. Hence in peacetime the ships would be disposed in both the Atlantic and the Pacific, but in an emergency they would normally be concentrated to form an integrated striking force.

The same report also discussed the distribution of the fleet, stating that this would be "determined by strategic considerations, and by the need for developing teamwork and experience in manoeuvres." It was recommended that normally the ships would be divided one "more or less equally between the Atlantic and Pacific," but would concentrate for an annual exercise.[8]

"The Continuing Royal Canadian Navy" also outlined the RCN's peacetime requirements for bases and other shore installations. Esquimalt was given importance equal to Halifax as a centre of naval activity. Each base, along with nearby civilian shipyards, was to be capable of serving at least 75 percent of the total peacetime fleet. This would make it possible to concentrate the fleet on either coast. The bases would have facilities for repair, manning, training, storage, and supply, as well as room to accommodate the reserve fleet. Near each base, a small naval air station would be established.

The report intimated that the navy would continue its wartime focus on the Atlantic. There would be no secondary base on the West Coast equivalent to Sydney, Nova Scotia, "until a palpable threat emerges," nor would there be any research facilities. The appendix of the report, which outlines the annual cash requirements for the peacetime navy, indicates that while Halifax would cost $700,000 per year to operate, Esquimalt would require just $280,000.[9]

By early 1946, Lieutenant-Commander E.E.G. Boak, the acting Assistant Director of Plans responsible for strategy, was able to solve one of the real conundrums for the RCN by identifying a credible threat to Canadian security. In a memorandum titled "A Naval Appreciation on Canada's Role in the Defence of North America," he singled out the Soviet Union as the one potential enemy until at least 1956. This was a far-reaching report that broached, for the first time, a number of important strategic concerns facing Canada over the next fifty years, particularly in regard to Arctic defence. There were considerable strategic concerns to be addressed in the Pacific. The only possible invasion route onto the North American continent was "by way of the Bering Straits." Boak outlined the strength of the Soviet Navy because there was "no doubt that the USSR intends to build a Navy of tremendous size and also implement [*sic*] her Air Force with long range bombers." It is worth noting that at the end of 1945, the Soviet Pacific Fleet was the largest of that nation's four fleets. It consisted of two modern cruisers, two flotilla leaders, nine modern destroyers, two old destroyers, and 101 submarines (although only eight of the latter were of modern wartime construction).[10]

The planners' belief that protecting the West Coast would be a major responsibility for the RCN in the postwar world was confirmed soon after the war. On June 4, 1946, the Joint Canadian–US Basic Security Plan was revised for peacetime. The RCN would be required to protect sea communications in Canada's Pacific coastal zone and to "co-operate with the United States Navy in the Protection of overseas shipping in the North West Atlantic and the Northern Pacific." This plan was approved by the American and Canadian Chiefs of Staff by the end of the year. The new security plan had other ramifications for the RCN, not the least of which was the need to continue wartime cooperation, as well as the standardization of equipment and techniques with the USN. As we shall see, moves were already well under way at Esquimalt to implement a close peacetime working relationship with the American Pacific Fleet.[11]

The dream of a balanced fleet equally divided between the two coasts did not long survive the realities of peacetime. The RCN had hoped for a fleet of two light carriers, four cruisers, and eighteen fleet destroyers, manned and supported by some 20,000 regular force personnel. As it turned out, that was wishful thinking. Budget cutting trimmed the navy's total complement to less than 10,000, not enough to properly man the one carrier, two cruisers, and a much smaller number of destroyers that would actually make up the fleet. With only one carrier, the dream of an equal fleet on both coasts became impossible. There was never any debate about basing the carrier at Halifax; still, the RCN saw that there were important strategic and practical reasons for placing a significant part of the fleet and its shore-based support at Esquimalt. The full extent of this commitment remained unclear at the end of 1946 because the entire operational navy was fully engaged in the complex and often painful process of demobilization.

Demobilization on the West Coast, 1945–47

If any situation in the history of the RCN caused more anguish than its rapid expansion during the Second World War, it was its even swifter contraction at the end of the conflict. A number of studies have pointed out that the RCN ceased to function as an operational military force as it dealt with the most precipitate dismantling of a navy in history. Between April 1945 and early 1946, the number of naval personnel shrunk from 92,529 to 15,624 – a decline of over 83 percent.[12] And the navy would continue to contract until, within two years of the end of the war, it stood well under the government-imposed ceiling of 10,000 personnel. Hundreds of ships, from the three armed merchant cruisers to dozens of escorts – destroyers, corvettes, frigates, and minesweepers – and many more smaller craft were decommissioned, to be either given away, placed in reserve, or, most likely, sold for scrap. Wilf Lund has called this period "The Doldrums," and Tyrone Pile has dubbed it a period of "turmoil." The navy and the West Coast went through all of the trials and tribulations of demobilization, which affected all aspects of its operations.

The first major changes for the Pacific Fleet came with the reorganization of the wartime command structure. In the spring of 1942, the COPC and his staff had been relocated from Esquimalt to the Pacific Joint Service Headquarters in Vancouver. The move was mandated at that time because "it was considered essential to the efficient prosecution of the war, and the Esquimalt–Victoria area was not thought suitable for this, since it was a 'forward' area in the coastal defence system."[13]

Even before the war with Japan had ended, in the summer of 1945 the Chiefs of Staff considered returning the COPC and his staff to Esquimalt. It was generally agreed that the move back to Vancouver Island would occur some time after the war because Esquimalt was to "be the only West Coast Naval base"; the only question was the timing. A move sooner rather than later was indicated because naval and other military activity in the Vancouver area was "dwindling in importance"; meanwhile, as a result of the Pacific war, activity at Esquimalt was increasing and likely to continue to do so.[14] In the upcoming assault on the Japanese home islands, Esquimalt was expected to be a "refit and training base" supporting fleet operations. So there was no pressing need to maintain geographically separate operational and base staff.

The driving force for a quick move back to Esquimalt was that it would allow a reduction in staff personnel. As one member of the Director of Plans staff outlined:

> One of the prime considerations of the transfer of COPC is the elimination of duplicate staffs, and the majority of the duplications occur on the respective staffs of COPC and N.O.I.C. [Naval Officer in Command] Esquimalt. If N.O.I.C. were absorbed by COPC, the following respective staffs would amalgamate and the surplus personnel be immediately available for other appointments or discharge, without interference with the set-up in Captain (D)'s organization.[15]

The end of the war brought added incentive to hasten the move. The transfer would allow for a significant reduction in staff; furthermore, the move "would effect a considerable savings in money." The other service chiefs voiced "no serious objections to the plan provided suitable liaison arrangements [were] made by the services." The move was formally approved by the Chiefs of Staff on September 12.[16]

On October 27, 1945, Admiral V.G. Brodeur, the COPC, struck his flag at Jericho Beach in Vancouver. The entire material content of his command, from office furniture to secret papers, was loaded onto thirty-five trucks, which in turn were loaded onto LST (3) *3534* for passage to Esquimalt. The large landing craft had been loaned to the RCN by the British Admiralty Technical Mission. The staff boarded the minesweeper HMCS *Grou* that same day, and by October 28 they had re-established headquarters in Building 70 at HMC Dockyard Esquimalt.[17]

The naval base that the COPC returned to was by October 1945 already fully involved in the demobilization process. Much of that task involved the decommissioning of ships slated for disposal or to be placed in reserve. Ships had to have ammunition and stores removed. If the ship was going into the reserve fleet, it had to be winterized and otherwise made secure for a long period of inactivity. If a vessel was slated for sale, all of its military and electronic equipment needed to be removed. This included guns, depth charge launchers and racks, minesweeping gear, radios, radio direction finders, loran, radar, sonar, and gyrocompasses. Everything removed from vessels had to be placed in storage at the base, shipped to other facilities, made safe for sale as scrap, or otherwise disposed of. In October 1946, three Bangor-class minesweepers, two corvettes, and two smaller minesweepers were made ready for disposal and towed to Vancouver. The decommissioning of ships peaked in November, when eighteen warships, frigates, corvettes, and minesweepers were declared surplus and made ready for disposal to the War Assets Corporation. In January 1946, among other ships dealt with were the three former Canadian Pacific liners of the Prince-class, which were demilitarized and towed to Vancouver for disposal. Although a few more ships would be withdrawn from service over the next few years, the massive postwar decommissioning of ships ended in February 1946 when the frigate HMCS *Matane* was handed over for disposal.[18]

After the defeat of Japan, it was not just ships that faced material downsizing. By the end of November 1945, many of the defensive installations protecting the approaches to Esquimalt harbour had been removed and placed in storage. The largest of these were the log boom defences and antisubmarine nets, which prevented unauthorized entry into the harbour, as well as their accompanying gate vessels and gate vessel moorings. Even bigger operations occurred outside of Esquimalt: many of the auxiliary bases set up during the war were closed, and all of their equipment and stores either sold or shipped to Esquimalt. The largest of these closures was of the naval base at Prince Rupert. This base had extensive boom and net defences as well as an antisubmarine loop detection system located off Ridley Island. Buildings had to be cleared out and anything useful loaded onto barges and towed down the coast to Esquimalt. Special cargoes included an entire tanker of oil and a large amount of munitions, which were sent south separately. There was not always enough time, money, or personnel for a complete and orderly dismantling of the navy. Many tons of obsolete equipment and ammunition were simply dumped into the ocean at designated sites.[19] Base closures continued until the end of 1946, when HMCS *Naden II*, the naval training centre at Comox, was shut down, and the Prince Rupert base was transferred to the naval reserve and reopened in a much reduced form as HMCS *Chatham*.[20]

Demobilization was as much about releasing personnel back to civilian life as it was about ships, bases, and material. The demobilization of personnel was as fast paced as the decommissioning of ships, but there was far less order and far more chaos. Much of the burden of demobilization fell on the special services organization, which saw a 40 to 100 percent increase in demand between July and October 1945 for the various types of assistance it provided sailors. Special services looked after the welfare of naval personnel, which included providing information and advice on discharge and payment of hospital bills and housing; it also ran or supervised privately run hostels and canteens and provided entertainment. The large number of ships being decommissioned placed many personnel ashore awaiting discharge or reassignment. This caused a huge increase in the demand for meals as well as entertainment. Hostels were filled to capacity. Hundreds of men wanted assistance to speed their discharge from the service or to find out why their return to civilian life was being delayed. The decommissioning of ships placed an additional burden on special service personnel, who were forced to work "overtime receiving and recording amenities belonging to organizations and sponsors."

Not surprisingly, the large number of sailors could not all be kept happy and entertained, and some serious problems resulted. In the autumn, there was a marked increase in cases of venereal disease, and a special meeting was called to discuss the situation. It was decided to ask all hostels to increase their entertainment programs and "to exercise more strict supervision of hostesses." This was supported by additional visits to hostels by the Shore Patrol.[21]

Every aspect of operations of the command was affected by the sudden discharge of key personnel and by the navy's inability to provide timely replacements. In the crucial month of October 1945, at the height of demobilization, the head of special services was unexpectedly discharged, and his replacement was not on the West Coast. As an interim measure, a reserve lieutenant who was acting as a liaison officer for a touring group of British entertainers was made acting head of the organization. The entire special services organization was shut down on March 31, 1946, before many wartime service personnel were released from the service. Many recreation facilities were also closed at this time, leaving no central body responsible for the welfare of sailors and warrant officers.[22]

On December 31, Commander P.E. Haddon, the senior officer for ships in reserve, reported that his efforts to prepare ships for entering the reserve squadron were being hampered by the personnel crisis. Particularly troubling was the situation in the five Algerine-class minesweepers under his command. He informed the COPC: "I regret to report that a state a little short of chaotic exists in these ships. This state is not due to the ships themselves or to any one person, rather it is caused by the difficulty of maintaining some sort of continuity and competing with the encroaching fingers of demobilization." As a result, the deterioration of ships in reserve was going to be "greater" than had been hoped.[23] The situation did not markedly improve during 1946. In May the Senior Officer for Ships in Reserve reported that a lack of personnel and equipment was leading to the deterioration of ships and a decline in morale. Seamen were being forced to spend their entire day chipping and scaling old paint and rust, and this led to a large number of requests for compassionate discharge, leave, or transfer.[24]

The organization of headquarters was also affected by the swift decline in personnel. Entire departments were closed down or amalgamated as reservists returned to civilian life. Some of these closures were predetermined by the winding up of the wartime organization responsible for controlling merchant ships and ensuring the security of ports. The routing of merchant ships by the naval authority mainly ceased in October 1945. On January 1, 1946, the Naval Control Service officers at Vancouver, Victoria, New Westminster, and Prince

Rupert were instructed to cease functioning and to disband their units by the middle of the month. The ports reverted back to the control of the National Harbours Board or the Department of Transport. As a result, the position of Staff Officer (Trade) was terminated on January 31, and the Staff Officer (Intelligence) was made the Staff Officer (Intelligence and Trade).[25] In March 1947, the acute shortage of regular force personnel compelled the navy to take the unusual step of continuing the appointment of Lieutenant-Commander R. Roberts (RCNR) as Staff Officer (Intelligence and Trade), even though he had been demobilized and was now a civilian. Roberts may have been a special case, in that he had been a civilian employee of the Department of National Defence prior to the start of the Second World War, and had served since August 31, 1939, in the intelligence staff on the West Coast. Still, it is reflection of the manpower crisis that befell the navy in the years after the war.[26]

As a result of the "reduction in the size of the Naval Service," a general reorganization of Pacific Coast Headquarters was initiated in Ottawa in January 1946. The administration of West Coast personnel was divided between two separate manning depots, HMCS *Naden* and *Givenchy*. The former became "essentially a training establishment and operational authority for seagoing tenders attached for training." The latter was responsible for administering communications stations, seagoing tenders, the ships in reserve and auxiliary vessels.[27] COPC retained operational control of all craft, other than harbour vessels. Where possible, senior officers were given multiple tasks. For instance, the Commanding Officer of *Givenchy* was also made "Senior Officer Ships in Reserve, Maintenance Captain and King's Harbour Master." [28]

The reduction and restructuring of the West Coast fleet organization continued for several years after the war. In March 1947, HMCS *Givenchy* was paid off, and most of its responsibilities were transferred to HMCS *Naden*. At the same time, HMCS *Rockcliffe* was commissioned as the depot and accommodation ship for the new position Senior Officer Ships in Reserve.[29]

Even Admiral Brodeur was forced to accept some temporary additional staff duties. On May 13, 1946, he assumed the dual appointment as Superintendent of the Dockyard. This proved to be unworkable, since running the dockyard was a full-time job, even in peacetime. In January 1947, a separate superintendent's position was re-established under the overall command of the COPC.[30]

Two aspects of demobilization brought the reminder that there had been a serious conflict in the Pacific, every bit as deadly as the European war. In the autumn of 1945, all three services on the West Coast were called upon to assist in the care of a large number of repatriated prisoners of war. Most of the POWs were British army, but there were also a number of RN and RCN personnel. The Staff Officer (Intelligence) acted as naval liaison officer and arranged to have RCN and Canadian Army teams, consisting of medical personnel and paymasters, placed aboard each vessel carrying POWs as they passed William's Head.

In early October, some 5,800 personnel were landed at either Esquimalt or Vancouver. HMCS *Prince Robert* brought nine officers and fifty other ranks to Esquimalt, all survivors of Canada's ill-fated force sent to defend Hong Kong in 1941. The largest number of repatriated prisoners arrived on two RN aircraft carriers, HMS *Implacable* and *Glory*. The *Implacable* arrived off William's Head on October 11 carrying 125 officers and 2,002 other ranks from POW camps in Japan, all of whom were landed in Vancouver. The *Glory* arrived on October 26 with 1,338 ex-POWs, who were landed at Esquimalt. "All the Vessels carrying repatriated personnel were accorded a tremendous ovation by whistles and syrens [*sic*] on entering Esquimalt Harbour and cheering crowds greeted them as they came alongside the Dominion Government's Landing Wharf." Such large numbers of personnel, many of whom required medical attention, overwhelmed the army base at Work Point barrack. RCN medical personnel were called in to assist. Many members of the public opened their homes to the British servicemen, offering a pleasant sojourn before they continued their journey home via train to the East Coast.[31]

Mines

In July 1945, the navy began to receive reports of floating Japanese mines sighted off the West Coast. Over the next four years, these mines would prove to be the most serious threat to West Coast shipping and coastal communities since Japanese submarines cruised in Canadian waters. Every month until the late 1940s, there were dozens of reports of mines that had been sighted at sea or that had washed ashore. Each report had to be investigated, which might mean a major sea search or the landing of a party to scour the shoreline. The problem was so serious that eventually a number of small, naval auxiliary vessels were sent on regular antimine patrols along the coast, and a full-time team of mine disposal experts was kept busy locating and destroying the mines.

On July 26, 1945, the first mine was sighted off the West Coast of North America by the Columbia River Lightship, operating some 50 miles out to sea. At first there were only a few scattered reports of mines, eight in October 1945, but their numbers quickly escalated, and over the following month some fifty-eight were sighted in the general Pacific area. The number of mines entering Canadian waters continued to grow until mid-1948, and there were still reports of mines through 1952.

In November 1947, the cause of this gradual escalation in the number of mines was assessed by Dr. John P. Tully, the oceanographer in charge of the Pacific

Oceanographic Group, located at the Pacific Biological Station in Nanaimo. Tully explained to Rear Admiral E.R. Mainguy, who had succeeded Admiral Brodeur as COPC, that the mines were being carried ashore to Canada by ocean currents. His group's studies of these currents indicated that most of the mines would near shore "in the approaches to Juan de Fuca strait [*sic*], and will land in the vicinity of Wickaninnish and Florencia bays. During periods of strong southwest winds (storm conditions) the odd mine may intrude Juan de Fuca strait, or Barclay sound, and drift to the northern side in each case." Tully concluded by telling Mainguy that the appearance of the mines came as no surprise to him, since he "had expected the Japanese to use this method of neutralizing this coast during the War, because they were conscious of ocean currents, and must have known our vulnerability to such an attack. We can expect a considerable proportion of the mines lost from Japanese mine fields to reach our area during the next twelve months."[32]

Two years later, Lieutenant I.G. Nelson, USN 13th Naval District's Bomb Disposal Officer, provided a further analysis of the mine threat. Nelson stated that the problem was caused by the Japanese Current, which captured mines that had broken off from their moorings in Asia and then carried them to the West Coast. If they did not drift ashore, the mines could make a circuit of the entire North Pacific three times in approximately four years.[33]

These scientific explanations for the appearance of the mines did not satisfy everyone. At least one concerned citizen from New Westminster warned the navy that the mines were part of a broader plot and that they had to have been "directed on the way." He feared that the mines "may fit into the plan of the seeming war of attrition being waged in Canada and the United States, where strikes in key industries, fires from unexplained causes cause enormous damage and property loss. The floating mines have all the earmarks of another Corfu incident." He believed that ultimately, the mines would cause another ship to never make port.[34]

The Staff Officer (Intelligence and Trade) had little time for such anticommunist paranoia, and replied to the concerned citizen that the mines were being brought here by ocean currents and that the USN and RCN had anticipated their arrival and set up procedures to warn shipping and to destroy any mines that came ashore. "Up to the present time," he assured him, "we have been fortunate that no marine disaster has been caused to any of our shipping by these drifting menaces."[35]

After January 1946, when the first mine was destroyed in the Queen Charlotte Islands, the navy investigated hundreds of reports of sightings and destroyed more than thirty mines. The public had to be kept informed of the menace to the coast, and in November 1946, 8,000 copies of a mine recognition poster

FIGURE 4 *Heatherton* at Esquimalt, July 1948. *Heatherton* was one of the small naval auxiliary vessels that undertook mine patrols along the BC coast. (CFB Esquimalt Museum)

were prepared by NSHQ for distribution throughout coastal British Columbia. "The poster described five types of mines likely to be encountered, the safety precautions to be observed and the correct procedure for reporting them."[36] Notices were also printed in newspapers about the correct procedures to follow if a mine was spotted. Most of these reports came from merchantmen, who spotted the mines well off the coast, or from fishing boats that sighted the mines closer to shore. A number of mines were located only once they had drifted ashore. Each offshore citing resulted in the issuing of a warning to shipping in the area, and if the mine was close enough to the coast, a naval search team was dispatched to perform the difficult task of finding and destroying the mine at sea.

The mines, while a worrisome threat to navigation, never sank or damaged any vessel. Since none of the mines detonated themselves, it is likely that they became inactive as soon as they broke from their moorings in Asian coastal waters. One American company, however, believed that its tug, the *W.H. McFadden*, might have been damaged by a mine in the Strait of Juan de Fuca on May 9, 1947, when an explosion rendered it a total loss. This was discounted by the RCN, for no mines had ever been sighted in the strait; the devices were generally spotted on the coast of northern British Columbia, mainly in the Queen Charlottes. Still, the reports of mines caused great concern among shipping companies, and several of them asked for assurances that their ships were safe. The navy reassured the shipping companies that the mines did not pose a serious threat to navigation, but always warned that "a sharp lookout should be kept as it is anticipated that such mines may be encountered at any time."[37]

The closest encounter with a floating mine at sea was reported by two RCN warships. On April 23, 1948, while returning from a southern training cruise, the cruiser HMCS *Ontario* and the destroyer HMCS *Crescent* spotted a mine in position 41° 31′ North 124° 56′ West. The cruiser was forced to make an emergency turn to avoid the mine, believed to be a type JA. The crew of the *Crescent* then managed to destroy it with gunfire.[38]

By May 1946 the navy had been forced to establish a regular mine patrol, generally with civilian-manned naval auxiliary vessels and tugs. The first such patrol was undertaken by the Motor Vessel *Kuitan*, which had been chartered by the navy to carry mine disposal teams. The first full-time mine disposal officer, H.G. Wood, RCNR, was appointed in June 1946. The article "Go West Young Men!" describes the procedures that were followed when a mine was reported:

> One might say the extra training has been forced upon us by the constant need to search out and dispose of mines, usually as the result of some vague report from a wandering fisherman or shore ranger. Great bustle is evident in the Ops. Room as cruising ships in the vicinity are immediately notified and "units" of the energetic mine-disposal fleet, consisting of CNAV *Heatherton* and *Glendon* are dispatched with all haste. In many cases the Japanese Current – the searcher's curse – has sent the mine south to the US coast, thus passing the buck to our good neighbours.[39]

By the spring of 1948, mine patrols required the deployment of three naval auxiliary tugs, the *Heatherton*, *Clifton*, and *Glendevon*. The main task of the ships was to locate the mines, which usually involved lengthy searches based on often scanty information from fishermen, provincial police officers, natives, and other civilians in the area. This cooperation with civilians was invaluable, although not everyone was cognizant of the threat posed by the mines.

In March 1947, a mine disposal officer was hastily flown to Massett in the Queen Charlotte Islands, where a Japanese type JB mine had been found on a farm. According to the incredulous mine disposal officer, the mine, "in a damaged condition with the horns broken off, had been recovered by a man who believed it to be a mooring buoy, and valuable as salvage. He had transferred it from the East Coast of Graham Island, a distance of 20 miles, to his farm on the north coast!" The mine was removed from the farm and then detonated by rifle fire. Alas, the records do not recount how the farmer recognized his mistake and decided to call in the authorities.[40]

Once located, destroying the mines was generally a simple affair for mine disposal specialists, usually requiring the firing of an armour-piercing bullet from a Lee-Enfield rifle into the explosive charge in the centre of the device. A few types of Japanese mines, however, needed to be detonated with a charge of TNT.

The decision to employ specialist search and disposal teams may have been the result of problems in some of the early mine disposals in 1946. In January a mine was detonated in Skidegate Inlet in the Queen Charlotte Islands. Although the officer in charge had moved the mine away from nearby buildings, it was not far enough away to avoid damaging the windows in buildings within a half-mile radius of the explosion. More serious was a tragic accident in March 1946, which marred another early successful mine demolition. On March 31, HMCS *Talapus* proceeded to Wickaninnish Bay at Long Beach on the west coast of Vancouver Island to destroy a mine that had washed ashore. The mine was swiftly located and disposed of, but on the return of the landing party from shore, their small craft capsized, "leaving the crew struggling in the water." What followed is best recounted in the official report on the incident:

> Mr. L.R. Whittington and his wife, local residents, at grave personal risk on the surf-swept rocks, dragged two of the crew to safety. Mr. Whittington then attempted to rescue a third man but was himself swept away and drowned. The evidence of the four survivors indicates that at least two of them owe their lives to the heroic efforts of Mr. and Mrs. Whittington.[41]

After the creation of regular mine patrols and permanent mine disposal teams, there was no repeat of these early mistakes. The effectiveness of these teams can perhaps best be seen in comparison to the efforts of other government agencies to destroy mines. While a mine disposal officer could generally detonate a mine with one or two shots from a Lee-Enfield, the crew of the Fisheries Patrol Craft *Howay* discovered that a mine could be an elusive prey. The *Howay* was patrolling in Kyuquot Sound on April 7, 1948, when it heard a radio message from the fishing vessel *Karsun* that it had spotted a mine floating in a kelp patch about 10 miles from Lookout Island. The *Howay* raced to the scene, a little more than an hour away, and spent the next two hours and twenty minutes looking for the mine. Having spotted it, the master of the fisheries vessel decided to unleash his main armament, an Oerlikon gun. Fifty-eight shots were fired in short bursts at a range of 200 metres, "but owing to the rolling of the vessel, and the mine only showing at short intervals on the tops of the sea no hits were made." Finally, a crewmen fired nine rounds with a .303 rifle at 150 yards range, hitting the mine four times. The mine then sank without having detonated.[42]

Mine patrols continued until early 1950, when the scarcity of mines led to abandonment of the patrols. In early June 1952, however, a fisherman reported seeing a mine washed ashore on Bonilla Island, 70 miles southwest of Prince Rupert. A demolition team, consisting of ordnance Lieutenant-Commander E.L. Borradaile and Petty Officer Donald Ross, was sent to dispose of the mine. Somehow there was an accident, and either the mine or a demolition charge exploded, killing Borradaile and wounding Ross. It was a tragic reminder of the very real danger posed by rogue mines. [43]

Conclusion

Mine clearance, reorganization, and demobilization were all part of the often difficult transition from war to peace. By 1947, the navy was a shadow of its wartime strength, with an uncertain mission and a limited number of trained personnel. The navy would now need to cope with rebuilding during the increasing tensions of the Cold War, and plan for the defence of the West Coast of North America with limited resources.

2

From Peace to Cold War, 1945–50

POSTWAR DEMOBILIZATION ENDED by 1946. While the mine menace lingered on for five more years, the navy's main issue was rebuilding the nucleus of a much smaller operational fleet than wartime planners had envisioned. There was a dearth of regular forces personnel to man the few ships retained in commission as well as shore establishments. The raison d'être for the navy on both coasts was training. Training involved everything from giving basic instruction to new entry seaman and officer cadets to specialty nonsubstantive training in everything from antisubmarine technology to manpower management.

By 1947, Naval Service Headquarters had determined that the wartime plans for a balanced fleet would, at least in the short term, not be realized, and that the navy's primary mission would henceforth be antisubmarine warfare. Operational exercises were limited by the lack of opportunities to train with large fleet units such as aircraft carriers; antisubmarine exercises were also restricted, because the RCN had no submarines. Only after 1947 did the USN provide limited opportunities for ASW training, which was becoming the main mission of the RCN.

From an operational perspective on the West Coast, the RCN had no clear mandate or doctrine, largely because defence planning with the Americans had been temporarily suspended. After the war, Mackenzie King's government was reluctant to continue wartime cooperation in the Pacific with the United States. His reasons for downplaying those defence ties are unclear, but they may have been tied to his desire to avoid any actions that would antagonize the Soviet Union.

Ship and Base Operations, 1945–50

The Esquimalt naval base was organized to serve this basic mission of training. The navy viewed HMCS *Naden* as being the centre of its efforts to transform itself into a well-trained professional force. In September 1945, as a result of the huge budgetary cutbacks experienced by the RCN after the war, the naval staff decided to transfer all new entry training from HMCS *Cornwallis*, in Nova Scotia, to Esquimalt. This was a poorly considered decision made in great haste at a time of fiscal crisis and rapid downsizing. There were insufficient accommodations and messing facilities for the 350 recruits transferred to *Naden* in December, let alone for the far larger number of new entrants who would be required if the navy was to man any ships in the coming years. Moreover, as Lund has pointed out, "*Naden* did not have enough officers and senior rates to supervise the recruits properly and to operate an effective divisional system for their welfare." The answer from headquarters for the shortage of supervisory personnel was to have existing members of the base staff undertake double-duty.[1] The problems of poor accommodations for naval personnel at Esquimalt would not be seriously addressed until the early 1950s. In the meantime, new entry seamen received a poor first impression of the RCN. In April 1947, Brooke Claxton called the living conditions at *Naden* "shockingly bad."[2] This situation was not rectified until January 1949, when the Naval Board decided to reopen *Cornwallis* in Nova Scotia to act as its recruit training centre.[3] In total, some 5,200 new entry trainees passed through *Naden*. Only after the transfer could anyone in the navy see any humour in the substandard living conditions on the West Coast. Reporting on the opening of *Cornwallis* in September, *The Crowsnest* reminisced: "Men who are new entries at *Naden* will recall some of the more familiar aspects of the base and training ... the luxuries of H Block and its 'air of being lived in' ... the water battles after hours ... the wet individuals who started them."[4]

While *Naden*'s role in new entry training did not last, the base would become and still is a centre for both officer and specialist training. Training facilities and sea training were required for cadets from the naval college, HMCS *Royal Roads* (after September 1947 the RCN–RCAF College), as well as for western Canadian RCNR officers and University Naval Training Division (UNTD) cadets. Specialized training centres were required for all ranks. In April 1946, nine different training centres or schools were authorized for *Naden*. These included schools for navigation and Action Information Centre training, electrical training, damage control and firefighting, communications, gunnery, supply and secretarial duties, torpedo and antisubmarine, physical and recreational training, and mechanical training.[5]

The government's decision in 1947 to reduce the ceiling on the total number of naval personnel from 10,000 to 7,500 had a direct effect on the training establishments on the West Coast. That spring, the mechanical and electrical training centres at *Naden* were shut down at the same time as HMCS *Givenchy*. This meant that West Coast personnel had to go to Halifax to receive specialist training in these areas.[6]

After the rapid postwar demobilization, the principal function of all warships that remained in service was to provide seamen and officers with seagoing training.[7] On the West Coast, during the two years after the war's end, only three major warships were regularly kept in commission: the light cruiser HMCS

Uganda (replaced by HMCS *Ontario* in July 1947), the C-class destroyer HMCS *Crescent*, and the frigate HMCS *Charlottetown* (replaced by HMCS *Antigonish* in April 1947). As well, the motor launch *ML 124* (renamed the *Elk* in 1954) was in commission during this period.

The number of major warships in commission on the West Coast did not increase until March 1948, when the destroyer HMCS *Cayuga* arrived from Halifax. Several months later, the Tribal-class destroyer HMCS *Athabaskan* joined the operational units on the West Coast. For a short time, the three destroyers were formed into the Canadian Destroyer Division, West Coast. The number of active destroyers on the West Coast was soon reduced to two in early 1949 as the *Cayuga* and then *the Athabaskan* were in turn given major refits and upgrades to carry the Squid antisubmarine mortar. The frigate HMCS *Beacon Hill* was reactivated from the reserve fleet in June 1949. *Antigonish*, *ML 124*, and *Beacon Hill* together formed the Pacific Training Force, which operated in the summer of 1949. The only other warship active on the coast during this period was the Algerine-class minesweeper HMCS *Sault Ste. Marie*, which served as tender vessel to HMCS *Malahat*, the naval reserve division in Victoria. The actual low point in numbers of ships in service occurred in November 1949, when only *Cayuga* and *Antigonish* remained in commission. That month, as a result of the wear and tear of almost four years of continuous service, *Crescent* was paid off into reserve. Her crew was transferred to HMCS *Sioux*, which was being recommissioned after a lengthy conversion into an antisubmarine destroyer. *Ontario* began a major refit that same month. Only in January 1950, when HMCS *Sioux* re-entered service, did the number of ships in commission in the RCN begin to increase. The number of operational vessels would continue to grow in the months ahead as a result of the growing tensions of the Cold War and the start of Canada's naval commitment to the Korean War.[8] The shifting of numbers of ships in commission makes a comparison with the Atlantic fleet difficult if not impossible. There were often more ships in commission on the West Coast than on the East, although with its carrier – *Warrior* until the spring 1948 and then the *Magnificent* – the Atlantic Fleet remained far larger in terms of firepower and number of personnel.

West Coast–based ships – *Ontario*, *Crescent*, and *Athabaskan* – were involved in three of the four mutinies or incidents that rocked the navy in the late 1940s and resulted in the appointment of the Mainguy Commission. The first incident occurred on *Ontario* on August 22, 1947, when the recently commissioned cruiser was at anchor in Nanoose Bay on the east coast of Vancouver Island. Some fifty men locked themselves in the mess deck and refused to report for duty. Captain J.H. Hibbard decided to defuse the situation by not directly challenging the men; instead, he used the ship's intercom to inform all personnel

FIGURE 5 Navy Week at Esquimalt, August 9, 1948. Left to right (foreground): HMS *Sheffield*, HMCS *Cayuga*, and HMCS *Ontario*. In the background is HMCS *Athabaskan* heading towards the fuel jetty. (Courtesy DND)

that in fifteen minutes he would address the entire crew topside. Hibbard listened to the crew's complaints, which focused on the rigid and "capricious" conduct of the executive officer, Commander J.V. Brock, who was responsible for the welfare of the crew. Hibbard's strategy worked; the crew returned to regular duties immediately after his talk. The only action taken was by Rear Admiral E.R. Mainguy, the FOPC, who removed Brock from the ship.

The incident on board the *Athabaskan* occurred eighteen months later, in February 1949, while the destroyer was at Manzanillo, Mexico. Once again, a group of sailors locked themselves in their mess deck and refused to report for duty. When Commander M.A. Medland, the ship's captain, arrived, he was allowed to enter the mess area. Like Hibbard, Medland sought to defuse the situation by listening to the men. He covered with his cap the list of complaints they had written down and instead listened informally while they spoke to him directly. Again, their complaints were directed at the rigid enforcement of uniform regulations by the executive officer, as well as the failure to go to tropical routine, which included not working at the height of the afternoon sun, and the difficulty in "maintaining self-respect and pride." Medland listened to the crew's concerns for fifteen minutes and left. A few minutes later, the crew responded to a pipe to resume normal duties. A few hours later this ship left harbour to resume her training cruise. Medland's only subsequent action was to charge several crew members with "slackness"; the only punishment handed out was a caution.

The third such incident, on the *Crescent*, followed a similar pattern, although the consequences were potentially more dire because the destroyer had been deployed close to a potentially hostile enemy. At the request of the Department of External Affairs, the ship had been sent to Nanking, China, in support of British efforts to protect their interests during the Chinese Civil War. On March 15, 1949, the crew locked themselves in the mess deck and refused the pipe to fall in. Lieutenant-Commander D.W. Groos, the ship's captain, refused to listen to the collective complaints of the crew, which included the failure to go to a tropical routine and the heavy demands on them to perform guard duties ashore. They also called for the executive officer to be removed. Instead, Groos informed the crew that those that wished could make individual complaints. After Groos heard the complaints of nineteen of the crew, they all returned to duty.[9]

After a fourth such "mutiny" on March 20 on board the Halifax-based aircraft carrier *Magnificent*, Brooke Claxton appointed a commission headed by Rear Admiral E.R. Mainguy to uncover the causes of these incidents. Mainguy was an interesting choice to head the inquiry, for he had a close connection to the events and may have even created some of the procedures that led directly to the work stoppages. Mainguy had captained the cruiser *Uganda* in 1946 before succeeding Admiral Brodeur as the second postwar COPC. When appointed to head the commission, he was the Vice-Chief of the Naval Staff; between 1951 and 1956, he would serve as Chief of Naval Staff. The Mainguy Commission's finding focused on poor living conditions and the failure of British-trained officers to connect with their Canadian crews. Claxton pushed for the Canadianization of the fleet, including the return of Canadian symbols such as the Maple Leaf on ships and uniforms. The Naval Board rejected these conclusions and tended to believe that the causes were tied to the poor qualities of wartime Royal Canadian Navy Volunteer Reserve (RCNVR) officers who had transferred to the regular navy after the conflict, as well as postwar turmoil within the service. Historians have extensively debated the causes, meanings, and consequences of the "mutinies" without coming to any agreement.[10] Marc Milner concludes simply: "They stemmed, as mutinies invariably do, from a simple failure of leadership."[11] An examination of the typical routines of Esquimalt-based ships and of their experiences has shed some new light on this controversial subject and tends to support the argument that personnel shortages and mismanagement were a major cause of unrest in the navy.

FIGURE 6 Captain Rollo Mainguy (centre) on board HMCS *Uganda* during its 1946 South America training cruise. Mainguy was later FOPC, 1946–48, and Chief of Naval Staff, 1951–56. Admiral Sir William Tennant, Commander-in-Chief, America and West Indies (Royal Navy) is on the right. (CFB Esquimalt Museum)

The desperate need for training in the immediate postwar navy, which Lund and Gimblett have examined closely from the perspective of high policy, can be seen in the experiences of the few ships retained in the Pacific Fleet. Acting Lieutenant-Commander C.P. Nixon, the first captain of HMCS *Crescent*, would have had a pleasant passage across the Atlantic and through the Panama Canal to Esquimalt had that voyage not been marred by a shortage of trained seamen. There were regular breakdowns in equipment, including the gyrocompass, steering, radar sets, and guns (which jammed), all "due to inexperienced personnel and not to deficiencies in equipment or construction." Reporting from the safety of Esquimalt harbour at the end of his trip, Nixon reported:

> It is considered not only hazardous to attempt to run a modern destroyer without the necessary number of experienced senior ratings; but it is strongly recommended that this ship is not employed operationally until an adequate number of such men are available. It is also considered that a Special Branch officer

> qualified in Radar is essential to the Ship's complement if the radar equipment is to be kept in efficient working order.[12]

By February 1946, the *Crescent's* situation had markedly improved; the complement had grown sufficiently that the total number of ratings roughly corresponded with the approved training complement. As well, the ratio of ship's company who were either regular navy or two-year volunteers had grown to 54 percent. This still meant that almost half the crew was waiting to be demobilized. As well, the ship remained short of "all of the higher non-substantive rates, particularly in the Gunnery and Radar branches." Despite these problems, Nixon believed "it was now possible for the ship to proceed on short-passages without having to borrow additional men for the occasion."[13] This came just in time, for in February the ship would be pressed into service as a full-time training vessel, conducting fifteen training cruises in the next nine months.

Unfortunately, Nixon's hope for a more stable personnel situation was misplaced. Three years later, on the eve of the *Crescent*'s operations in China,

FIGURE 7 *Crescent*'s ship's company in 1948. The problem of maintaining trained personnel was a key factor in the work stoppage on board this ship in 1949. (CFB Esquimalt Museum)

manning problems persisted and were in some ways even worse. When the orders to proceed to China were received at Esquimalt, twenty reservists, on board for a training exercise in the Caribbean, were quickly exchanged for twenty-five regular force seamen from *Ontario*. The ship's complement totalled 14 officers and 187 other ranks, just shy of its nominal peacetime complement but 56 below its wartime requirements. Given that the ship was going into a potential combat situation, the vessel was significantly undermanned. Three-quarters of the crew and all but one of the officers had been on the ship less than a year. Less than 10 percent of the crew had been in the navy prior to 1939, slightly more than 40 percent were wartime entries, and over 50 percent had joined in the postwar period.

As Gimblett has pointed out, the personnel situation was made much worse by the major restructuring of the rating and warrant officer rank structure imposed by the Defence Department in early 1949 in order to standardize the service's rank structure with those of the army and air force. As a result, the *Crescent* sailed with far too many chiefs and petty officers and a shortage of junior ratings. Much of the tension on board was the result of forcing a smaller number of seamen to take on time-consuming duties such as standing watch guarding the jetty or the wet canteen while at Nanking.[14]

The reality of the RCN between the end of the Second World War and the Korean conflict was of perpetual training, as the service struggled to maintain even the small number of personnel authorized by the government. Until 1948, the training cruises of West Coast warships were carried out mainly (although not exclusively) in Canadian waters. These cruises could be as short as a weekend cruise for cadets from *Royal Roads*, which might take the ship as far as James Island or Saanichton Bay, just a few miles down the coast, as carried out by *Crescent* in the winter of 1945–46. Longer training cruises of up to six weeks were regularly undertaken, however, particularly during the summer. The ship regularly travelled through the Strait of Juan de Fuca along the west coast of Vancouver Island to visit Port Alberni or along the east coast of the island to Nanoose Bay or Comox. Cruises then often proceeded up the Inland Passage as far as Prince Rupert or the Queen Charlotte Islands. A few trips went farther north to Alaska, to places like Kodiak, Dutch Harbor, and Juneau, which soon became regular ports of call.

Normally, the training on board ship included basic seamanship skills, such as boat handling and anchoring and mooring practice, more advanced seamanship, such as watch keeping and ship handling exercises, and use of the ship's weaponry. The programs for cruises varied to a certain extent depending on the personnel being trained, but there was generally a consistent list of activities, both naval and social.

One typical training cruise of the period occurred in April 1947. On April 1, *Crescent* received a party of forty-six naval cadets of the senior term, along with three of their instructors. At the same time, thirty-seven cadets of the junior term and three instructors boarded *Uganda*. The ships spent the next three days sailing near Esquimalt before returning for an inspection by the Minister of National Defence, Brooke Claxton, and a brief period of leave over the Easter weekend. On April 8, the vessels proceeded northward to Prince Rupert, arriving there on April 10. Two days of social and sports activities followed, including dances, boxing exhibitions, and basketball and soccer games. The ships then gradually worked their way back to Esquimalt, stopping at Alert, Oyster, and Nanoose Bays along the way. At each stop, training was undertaken and shore parties were allowed to explore the shoreline. On April 16 the ships returned to Esquimalt for a refuelling stop of only a few hours before proceeding out to sea, headed for San Diego. They arrived there four days later. The stay in San Diego lasted just seventy-two hours. Before departing, the cadets exchanged ships. The *Crescent* arrived back in Esquimalt on April 27 carrying the junior term cadets.

What is unusual about this trip is that a record of the actual training activities has survived. The cadets were instructed in their schoolwork, as well as in "technical training on ship's equipment, gunnery, torpedo, engine room and AIC [Action Information Centre], and practical work in parts of the ship." As well, "the cadets kept watch on the bridge, in the AIC and in the engine room daily from 1600 to 2200. When manoeuvring, they were allowed to keep station and con the ship." This practical work was considered extremely useful by the *Crescent*'s new captain, Acting Lieutenant-Commander J.C. O'Brien, who reported: "It is regretted that all the Cadets did not have a chance to do this owing to their numbers, as the feeling of importance and responsibility imparted by these simple acts is tremendous."

To provide the cadets with a complete naval experience, the ships carried out a series of special exercises. These included main armament subcalibre firing and close range firing at target smoke bursts in which the cadets made up the control and gun crews. The ships also engaged in surface plotting and in dummy blind torpedo attacks, torpedo firing exercises, officer-of-the-watch manoeuvres, night encounter exercises (during which starshells were fired), and the refuelling of the *Crescent* from the *Uganda* by the oiling-by-trough method. The cruise was considered "a very good experience" for the cadets, although it was judged too short to give a good indoctrination into "general drill, boatwork, landing party and harbour drills."[15]

One atypical training cruise of this period also requires some scrutiny. From February 5 to May 17, 1946, *Uganda* undertook a rare, lengthy South American cruise. The ship was under the command of then Captain Mainguy. The voyage was a great adventure, for, as Mainguy reported, "to most of us [South America]

FIGURE 8 The cruiser HMCS *Uganda* in Uruguay in 1946. (CFB Esquimalt Museum)

was a rather a large piece of land with some mountains to the Westward, the Amazon, Inca remains, Rio and the Copacabana, and Cape Horn at the bottom end. We all learnt a great deal." Mainguy would remember the South American cruise as a tremendous success in terms of training and diplomacy. People in all of the countries they visited were anxious for "much closer ties with Canada" as a means to counter American domination of the continent. Mainguy believed that for this reason, there should be regular cruises to the region. He "suggested that Spanish should be taught in the RCN College," since it would be easier to learn and "would be of more use than French."

While on board, midshipmen "completed a course in Torpedo and Electrical Engineering and Engineering." They also learned about signalling, navigation, boat work, and watch keeping. However, there were some important limitations on the training opportunities. These were likely a factor in the navy's not returning for another extensive cruise to this region during this period. There were no shore-based training facilities, except at Stanley in the British-controlled Falkland Islands. Nor were there aircraft for anti-aircraft training or targets for main gunnery practice.

Another issue concerning training, which was often mentioned by other captains before 1950, was the limitations imposed when a vessel sailed unaccompanied by another warship. Mainguy advised:

> It is very strongly recommended that if it can possibly be arranged we should have at least one other ship in company. Opportunities could have been taken to exercise manoeuvring, throw-off and throw short shoots, night encounter, range

> and inclination exercises, torpedo control, etc. As it is, officers of the watch have had practically nothing to do, as we have normally been out of sight of land, and signallmen have no one to signal to. A destroyer, frigate or castle class corvette would be of tremendous help. Anything that can do 15 knots. She could refuel from us, if necessary.

Mainguy also provided some important insights into the nature of the postwar navy. For many of the 733 ratings who made up the ship's company, this was their first cruise and "the first time they have encountered such a variety of temptations." Yet Mainguy found the conduct of the crew to be "remarkably good." The only source of trouble was a group of about fifty, most of whom were getting out of the service. Mainguy urged caution in allowing any of these troublemakers to re-enter the service, which he "had no doubt many will want to when they had a taste of the rigours of civilian life." The fact that only twenty-three cases of sexually transmitted diseases were reported from the crew was presented as an example of the crew's good conduct. "Offhand," wrote Mainguy, "considering we have visited what is probably the worst part of the world for these diseases, containing very large numbers of good-looking and extremely willing girls, I should not be surprised to learn that we have set something in the nature of a record low!"

To keep crews happy and in order, Mainguy strongly recommended that officers act in a strongly paternalistic fashion and that the men be treated firmly but fairly. He reported: "Every effort has been made to encourage the men to think of the ship as their best friend, and when in trouble, doubt or difficulty to make for her." The only difficulty encountered was that inexperienced officers sometimes did not enforce discipline when dealing with minor infractions. This only allowed the men to commit more serious offences, which resulted in more serious punishment.

Finally, Mainguy implemented certain procedures for cruising in tropical waters that may have had some influence on the later incidents on the *Athabaskan* and *Crescent*. He authorized the issuing of beer rations and strongly urged headquarters to ban the issuing of rum, which he believed was the cause of most crime on board ship. However, he chose not to return to the prewar peacetime routine when steaming in hot climates. He reported: "'Tropical routine' is not necessary and has not been carried out. If men can work and fight in the tropics under wartime conditions they can certainly work in the afternoon in peacetime." Given that Mainguy's next posting was to COPC – a position he would hold from August 1946 to August 1948 – it is possible that his policy, instituted on the *Uganda*, became standard procedure on all West Coast ships and remained in force in 1949.[16]

While this is speculative, it is documented that in November 1946, during Mainguy's tenure as COPC, the captain of the *Crescent* requested a few changes in the ventilation system to improve the hot weather living conditions for crew serving in the tropics.[17] Apparently these changes were not made, since poor hot weather living conditions were one cause of complaint among the crew of the *Crescent* during her mission to China in 1949.

The West Coast ships undertook no antisubmarine warfare training between the end of the war and November 1947. No training submarines were available, and Canadian warships had no access to USN submarines or to training facilities. In May 1947, discussions with USN authorities in Washington led to the promise that the submarine that visited Alaska every two months would be made available for training at Esquimalt for a few days on each trip.[18] This promise was followed by discussions with USN officers and Admiral Mainguy on August 21 to establish the procedures for the first West Coast antisubmarine exercises. These exercises took place between October 30 and November 8, with *Crescent* and *Antigonish* using USS *Queenfish* as their underwater prey.[19]

During these exercises, teams from both ships and *Naden*'s ASW training school tracked the submerged submarine. The teams were under the direction of Lieutenant P.S. Booth from *Naden*. The *Queenfish* also provided an opportunity for six RCN officers and twenty men per trip to experience what it was like to be hunted while on board a submerged submarine. One exercise gave the submarine an opportunity to launch an attack on *Ontario* while the cruiser was being screened by *Crescent* and *Antigonish*. The captain of the *Crescent* reported that "the ship's officers and A/S team derived great benefit from the exercises."[20]

The visit of the *Queenfish* finally gave Esquimalt-based ships an opportunity to practise on a live submarine. However, before the Korean war the USN provided submarines infrequently. It appears that between December 1947 and December 1950, RCN ships had only twelve opportunities to exercise with US submarines, and one of these was an unscheduled encounter in which only one hour of training time was provided. Almost all of these ASW sessions involved practical training for students finishing their TD (torpedo detector) course at *Naden*. Only three of the missions involved firing antisubmarine weapons, including hedgehogs and depth charges. On four occasions RCN vessels had an opportunity to work with USN aircraft in a combined hunter-killer exercise. There were limited opportunities for ship's personnel to practise their submarine tracking skills while the trainees completed their courses.

Only twice did crews have an opportunity to practise their own ASW skills in an operational exercise. The first of these occurred during the joint RCN/RN exercises in the Caribbean in the spring of 1949. On March 30, *Athabaskan* and *Antigonish* joined with other Canadian and British destroyers and frigates in forming an ASW screen around the carrier HMCS *Magnificent*, the cruiser HMS *Jamaica*, and RFA *Cold Ranger*. For thirty hours the submarine HMS *Tudor* attempted to break through the defences.

The second opportunity to test ASW combat skills took place on May 16–17, 1950. This was the largest ASW exercise on the West Coast prior to Korea and the first to attempt to simulate the new realities of the Cold War. The first day's program involved the *Cayuga*, *Sioux*, and *Athabaskan* screening *Ontario* as the ships passed through a corridor of 20 miles in width and 100 miles long patrolled by USS *Ronquil*, *Volador*, and *Razorback*. The destroyers managed to successfully shield the cruiser from a submarine attack; the *Cayuga* detected and launched a simulated attack on the *Ronquil*.

The next day's program was much more sophisticated. The submarines were instructed to simulate a guided missile attack on the Washington coast between Cape Flattery and the mouth of the Columbia River. The three Canadian destroyers, supported by aircraft from USN's Fleet Air Wing Four based at Whidbey Island, would attempt to intercept the submarines before they could reach firing positions. Unfortunately, rough seas interfered with the sonobuoys dropped by the aircraft, and it appears that none of the submarines were prevented from reaching their launch positions.

On May 27, senior officers from all four RCN vessels and senior staff officers from the FOPC staff attended a debriefing conference on this series of exercises at Whidbey Island. It was the first time that such a detailed analysis of a sea exercise was undertaken on the West Coast.[21]

As with ASW, while ships focused on basic and nonsubstantive training there was little time for operational training to improve the fighting efficiency of the ships' crews. There were only a few substantial exercises in which the focus was on improving operational readiness.

In August 1948 there was a rare break from training cruises for a number of ships to engage in two operational exercises. On August 16 and 17, five ships were involved in Operation Nootka. This was followed on August 22 to 23 by Operation Soldier, which involved personnel from three destroyers. These operations were considered important enough that extensive reports on each were prepared for the COPC staff.

Operation Nootka was held in Nootka Sound, an area of small islands divided by steep channels in which the ships never had more than two miles of sea room to manoeuvre. The operation was intended to simulate one of the major security threats believed to be posed by Soviet forces along the West Coast – a surprise raid. The ships were divided into two forces: an enemy raiding group, consisting of *Antigonish* and *ML 124*; and the defenders, made up of *Cayuga*, *Athabaskan*, and *Crescent*. The *Antigonish* was to act as a fast enemy raider supported by a

Motor Torpedo Boat (MTB), played by *ML 124*. Their objective was to land fifth columnists, pick up escaping POWs, lay minefields, create alarm and despondency along the coast for a twenty-four-hour period, and then return from whence they came. The defenders were to wait in Esquimalt until they received a report of the raiders, supposedly from a patrol aircraft.

On his arrival in Nootka Sound at 0730 on August 16, Lieutenant-Commander C. Anthony Law, the captain of the *Antigonish,* set up an intricate trap for the approaching defending force. He landed four teams, equipped with radios, in strategic positions around the sound so that "they would keep the raider constantly informed of all movements of any pursuers." The radio teams were instructed to operate on frequencies usually used by fishing boats. Each radio party and ship was given a code name that sounded like the name of a fishing boat, like *Tuna King* or *Mary Ann*.

A party of fifth columnists then took over San Rafael Lighthouse and the nearby village of Friendly Cove. The fifth columnists used government telephones to convince Estevan Lighthouse and Refuge Cove that the *Antigonish* was a friendly vessel and that the three approaching destroyers were the enemy. Meanwhile, *Antigonish* laid a simulated minefield at the entrance to Plumper Harbour and landed a party with a smudge pot on a nearby island. The smudge pot was to be lit in an effort to draw the unsuspecting defenders through the minefield. As this was going on, *ML 124* laid a second minefield at Tsowin Narrows to guard *Antigonish*'s escape route.[22] The motor vessel then found "a drydock-like cove in the south-western end of Jewitt Cove in Strange Island" in order to lie in ambush for any approaching destroyer.

At 0730 the following day the three destroyers were spotted approaching the sound. Despite approaching cautiously and sending in their motor launches to scout ahead, the attackers soon fell into the carefully laid traps. The *Crescent* ran into the first minefield and judged herself to be badly damaged. Then just after 1030, the destroyers unknowingly approached the MTB's hiding place. The executive officer of *ML 124*, a young RCNR midshipman named T.W. Creery, recounted what then unfolded:

> All signals were now being sent to the fish boat *Hecate* (code word for *ML 124*) who was preparing to torpedo the enemy the moment he should come in sight. We in *Hecate* waited as the moment seemed minutes. Then a lot of things happened at once. *Cooperator* (code word for a radio team) reported *Cranker* (code word for *Crescent*) to be passing between Strange and Canal Islands. The time was 1043. Then the lookout on our foc'sle sighted *Cranker*. Slowly she crept into view. We fired a green very's light and our torpedo was away. Then two more light and the enemy had been struck and was sinking. At high speed we dashed out so

> as not to remain a sitting duck in case he should use his close range armament on us. Quickly we signalled *"you have been sunk return to rendezvous." Crescent* made no reply and we sped away past her stern. She had had no lookout on the fo'c'sle [*sic*] while coming up the channel and indeed our torpedo must have struck her just as she sighted us, so that she was unable to fire any of her armament at us even though it was trained in our direction.[23]

Just six minutes after being torpedoed, the luckless *Crescent* sailed past the concealed *Antigonish* and was subject to fire from point blank range of 900 yards. The destroyer was now considered by the raiders to have been sunk "for the second if not the third time."

Antigonish spent the next two hours in a cat-and-mouse game with *Athabaskan* and *Cayuga*. At 1245, the frigate managed to draw the two destroyers across the minefield at Tsowin Narrows. The exercise then concluded. As the captain of the *Antigonish* reported: "Then we proceeded to Esperanza Inlet after having created alarm and despondency along the coast for a 24 hour period and then return from whence we came. (That is returned to Russia)."[24]

Although the destroyers disputed the scope of the raiders' victory, there was little doubt that the smaller vessels had humiliated the defenders. However, the captains all agreed that operational training was sorely needed and that exercises like Operation Nootka were invaluable. Lieutenant-Commander Law reported that "this is the most successful exercise HMCS *Antigonish* has taken part in. It is a great up lift in the ship's morale, also since *Antigonish* has joined the 2nd Destroyer Division the morale and efficiency has gone to a new high with a new spirit of enthusiasm."[25] Commander O.C.S. Robertson, captain of the *Cayuga* and commander of Canadian Destroyer Division, West Coast, concluded:

> It is considered that the operation was eminently successful in that mistakes in tactics, employment of forces in coastal and inland waters and the standards and efficiency required in a task force were sharply brought home to all who participated. The lessons learned have brought forward a genuine desire on the part of the officers and men to improve the fighting efficiency of their ship, and of the Division and a healthy spirit of competition within the Division to produce the most efficient ship.
>
> It is considered that operations of this type produce a measuring rod against which our normal routine training can be checked.[26]

The second exercise, Operation Soldier, was intended to test the ability of the *Cayuga*, *Athabaskan*, and *Crescent* to land a force of sailors, who were ordered to dislodge an imaginary enemy force landed by a raider in the vicinity of Naden

FIGURE 9 The River-class frigate HMCS *Antigonish*, circa 1949, one of the few warships remaining in commission on the West Coast after the end of the war in 1945. (CFB Esquimalt Museum)

harbour. The exercise degenerated into a farce as soon as the sailors touched shore several miles from the harbour. Almost immediately, one platoon and a company commander became separated from the main force, not to be seen again until they were rescued from a beach by ship's boats. The main force's compasses, apparently purchased from Woolworth, failed, and the portable radios proved useless. The landing party continued, trying to navigate by the sun (which often disappeared behind clouds), by sending men up trees to survey the lay of the land, and by examining the moss on trees to determine north. Needless to say, the main force was soon hopelessly lost in the woods. After more than five hours stumbling through the thick underbrush, the increasingly exhausted sailors managed to attract the attention of a hunter by firing shots into the air. The hunter directed them to a small bay northeast of George Point, several miles from their intended objective. They were then able to hail one of the ship's motor cutters, which rescued them and carried them the rest of the way to the base camp at Naden harbour. They were not the last to arrive: one section was only found at 2030 in the evening, having been lost in the woods for almost eleven hours.

The report of Lieutenant J.S. Gill of the *Cayuga* conveys the depth of the fiasco:

> Of the lessons learned, the one most firmly impressed on number one section was that reliable equipment, especially compasses, is essential for such a type of landing operation. It is felt too that there was insufficient briefing and too little information given to the men. Maps of the area of operation should be issued to each body of men that is advancing independently, in this case each section. It is my opinion that such a large scale landing operation should not have been attempted without previous training. I felt the degree of fatigue was so great that had the camp been attacked the night of our arrival the resistance we could offer would not have been of the desired calibre.[27]

While Operation Soldier was a debacle, no one begrudged the opportunity to improve the operational efficiency of the crews. It was well recognized that the dearth of opportunities to engage in realistic operational exercises had a profoundly negative effect on the morale of ships' companies prior to the Korean War. The focus on basic training meant that RCN warships were not usually ready for operational deployments, but between the end of the Second World War and the beginning of the Korean War, only once was a ship sent into a potential combat situation: the *Crescent*, on its turbulent mission to China in 1949. *Crescent*, along with the other ships in Pacific Command, was just about to leave for joint exercises in the Caribbean with Halifax-based RCN and RN warships (see below) and was, therefore, far more ready for a prolonged operation than she would have been at any other time. The decision by the Department of External Affairs to ask the navy to send the ship to China was made very quickly, in large part because the department knew that Pacific Command's ships were about to sail and that any delay would have meant that no vessel was available for the mission.

Note that immediately after the incidents on the *Athabaskan* and *Crescent* in February and March 1949, both ships were given the opportunity to engage in operational training. The captains of both ships noted a marked improvement in the behaviour of their crews when they had a chance to practise their skills and compete with other ships in environments that simulated wartime operations.

Lieutenant-Commander D.W. Groos, the captain of the *Crescent*, in the weeks after the mutiny on his ship, made a special point of taking every opportunity to participate in exercises and practices to increase "the confidence and pride the Men have in their weapons and their ship."[28] After the incident in Nanking, *Crescent* sailed to Hong Kong at the end of March and was almost immediately called upon to participate in Operation "Lancer," a joint RN, RAF, and British army exercise to test the defences of the Crown colony. By early April, the ship was at dockside in Hong Kong, where the crew enjoyed a three-week dose of unrestricted shore leave, an active sports program, and a well-managed program of ship's maintenance. He observed that in the month after the incident on board his ship, "during the month, circumstances, weather, practices and events have combined to effect a general heightening of ship's spirit. It has become noticeable in walking around the ship. The equipment shines, the men are content and their efficiency is rising to a marked degree. I am very happy indeed with the way things have progressed on all counts."[29]

Crescent also supported British ships involved in attempting to rescue HMS *Amethyst*, which had been trapped by Chinese Communist guns on the Yangtze River. This was the closest a Canadian warship came to combat between 1945 and the Korean War. When word reached Hong Kong of the *Amethyst*'s plight on April 20, Groos, on his own initiative, cancelled an impending port visit to Manila and placed his ship at the disposal of the British Admiral in command of RN forces in the region. Groos reported: "The Ship's Company was obviously pleased when I informed them that I had done this. They now feel quite a bond

FIGURE 10 The destroyer HMCS *Crescent*, circa 1948–49. She was usually the only destroyer in commission in the Pacific from 1946 to 1949. (CFB Esquimalt Museum)

of fellowship between themselves and the other ships in the flotilla and it is evident in many ways."[30]

Groos's offer of support was made without the approval of either External Affairs, Naval Service Headquarters (NSHQ), or the Canadian Ambassador to China, who was now somewhat isolated in occupied Nanking. After an initial attempt to rescue *Amethyst* failed, with another RN warship fired upon and damaged, it became clear that his ship might be drawn into an "imperial" war, and Groos sought clarification from Ottawa. Fortunately, no clarification was needed, since the British admiral was well aware that he did not have the authority to send the Canadian ship into harm's way. The admiral even rejected Groos's offer to loan a Chinese Canadian naval reserve officer to act as a negotiator with the Communists, because without permission from Ottawa he could not send even a single Canadian sailor into danger. Well aware of the slow pace of political, diplomatic, and naval decision making, the admiral informed Groos that by the time he received permission from Ottawa, "*Amethyst*, and all those surviving on her would be beyond help."[31]

After some procrastination in Ottawa, *Crescent* was ordered back to Esquimalt in early May. Ottawa's decision was only partly motivated by the Canadian ambassador's belief that her help was not needed to evacuate Canadians from China. NSHQ also pressed for the ship's early return so as not to risk the fragile happiness of the crew by constantly changing their departure date, by the need to have the ship available for the summer training session, and by the desire to have members of the crew available to testify before the Mainguy Commission. *Crescent* arrived back to a hero's welcome at Esquimalt on June 4. Her ambiguous mission of rescuing Canadians remained unfulfilled, except for a dog owned by a Canadian diplomat. The government was fortunate it was not *Crescent* trapped on the Yangtze, for that would have provoked a far greater political crisis than had been posed by the "mutinies" onboard RCN vessels. Still, the mission had the unintended effect of turning the unhappy and near-mutinous crew into a combat-ready one, albeit far short of her war complement. This went unnoticed by the RCN (even though the transformation was reported by Groos); it was, however, noticed by one well-placed observer. The RN captain in command of the British destroyers operating in Chinese waters noted:

> On arrival on the Far Eastern Station it was realized that her ship's company who were practically all borne for training only were most inexperienced, and the same was apparent of most of her officers ... thus naturally to start with she was backward in most things ... By the time she left the station the whole picture had changed, she was smart, ready for action, competent at sea manouvers, and had

a cheerful balanced ship's company. The ship was as much liked ashore as it was by the rest of my flotilla and it was with regret that we saw her depart.[32]

Unfortunately, when this report was received in Ottawa, it was buried in Groos's personnel file, likely unread until it was discovered by Gimblett during his research on the *Crescent's* cruise.

The exercise that dramatically improved the situation on the *Athabaskan* was held between March 16 and 31, 1949. It involved RCN vessels from the West and East Coasts joining with the RN's America and West Indies Squadrons and some American vessels in the Caribbean. *Ontario* and *Antigonish* rounded out the rest of the Esquimalt-based ships; Halifax provided the aircraft carrier *Magnificent* and the destroyers *Nootka* and *Haida*. The British squadron included the cruisers HMS *Glasgow* and *Jamaica* and the frigates *Snipe, Whitesand Bay*, and *Bigbury Bay*, as well as the submarine HMS *Tudor*. For the West Coast ships, it was the first major opportunity since the war to test all their military skills. This included major ASW tests (see above), night encounter exercises, full-calibre gunnery shoots, and plane guard duties. On March 22, the *Athabaskan* had to rescue a Firefly pilot who had ditched his aircraft. Ironically, it was during these exercises that the *Magnificent* recorded the third of the "incidents" that rocked the navy in the winter of 1949.

Commander M.A. Medland, the captain of the *Athabaskan*, was given the opportunity to command a squadron of all seven of the destroyers and frigates. He reported that this responsibility "caused some headaches, hard work for communications, some loss of sleep and a considerable quantity of invaluable experience for several officers and men." Overall he judged that the crew's morale and efficiency had improved as a result of the exercises; he believed, though, that much more training time was required. For instance, while the Firefly pilot was rescued, it had taken far too long to get to him.

To improve skills was only one reason why additional operational training was needed. Medland argued that the RCN ships had barely had time get acquainted with one another and had not had the opportunity to develop really efficient teamwork or to discuss common interests and problems. Moreover, the ships of the RCN squadron had marked differences in routines and habits, "some of which were most noticeable and divergent." Unfortunately, he provided no further details on this subject. Finally, Medland mentioned that frequent changes in personnel and the reduced peacetime complement limited the effectiveness of all RCN destroyers.

In the months ahead, Medland would continue to cite the problems caused by massive personnel turnover, especially among seamen. In the two months after the return of the *Athabaskan* from her spring cruise, over 25 percent of the seamen left the ship, all but nullifying any performance gains from the Caribbean exercises.

In the autumn, Medland was promoted to captain and placed in command of the recently recommissioned *Cayuga*. Again, the drafting of a large number of personnel from the ship affected performance – a problem made worse by the fact that the ship was still working up. Medland stated that there were several reasons why men left the ship, including the need to attend courses, compassionate and medical leave or discharge, and for substantive and nonsubstantive adjustment to the complement. In November, 14 percent of the crew and 25 percent of the seamen were drafted away. A month later, ten men from the seaman branch, two from the engine room branch, and two from other branches left the ship. This represented a monthly turnover rate of nearly 10 percent of the total crew and 20 percent of the seamen.[33]

By the time the first three Canadian destroyers were sent to Korea in the summer of 1950, there was no improvement in either the size or the stability of crews. In the beginning of July, the *Cayuga*'s crew consisted of 13 officers and 197 men – almost identical to the complement born by the *Athabaskan* in February 1949. Before sailing for Asia, the crew was augmented by emergency drafts of 2 officers and 74 men. Only then was the destroyer considered ready for war.[34]

Relations between the RCN and the USN on the West Coast, 1945–47

After the Second World War ended, RCN officers on the West Coast anticipated a close working relationship with the USN. In October 1945 the Pacific Command, apparently on its own initiative, undertook a "complete changeover to USN Communications System." This entailed "changes in procedure, cryptographic aids and publication accounting procedures."[35] In November 1945 the National Research Council supervised joint American–Canadian experiments designed to help NRC scientists design a deep underwater target capable of being towed at high speed. A scientist from the USN's Radio and Sound Lab joined his Canadian colleagues, and the US Navy supplied a submarine and a patrol craft to work alongside three RCN vessels during the experiments.[36] This would prove to be the last joint RCN–USN operation on the West Coast for the next two years.

After November 1946, joint exercises and missions ended, and no immediate effort was made to extend wartime mutual cooperation agreements to encompass a peacetime environment. Contact with the USN remained very friendly, but officially, with limited exceptions, relations returned to those that had existed in the prewar period. USN vessels were treated as warships of a foreign power and were required to ask for permission each time they entered Canadian territorial waters. USN ships did continue to use the Esquimalt degaussing range to calibrate their antimagnetic mine defences. The only other USN visits to Canada on the West Coast were made while American vessels were in transit to Alaska or to provide ships (generally from the reserve fleet) with a friendly foreign port of call. Similarly, RCN vessels, while making regular visits to American ports for social purposes, did not utilize USN training facilities on the West Coast.[37]

Between V-J Day and the commencement of joint ASW exercises in November 1947, there were very few episodes of direct USN–RCN cooperation. On September 1, 1946, HMCS *Uganda* and *Crescent* were at Kodiak, Alaska, on a training cruise when the Commander Alaska Sea Frontier received a distress call from the tug *Apache*. The tug reported that it was towing a large floating dry dock and that in heavy seas, its charge was taking on water and was in imminent danger of sinking. The Americans requested that the *Crescent* assist the *Apache*. Despite heroic efforts by the crews of the Canadian destroyer and the American tug, the dry dock went down during the night.[38]

The failure to continue the special wartime alliance flowed out of decisions made at the highest levels of the Canadian government and reflected the uncertainty that existed in Canadian foreign policy in the last years of the Mackenzie King government. Jamie Glazov contends that after the war, the prime minister abandoned his earlier anti-Communist stance in the forlorn hope that the wartime alliance between the West and the Soviet Union could be maintained and that a nuclear arms race could be avoided. "King's concerns," argues Glasov, "led to a naiveté that distorted his relationship with the real world. He assumed a public posture toward the Soviet regime that was laden with contradiction."[39] So the prime minister refused to sanction the continuation of the wartime formal alliance with the Americans, even though this was a vital pillar of Canadian security in the Pacific.

This can be seen in the Canadian response to the request made by the US Army to conduct amphibious warfare exercises in the Strait of Georgia and the Inland Passage in summer of 1947. On June 27, General Guy Henry, the US Army's representative on the Permanent Joint Board of Defence, asked permission for the Second Engineer Special Brigade, along with elements of the Second Infantry Division, to conduct operational training in Canadian waters from April 1 to July 1, 1948. The brigade was based at Fort Worden in Port Townsend, Washington, near the junction between the Strait of Georgia, the Strait of Juan de Fuca, and Puget Sound. It had been given a training mission to operate its landing craft over long distances at sea, to be prepared for combat upon arrival, and to operate these units for protracted periods under field conditions. The War Department offered to make this exercise a joint operation with the

Canadian Army, since it was "believed this would assist in developing uniform methods and foster relationships of the ground forces of the two nations." Initial permission was sought so that an air and water reconnaissance could be undertaken, in order to determine sailing routes and overnight stopping points for the training program.[40]

The Canadian Chiefs of Staff considered the matter on July 30. They determined that Canadian service participation in the exercise would be limited to a dozen army personnel already on an amphibious warfare course in the United States and a single RCN liaison officer. Despite the lack of Canadian participation, the Chiefs of Staff saw no reason why the American training mission should not go ahead. They recommended that Brooke Claxton, the defence minister, authorize the preoperation reconnaissance to commence immediately, prior to approval of the scheme by the Cabinet Defence Committee.[41]

Claxton quickly approved the Americans undertaking the preliminary reconnaissance for the exercise, pending the anticipated endorsement of the whole operation by the Cabinet Defence Committee on August 12. The Americans were informed by phone of the minister's decision. They immediately began appointing officers to undertake the survey of Canadian waters.

At the Defence Committee meeting, however, the American operation came under unexpected criticism from Louis St. Laurent, the external affairs secretary. St. Laurent "expressed some apprehension that the exercise would give rise to publicity, and inquired as to the scale of the exercise and as to whether Canadian participation could be increased." After the Chief of Staff explained that the army had no suitably trained personnel to join the exercise, it was agreed to defer a decision on the American request until a special meeting with the Canadian members of the PJBD scheduled for that afternoon. The topic for this meeting was, appropriately, the sovereignty and financial implications of defence cooperation and planning with the Americans.

After Lester Pearson, St. Laurent's under-secretary, outlined Canadian–American defence arrangements, the discussion turned to the specifics of the Strait of Georgia exercises. Claxton, who had previously supported the position of the Chiefs of Staff, now made a dramatic about-face. The defence minister "expressed concern about the public reaction to US troops manning installations and carrying out exercises in Canadian territory": "At present, the Canadian people would not like to see US formations or units in Canada." The proposed exercise was clearly not a joint operation, since Canadian participation would be limited.

The Vice-Chief of the General Staff tried to defend the exercise, explaining that Canadian officers would be participating in planning it and that while there were insufficient trained Canadian personnel to participate, "full reciprocity existed with US forces in regards to use of facilities and the exchange of information."

After further discussion, the details of which are not provided in the minutes of the meeting, it was decided "that the United States authorities be informed that in the present circumstances the Canadian government would prefer that the exercises planned [for] Georgia Straits" not proceed as "obviously they were not a joint undertaking."[42]

The Americans were informed immediately of the Canadian about-face, and they promptly terminated preliminary preparations for the reconnaissance mission. The Americans were not happy with the cancellation of the exercise. The Canadian Ambassador in Washington complained to External Affairs that there seemed to be "some crossed wires somewhere in Ottawa."[43] To ease American concerns, at the next meeting of the PJBD on September 11, General McNaugton, the chairman of the Canadian Section, offered the full rationale for Ottawa's decision. McNaughton explained that the large population in the area in question was in itself a justification for rescinding permission for the training scheme. However, the primary reason was that as the "principles of joint Canadian–United States military cooperation were not as well established in the public mind as they some time no doubt would be, it was felt that on balance the manoeuvres might do more harm than good to the over-all defence programme."[44]

When McNaughton informed the Americans that the Canadian government feared the negative publicity if an exercise dominated by US troops were to take place in Canadian waters, he was being, to say the least, disingenuous. The government's concerns extended to operations that primarily involved Canadian forces. On October 30, NSHQ provided Pacific Command with the guidelines governing the publicizing of the first postwar ASW exercise with a USN submarine. The command was informed by telegram that "no publicity [was] to be given to these exercises and no broadcast navigational warning should be issued. Exercises should take place as clear of shipping as possible. A simple statement to the press on the same lines as for any courtesy visit of US ships may be made if you consider this necessary."[45]

It is a remarkable tribute to the US Navy that despite the Canadian government's refusal to continue wartime cooperation, it agreed to provide submarines for RCN training. Fortunately for the RCN, the Canadian government under a new prime minister would soon give permission to begin negotiations for a comprehensive American–Canadian maritime defence agreement on the West Coast.

Conclusion

From 1946 to the Korean War, the RCN in the Pacific struggled to rebuild the service after the rapid and massive postwar demobilization. The few ships in commission were almost exclusively involved in the training of crews. A lack of stability in crew composition, poor morale caused by the new rank structure, and poor leadership led to the brief work stoppages that rocked the RCN and led to the Mainguy Commission. Exercises were confined primarily to rather imaginary scenarios as such Operations Nootka and Soldier. On the rare occasions when RCN vessels had an opportunity to practise their craft in major exercises, crew morale dramatically improved. However, the continuing problem of stability and numbers limited the operational readiness of every Canadian warship.

3

Defending the West Coast in the Nuclear Age

BY 1948, THE Canadian military had begun serious efforts to develop its first national defence plans in light of the growing danger of the Cold War. Concerns over American dominance were quickly superseded by the acceptance that an adequate plan for West Coast defence had to include US commands in the western states and in Alaska. The first ALCANUS defence agreement, designed to provide a framework for effective US–Canadian defence planning, was signed in 1949 and expanded over the next few years.

But the RCN could not provide sufficient ships and resources to turn the broad outline of a strategic plan for the Pacific Coast into a workable defensive scheme. The Canadian government and the RCN emphasized their defence commitments to NATO. The navy's priority was providing ships to keep the Atlantic sea lanes open so that North American reinforcements could be rushed to Europe if the Red Army attacked. In the early 1950s, the RCN promised NATO it would supply its carrier and twenty-four ocean escorts on D-Day within twenty-four hours of a Soviet attack. The navy also committed itself to provide a further two cruisers and eighteen escorts within six months of the start of a war. Despite beginning a program of rebuilding wartime destroyers, frigates, and minesweepers into more modern escorts, and despite the construction of a new generation of cutting-edge St. Laurent-class antisubmarine vessels, the RCN could never hope to fulfill its commitments to its North Atlantic partners, let alone have adequate forces to devote to Pacific defence.[1] West Coast defence planners, knowing that in the advent of war, NSHQ planned to strip the Pacific coast of almost every available warship, turned to desperate and unworkable schemes. For instance, the RCN requested that the army return to its traditional role of providing coastal defence artillery to secure the northern approaches to Vancouver. All of the Pacific defensive plans were exposed as unworkable and inadequate. Meanwhile, the RCN kept a close watch on potential security threats, both external threats posed by possible Soviet submarine operations in Canadian waters and the internal threats they believed might exist from Communist agitators.

The Creation of the First ALCANUS Defence Agreement on the West Coast, 1948–51

The Joint Service Committee, Pacific (JSCP), was responsible for securing "the fullest measure of co-operation between the Services and to co-ordinate all details respecting the defence of the Pacific Coast."[2] It mirrored similar Joint Service Committees established to coordinate defence planning on the East Coast and in Newfoundland. The JSCP was the primary body responsible for developing postwar plans for the defence of the West Coast, eventually including planning with the American armed forces. The JSCP consisted of representatives from all western commands of the three services and included as its principal members the COPC, the General Officer in Command of Western Command (GOC WC), and the Air Officer in Command, North West Air Command (AOC NWAC).

Postwar defence planning for western Canada began in 1948. Plans were drawn up stating the priority given to each area to be defended and the resources to be allocated for its protection. Some aspects of defence planning were decided by the JSCP in isolation from other bodies, such as the maintenance, for the time being, of the coastal defence batteries protecting the approaches to Esquimalt. It soon became apparent that it would be difficult, if not impossible, to develop a meaningful plan without reference to the Americans. The defence of Vancouver and the Esquimalt–Victoria area was listed as of primary importance, because of the significance of both to Canada, but determining the priority of other locations required consideration of American defence requirements. At the JSCP meeting on December 8, 1948, in which a scheme for defending ports on West Coast was agreed to, Major-General M.H.S. Penhale pointed out that Prince Rupert should be included as a class B port because "the United States places some importance on it for supply of Alaska." A lack of resources, however, meant that it was impossible to provide any meaningful defences for the northern port.[3]

By February 1949, the JSCP had decided that more detailed knowledge of US plans in the Seattle area was necessary in order to coordinate defence planning. The western commanders asked the Chiefs of Staff Committee to authorize the members of the JSCP to initiate discussions with their US opposite numbers.[4] On April 28, the committee met to discuss the Pacific Coast Emergency Plan, which had been approved by the COS's Joint Planning Committee. Prior to the meeting, the JSCP had asked whether this approval of the plan by the Planning Committee meant that the western services commanders were authorized to begin discussions with their US opposite numbers at a working level. The Chief of Staff replied that it did not, but "it was felt [by the Pacific committee] that such arrangements were necessary, and the Committee instructed the secretary to request clearance so that Canadian and US commanders on the Pacific Coast could discuss their [defence] arrangements."[5]

Not until the spring of 1949 did the JSCP finally receive preliminary permission from the Chiefs of Staff Committee (CSC) to begin joint defence planning with the American armed forces responsible for West Coast and Alaskan defence. This change in policy is undoubtedly linked directly to Louis St. Laurent's becoming prime minister and the consequent dramatic shift in foreign policy. Canada's decision to become a founding member of the North Atlantic Alliance is the best known of Canada's decisions that marked the nation's resolve to join in the Cold War. But equally important steps were taken to defend the North American continent. At the end of the Second World War, both Canada and the United States recognized that the wartime continental defence plan (ABC-22) required significant revision. In March 1946, the US Joint Chiefs of Staff and the Canadian CSC created a combined US–Canadian planning body to create the new defence scheme; this committee eventually become known as the Military Co-operation Committee (MCC). It took the MCC two years to create a basic security plan, MCC 100/1. To provide a more detailed plan in the event of a future war, the MCC quickly followed up MCC 100/1 with a new Emergency Defence Plan. The Emergency Defence Plan, MCC 300/1, was completed and approved by both governments on March 25, 1949. Included in MCC 300/1 were various appendices designed to provide specific details of each aspect of the plan. Appendix E authorized regional operational commands "to prepare such combined plans as were necessary to execute operations implicit in the tasks of the overall Emergency Defence Plan."[6]

Once the details of MCC 300/1 were circulated to operational commands, the COS authorized the various regional planning committees, including the JSCP, to commence discussions with their American counterparts. The American and Canadian operational commanders on the West Coast viewed it as urgent to create a West Coast regional defence plan – a task that had long been delayed. Largely, this reflected the appreciation that the region faced a credible military threat. The primary concern was the USSR's Far Eastern Fleet. In October 1948 the MCC produced an agreed estimate of the military threat to the continent, "Soviet Capabilities and Probable Courses of Action Against Canada, the United States and the Areas Adjacent Thereto." The document estimated there were 50 ocean patrol and 45 coastal submarines in the USSR's Far Eastern Fleet. This would allow the Soviets to keep 23 submarines on patrol stations, attacking shipping, mining approaches to ports, and so on. The same document speculated that Soviet forces might take action in the Aleutian Islands or Alaska.[7]

On September 7, at McChord Field–Fort Lewis, Washington, the JSCP met with the commanders of Western Sea Frontier, the 6th US Army Group, and representatives of the US Air Force. The committee was introduced to the document ALCANUS-EDP-49, the outline of an Alaska–Canada–US emergency defence plan, as envisioned by HQ 6 US Army Group. "After a brief discussion, the committee agreed that certain changes and details might be required in the appendices." Discussions continued to integrate the various emergency plans of all the commands involved in West Coast continental defence. After a series of amendments to the draft plan, the JCSP approved EDP-49 on January 16, 1950. The committee, however, was not completely satisfied with the plan, largely because the intelligence estimates of enemy forces contained in it were low as a result of the USSR's having the A-bomb and "new major surface units."[8]

In fact, EDP-49 entailed no more than the American and Canadian commands crudely linking together their separate pre-existing emergency plans. Still, the document was an important first step towards establishing a defensive scheme for the West Coast. On January 10, 1950, the Director of Naval Plans reported to the Chief of Naval Staff (CNS) that "the purpose of the plan is to provide for the mutual defence of Western Canada, Alaska, and the Western United States against a common enemy and is based on forces currently available." The plan is basically divided into three combined tasks:

1) Defence of Vital Areas Against Air Attack
2) Protection of Coastal Sea Line of Communication
3) Reduction of Enemy Lodgements[9]

The RCN's specific contribution to EDP-49 was not outlined until an appendix to the plan was completed in March 1950. What is surprising is the limited naval resources committed to West Coast defence. None of the major fleet units – the light cruiser, destroyers, or frigates – were assigned to the scheme. Instead, the RCN was only expected to provide for the naval control of shipping and local harbour defence. The control service consisted of a patrol on the Canadian side of the Strait of Juan de Fuca, with a single small striking unit, HMC *PTC 724*, and a single control vessel on the Canadian side of the boundary line. Harbour defences involved the laying of antisubmarine nets at Esquimalt and Prince Rupert. Minesweeping was to be provided by two reserve minesweepers. Two additional patrol vessels were necessary, one based at Prince Rupert, the other at Vancouver. An examination service was to be created using a fisheries patrol vessel. As for working in conjunction with the USN, the appendix simply stated that the "Naval Officer in charge, Esquimalt, will coordinate with the Commandant, 13th Naval District, who will take complementary action in providing Control Vessels and striking units on the American side of the international boundary line."[10]

The Creation of ALCANUS EDP-51

Almost as soon as EDP-49 was approved, senior West Coast commanders began raising doubts about the plan's completeness. At the first meeting of the JSCP after the naval component of EDP-49 was approved, Admiral Harry DeWolf, the FOPC, suggested that the committee should be doing long-term defence planning, to improve on the just-approved document. DeWolf pointed out that EDP-49 did not include anything about the long-range defence of the coast. The other members of the JSCP agreed on the need for long-term planning but decided that they did not have sufficient information to do so.[11]

This did not stop the RCN from continuing to flesh out the rather scanty details in the emergency defence plan. By July 1950 the navy, using its wartime experience, had created a plan for the Control of Merchant Shipping in Canadian Coastal Waters (CANCON) in the advent of war. The USN, however, had no similar system in place, nor was it clear who would be responsible for protecting offshore shipping that travelled through waters that the Canadian services were assigned to protect. These issues became the subject of a lengthy discussion at the meeting of the JSCP on July 7. DeWolf asked his colleagues on the JSCP, and the visiting representatives from NSHQ, to establish a unified Canadian position on convoy routing. These views would then be presented to the USN at a meeting on the subject to be held the next day at the Headquarters of the Commander, Western Sea Frontier, at Treasure Island, San Francisco. The committee agreed that convoy protection of shipping should follow Second World War models used in the North Atlantic and that they would advise that the United States adopt the Canadian CANCON plan for control of coastal shipping, since the Americans had no equivalent scheme. The JSCP also decided to take the opportunity to get information needed from the Americans in order to finalize the Canadian emergency defence plan. This included estimates of the volume of shipping to and from Alaska, and whether the USN would require that Prince Rupert be available in a future war, since at that time the city had no defences.

After the JSCP agreed to these points, DeWolf initiated a discussion that reveals the still embryonic nature of RCN–USN defence cooperation on the West Coast:

> The Chairman felt that the relationship between the Commander WSF and FOPC should be discussed at the Treasure Island Conference, since the Canadian area of responsibility in the Pacific is small and actually resembles a sector of an American Sea Frontier, except for the question of sovereignty. In this respect, Lt. Commdr Jones [from NSHQ] suggested that the feeling at Naval HQ was that local area CHOP should not apply to ocean-going ships. Clarification of this

problem would require a decision at the highest level. The problem actually to be resolved, in the opinion of the Chairman, was whether the Canadian Coastal Zone was to be a sector of the overall plan, or the equivalent of a sea frontier. This question was complicated by the fact there was an argument for common operational control of the entire Pacific area.[12]

Unfortunately, the details of the meeting on Treasure Island have not been located, but it is apparent that DeWolf's concerns about command relationships were addressed in part. On August 15, an annex was added to the plan which stated that upon implementation, after the start of hostilities, joint communications would be established among the following: the western area joint operations centre in San Francisco; HQ Alaska Command, Anchorage; the Joint Operations Centre Pacific Coast, Vancouver; HQ Western Command of the Canadian Army; and NW Air Command, RCAF, the latter two in Edmonton. Note that the annex's approval indicates that the JSCP intended to move the RCN's command centre and the RCAF's maritime patrol aircraft to Vancouver in times of war. This was in keeping with what had occurred in the Second World War. However, the re-establishment of a joint operations centre in Vancouver remained a point of considerable debate within the JSCP.

The same annex contained the first postwar definition of the Canadian area of responsibility in the Pacific. The CANFLAGPAC area went out as far as 54° 40′ North 140° West, then south to the 49th parallel and 138° West. The use of the American designation CANFLAGPAC for FOPC should be noted here, for it represents a further step in the integration of American and Canadian naval forces on the West Coast.[13]

By August, it was apparent that EDP-49 needed a complete overhaul. A series of discussions between American and Canadian staff officers took place for the purpose of drafting a revised emergency defence plan. The decision to begin a major renewal of the plan was inspired by the realization by senior commanders on both sides of the border that it was necessary to re-evaluate the growing Soviet naval threat, to provide for naval forces in support of army and air force efforts to dislodge enemy forces in Alaska, and to consider joint US–Canadian plans to provide air and naval protection for convoys in the Pacific.[14]

A draft of the new defence plan, ALCANUS EDP-51, was completed by March 1951. It provided "more details of operations and better and more current intelligence on Soviet capabilities in the region." For the first time, the RCN was committing itself to wartime defence; it also provided a timetable for mobilization. In addition to harbour defence, the RCN's responsibilities would include providing naval forces for convoy escort, ASW operations, and army and air force operations. For harbour defence, the RCN was expected to provide four coastal escorts by D+3 months, three coastal minesweepers by D+6 months, and one patrol craft. For the expanded responsibilities assigned to the RCN, these forces were to be augmented by four coastal escorts by D+3 months and one patrol craft. This shows considerable growth in the Canadian commitment, reflecting the increase in the size of the navy since just before the Korean War. Still, the forces allocated to West Coast defence remained relatively small, without a single major warship. They would require three months after the commencement of hostilities to become effective and six months to be complete.[15]

The new defence plan was an improvement over the previous one but still did not provide adequate forces to protect the West Coast. That was the gist of a memo written by Lieutenant General A.C. Wedemeyer, the commander of the US 6th Army, on March 14, 1951. Wedemeyer was critical of most aspects of EDP-51 and was particularly scathing about Canada's contribution. The RCN, Wedemeyer argued, needed to provide additional vessels to augment inadequate USN forces dedicated to protecting the sea lanes of communications to Alaska. The general wrote:

> Insofar as the RCN and RCAF are concerned, the plan for the protection of sea lines of communication covers the Canadian Coastal Sea Area, only. Therefore, further planning is required ... to define the responsibilities of the RCN and RCAF relating to the protection of shipping and long range maritime air-sea operations beyond the limits of the Canadian Coastal Sea Area, as defined in ALCANUS EDP-51.[16]

In Ottawa, Wedemeyer's memo went over like the proverbial lead balloon. It seems to have led to a lengthy delay in the CSC's approval of the plan, even though the American Joint Chiefs of Staff finally approved it in the spring. Only on December 8 did the RCN respond to Wedemeyer's concerns. Lieutenant H.G.J. Walls, the Staff Officer (Policy), concluded that while Wedemeyer might believe that the RCN's forces committed to West Coast defence were inadequate, this opinion was not shared by the FOPC. After all, Walls concluded, "regardless of how plans are made we cannot grow ships on trees. Therefore, we cannot make a reply to the US general's concerns."[17]

However, Captain A.H.G. Storrs, the naval member on the Joint Planning Committee (JPC), disagreed with Walls's conclusion. On December 13, Storrs urged the JPC to take a different tack in replying to Wedemeyer's letter. He suggested that the general be informed that, as with the USN, the forces available to the FOPC were also inadequate. Storrs, though, wanted to offer some hope that the RCN could make a more meaningful contribution to Pacific defence in the not too distant future. He wrote that Wedemeyer should be informed that

> The RCN agree with this statement and are taking steps, as far as is possible within the limitations of the approved Four-Year Programme to augment the forces available to the Pacific Coast. These forces by 1954 will be augmented by 2 coastal escorts, 4 patrol craft and 4 coastal minesweepers. It is proposed that the RCN take unilateral action in this matter to make available to the Flag Officer Pacific the forecast of these increased availabilities.

Storrs realized that even this expanded force would be inadequate to safeguard the Pacific area, but that this was all Canada could provide in the next five years. The FOPC should therefore be instructed to so inform his American counterparts.[18]

On January 10, 1952, the JPC sent a memorandum to the Chiefs of Staff Committee urging it to quickly approve EDP-51, particularly since the Americans had already done so. The committee also suggested that Storrs's suggested increase in naval forces committed to Pacific defence also be approved forthwith.[19]

The response of the chairman of the CSC to the JPC reflected the difficulties of providing even a marginally adequate force to provide for Pacific coast security at a time when priority had been given to supplying forces to meet NATO commitments. On March 22 the JPC was informed that the chairman of the CSC was disturbed by its proposal that additional forces be provided to the FOPC under EDP-51. Colonel R.L. Raymont, the CSC secretary, explained to the JCS:

> It is pointed out that the D plus 180 commitments for CUSRPG 1954, for both Atlantic and Pacific Coasts, already total 25 coastal escorts and 14 coastal minesweepers which are the total number of coastal minesweepers and escorts that have been authorized by the Government in the RCN phased build-up programme. Because of this, it is obvious that the additional escorts, minesweepers, and patrol vessels cannot be made available unless they are taken from the Atlantic Coast.

Storrs's proposal to reallocate forces to the Pacific had been noticed by Canada's defence minister. Raymont informed the JPC that "the Minister has instructed that Canadian Planners, particularly when drawing up plans with other nations, must not agree to a plan which requires more forces to implement than those which the Canadian Government has already authorized in the Service phased build-up programme."[20]

The CSC finally approved EDP-51 in early 1952, but without the additional forces the JPC had recommended. Well before the CSC's action, however, the FOPC's staff and related army and air force officers were engaged in making detailed plans for defending the West Coast.

Coastal Defence Planning, 1950–54

Even while the specifics of a working relationship with the American forces were being worked out, the FOPC's staff were trying to deal with the almost insoluble issue of how to defend the West Coast. On May 16, 1950, the CSC assigned the FOPC overall responsibility for planning the coastal and seaward defence of Canada's West Coast.[21] The problem confronting naval planners was how to defend that coast with very limited forces, even as the Soviet threat in the Pacific was growing. One naval planning document written in the spring of 1951 explained that commitments to NATO meant "that practically all vessels of A/S value will be withdrawn from the Pacific Command in the event of war and the defences of such important areas as the Straits of Juan de Fuca and Yorke Island will be left to the care of small auxiliary craft." Even after the planned build-up of the navy in 1954, the total naval forces available to the FOPC by D+6 months were expected to be no more than four Algerine-class and two Bangor-class coastal escorts, three new-construction coastal minesweepers, and six new-construction "Seaward Defence Patrol Craft." Moreover, there is no mention of any Canadian air support being available.[22] So West Coast defence planners had to set themselves very limited goals, ones that would rely as little as possible on naval forces.

An intelligence assessment made in November 1950 indicated that a sea offensive against the West Coast of North America would pose a formidable challenge. Such an attack might include the following:

- Mining of ports and approaches by merchant ships and submarines on or before "D" day, and by submarine after "D" day.
- Submarine and surface raider attacks on shipping. It is estimated that 15 ocean-going submarines are now available for this work, and that many of these will be on station before "D" day.
- Long range attacks on ports and vital areas from submarines, some of which were fitted with equipment capable of launching both water-borne and air-borne guided missiles fitted with conventional or atomic warheads.
- Introduction into vital waters of atomic bombs by submarines or merchant ships on or before "D" day.
- Midget submarine attacks on shipping.
- Small amphibious operations to land sabotage teams from submarines or raiders up to a maximum of 50 men per vessel.[23]

The threat of guided missile attacks, which in the early 1950s were believed to have a range of up to 75 miles, and the fear of marauding submarines operating in the approaches to harbours, led West Coast defence planners to conclude that an outer defensive perimeter was required. Fortunately, the geography of the West Coast meant that the two most important areas, Esquimalt–Victoria and Vancouver, could be safeguarded by blocking the entrances to the Strait of Juan de Fuca and the Johnstone Strait. This had the added advantage of involving the Americans in collective security, since these defences would also safeguard Puget Sound.

An "inland sea" could be created by denying entry through the straits to enemy naval forces. In the Second World War, the entrances had been protected by "a constant patrol by air and A/S vessels." This option, explained a December 1950 FOPC planning paper, was no longer viable:

> In view of the width of the *Straits of Juan de Fuca,* the necessary air and surface craft to provide an effective patrol would not be available. Moreover, under stormy conditions and at other times when ship-borne asdics are not 100% effective, there would be no guarantee that submarines would not be able to penetrate such patrols and therefore, some seaward defences in ports within the area would be required.[24]

Since the approaches to West Coast ports could not be secured, defending the coast would involve restoring many of the wartime fixed harbour defences. At Esquimalt, this included the deployment of indicator loops, harbour defence asdics, surface search radar, shore batteries, and antisubmarine or torpedo nets so that they could be in service at the start of a conflict. Vancouver and Prince Rupert would have less extensive defences available on D-Day; secondary ports, such as Port Alberni and Nanoose Bay, were to be provided with no defences.[25]

The FOPC staff appreciated that securing the outer approaches was the best defensive scheme. If adequate naval and air forces were unavailable, they hoped that passive detection and defence technologies, combined with conventional coastal defence artillery, would be able to close the gap.

The key position in the northern defence barrier was Yorke Island, north of Campbell River, which dominated the narrowest point of the Johnstone Strait. In late December 1950, initial proposals for sealing the strait called for the laying of a series of detection loops and harbour defence asdics (sonar) to provide warning of submarines to an antisubmarine patrol vessel. A coastal artillery gun, either a 25-pounder or an old 6-inch gun, would prevent a surface ship from avoiding inspection by the traffic control service.

Sealing the Strait of Juan de Fuca would prove far more difficult. That strait was considerably wider and deeper and had a considerable current. The FOPC staffs were uncertain whether any passive defence technology available could substitute for a large naval and air presence. Initial suggestions included the laying of antisubmarine and anti-surface-vessel minefields between Otter Point, on the southern coast of Vancouver Island, and Tree Bluff, on the Olympic Peninsula in Washington State. The planners proposed establishing antisubmarine nets and gates at both ends of the minefield to allow for the passage of friendly vessels.[26]

On December 19, 1950, Rear Admiral W.B. Creery, the FOPC, and his staff met with their counterparts in the USN's 13th Naval District in Seattle to discuss defending the strait. The Canadian officers confessed to the Americans that they had little technical expertise with either fixed detection systems or minefields, and they asked the Americans for advice on the feasibility of their scheme. The Americans informed Creery that while they too lacked data on the latest technologies, they doubted the effectiveness of either minefields or indicator loops, because of the depth and current of the water and the ability of modern submarines to steer through minefields.[27]

Creery was surprised by the Americans' information, and he asked NSHQ to have its technical experts assess the planned defensive scheme. In early January 1951, Creery received two reports that confirmed his worst fears. Commander J.P. Singleton, the Director of Seaward Defence, reported that while loops or harbour defence asdics (sonar) could be laid in the Strait of Juan de Fuca, "the chances of detection, due to the broad front, depth and tidal effect [*sic*] do not warrant the expenditure involved." Mines would be equally ineffective, for they had only an 8 to 10 percent chance of sinking a submarine. Captain E.P. Tisdall, the Director of Weapons and Tactics, agreed with Singleton and provided details on the futility of mines. According to Tisdall, an effective minefield would require some 98,000 mines and cost $25,000,000. Moreover, it was impossible to cover the upper 75 feet of the ocean at high tide and the current made it impractical to lay mines at more than 40 fathoms. Given that the average depth in the strait was over 100 fathoms, a minefield simply could not work. Although Singleton held out hope that something called an "acoustic fence," then under development, might plug the gap, both officers reported that the only effective defence in the strait would depend on surface vessel and aircraft patrols. One can only imagine Creery's reaction – his command faced a classic catch-22 situation: NSHQ would not allocate enough ships or aircraft to control the strait, but its technical experts had debunked all proposals for an alternative defensive scheme.[28]

On January 23, 1951, Creery held a joint service meeting to examine what could be done to defend the coast, based on the qualitative and technological limitations placed on his command. The officers at the meeting agreed that they would have to provide harbour defences for Esquimalt–Victoria, Vancouver, and Prince Rupert. The Johnstone Strait would be defended by an examination vessel, marine radar, and a 25-pounder. The gun would "function both as the Examination Battery and for close defence until such time as a more suitably-armed Examination Vessel could be provided, after which the shore battery could be withdrawn."[29] No mention was made of defending the Strait of Juan de Fuca, which presumably required further study.

On April 16, Creery felt compelled to tell NSHQ that adequate defences could not be provided for the West Coast. He stated that since practically all vessels of A/S value would be withdrawn from the Pacific Command in the event of war, the defences of important areas such as the Strait of Juan de Fuca and Yorke Island would be left to small auxiliary craft. On May 28, NSHQ informed Creery that while nothing could be done immediately about the lack of resources, by 1954 the RCN expansion plans called for four Algerine-class and two Bangor-class coastal escorts to be available on the West Coast by D+6 months. These ships would be rearmed "to make them suitable for their role." In addition, Pacific Command would have at its disposal three new-construction coastal minesweepers and six small seaward defence patrol craft. According to NSHQ, all six of the coastal escorts would be required to fulfill the RCN's share of the task of patrolling the Strait of Juan de Fuca, while the smaller craft could be used at Yorke Island and for coastal convoy escort duties. NSHQ bluntly informed Creery to expect nothing more:

> In view of the urgent requirements for Coastal Escorts and Seaward Defence Patrol Craft to escort coastal convoys and defend East Coast ports, which it is considered are exposed to relatively greater enemy threat than are the West Coast ports, it will not be possible to augment the forces allocated to your Command to a greater extent than is indicated ... for the first 6 months of war, nor can this augmentation be achieved until 1954.[30]

For Pacific Command, therefore, the issue became how to maximize the utilization of very limited resources. Key to this was sealing Johnstone Strait at Yorke Island, primarily through a combination of indicator loops to detect subsurface targets and a coastal defence gun to control surface shipping. One, or at most two, small naval craft would conduct subsurface searches to augment the loops and would be available to hunt down any submarine attempting to breech the defensive barrier. This would allow, as NSHQ required, the concentration of all coastal escorts in the southern approaches.

By the summer of 1951, however, the army was beginning to cast doubt on the plans for Yorke Island. In earlier discussions with FOPC, officers from the army's Western Command had indicated their support for mounting a gun on the island as long as a suitable weapon was available. In lieu of anything better, the navy agreed with the army that an old 6-inch coastal defence gun, in storage in Victoria, could be mounted in a pre-existing gun mount on the island. The navy even agreed to provide the heavy lifting equipment necessary to move the gun, which could be ready for action within six weeks after an emergency was declared. In August, the GOC WC informed FOPC that he did not consider the expense involved in providing the gun warranted.

Creery saw the army's decision as an opportunity to request additional patrol vessels from NSHQ. In Ottawa, however, staff officers saw something much more sinister in the army's desire to be relieved of its responsibilities at Yorke Island.[31] Commander Singleton expressed alarm that any agreement to allow the army to withdraw from providing coastal artillery on the island might set a "precedent" that would allow the army to shut all other examination batteries. This would force the navy to "create a fleet of *Armed* Examination Vessels in Canadian Waters." Moreover, Singleton believed that the lack of a gun at Yorke Island would reduce the effectiveness of asdic patrols, since ships would have to interrupt ASW work to deal with potential surface threats.[32]

This began a prolonged and often bitter debate between the army and the navy about who was responsible for defending the Johnstone Strait and, as Singleton predicted, about the continuation of all coastal defence artillery. The navy argued that the mounting of one gun on Yorke Island, even an obsolete 6-inch piece, was far more economical than being forced to provide the additional ships that would be needed to substitute for it. The army's position was that it had more pressing requirements than providing coastal artillery. In 1951 the two services agreed to continue to study the issue. After nearly three years without any resolution, Lieutenant General G.G. Simonds, the Chief of the General Staff, decided it was time for the army to get out of the business of coastal defence altogether. On March 31, 1954, Simonds told the chairman of the Chiefs of Staff that

> while I appreciate the Army's responsibilities to support the Navy in seaward defences, nevertheless having in mind the considerable effort which this country has put into coast defences over the past many years without these defences ever having to perform a useful function, it is my view that we should endeavour to eliminate the coast defences to as great an extent as possible. Moreover, since Yorke Island is an isolated location remote from any harbour and in narrow

> waters, it seems to me there must be some more economical means of control than the provision of static coast artillery of doubtful value.[33]

The navy's response to Simonds's broadside was led by Captain D.G. King, the Director of Naval Plans and Operations. In several memorandums beginning in June, King emphasized the vital significance of Yorke Island to West Coast defence and the important role that coastal defence guns would play. King also emphasized that any purely naval-based scheme of sealing the Johnstone Strait was uneconomical.[34]

King expounded on all of these and additional arguments against the army's plan to abandon Yorke Island in a thirteen-page report completed on December 2. King expanded on then current thinking about why it was necessary to seal the Johnstone Strait. It is interesting to go into this in some detail, since some of King's concerns are highly relevant in today's security environment. King pointed out that "a recognized threat in wartime is the attempted introduction into Canadian and US ports, by surface craft, of *weapons of mass destruction* and saboteurs or agents, especially in the early stages of war." A system for controlling shipping would greatly diminish this threat, and a coastal at Yorke Island was required for this purpose.

King, in essence, was accusing the army of shirking the coastal defence responsibilities that had been assigned to it by the CSC. Moreover, the army was failing to live up to the terms of joint American–Canadian defence plans, including MCC 300/6 and ALCANUS-EDP-52, which required that Yorke Island be adequately defended. King then provided a thorough technical, strategic, and economic rationale for forcing the army to provide a gun on the island. Since all frigates were required for duties with SACLANT, the only ships that could be used were Bangor- or Algerine-class coastal escorts. The former were being rearmed with only 40mm guns, which were too small to deal with surface threats. The navy was desperately short of *Algerines*, two of which would be required to maintain a constant watch – fully one-half the ships of that class available on the West Coast in the advent of war. King believed that using these ships in this way was a "maldeployment" of resources. He pointed out that the cost of providing additional *Algerine* escorts was "between eight and ten million dollars" and "that the costs of fuel and maintenance for two Algerines would be far higher than the cost of maintaining a shore battery." As well, the crew of a single *Algerine*, consisting of 135 officers and men, was far larger than the army personnel needed to man and support a coastal defence gun. Unlike shore-based artillery, neither *Algerines* nor even frigates were capable of blind firing at targets sighted by shore-based radar or observation stations.[35]

It remains unclear whether and how the navy and army resolved the dispute over Yorke Island. It is known that beginning in fiscal 1952–53, money was allocated for the harbour defences at Esquimalt, and later on some work was carried out at Yorke Island and Prince Rupert to implement the defensive scheme laid out by Creery in 1951. Yet most of the plan for West Coast defence, as inadequate as it was known to have been, was never implemented. When it next came time to visit the issue of West Coast defence, beginning in 1957, the nature of the threat, the resources allocated to deal with it, and the organization of the defences would be radically changed. These changes will be explored in Chapter 6.

Submarines Sightings and Other Security Concerns in the Early Cold War Period

While planning for West Coast defence had an air of unreality about it, there can be no doubt that the RCN felt there was a real threat to Canadian coastal security. In August 1950, NSHQ informed its operational commanders that reports had been received of "unidentified submarines in Canadian waters" and issued an instruction on how to deal with any such encounters. The instruction laid out specific procedures to be followed. If a submarine was sighted by a Canadian warship within the 3-mile territorial limit, the ship should first verify the submarine's position by all available means and make every endeavour to identify it positively and to take photographs. If the submarine belonged to the Soviet Union or to one of its satellites, the ship was to report the situation to Canadian Naval Headquarters (CANAVHED) and the appropriate HQ and escort it to nearest suitable port, using force if necessary. If a submerged submarine in Canadian waters remained unidentified, the warship was authorized to make every effort to force it to surface. On the other hand, if a submerged submarine was detected outside Canadian territorial waters but inside the Canadian defensive zone, NSHQ's policy was for RCN vessels to "track submarine as long as possible using asdic." A sign of the growing integration of Canadian and American forces in continental defence was that any indications of submarine activity reported to the FOPC were to be forwarded immediately to the C in C Pacific and to the USN's Commander Western Sea Frontier (COMWESTSEAFRON).[36]

In the early 1950s on the West Coast there were no verified sightings of unidentified submarines. Only three incidents are recorded in the files of the FOPC's Staff Officer (Intelligence). The first did not even directly involve Canadian forces; however, it shows that the passage of information between American and Canadian commands on the West Coast went both ways. On December 17, 1950, the USN's Commander of the Western Sector of the Western Sea Frontier reported to the FOPC that the merchant ship *Atlantic Star* had reported sighting a submarine. Subsequent searches by US aircraft had reported only detecting a Canadian corvette nearby, which perhaps had been confused with a submarine. The USN then called off the search.[37]

The Canadians replied that there were no Canadian warships in area but that the Department of Transport weather station vessel on Ocean Station Peter had not been far from the location reported by the aircraft.[38]

The Americans then received further information from the captain of the merchant ship. He denied that his crew could have mistaken what they had seen. They had sighted the sub when it was only 200 feet from ship, and the sub had submerged immediately after it was detected. It had been possible to make the sighting at night because there had been some moonlight.[39]

The US Navy continued its air search the next day, and the aircraft made two disappearing radar contacts. After some analysis, the sightings were judged to be of whales. Tragically, just after determining this, the patrol aircraft crashed into the ocean and the crew was lost.[40]

Five months later, the Pacific Command had its own submarine scares. On May 5, 1951, F. Corneille, Chief Officer MV *Imperial Nanaimo* and a RCNR lieutenant, reported to the FOPC that on the morning of April 10–11, while his ship was at anchor under Tow Hill, Graham Island, in the Queen Charlottes, he observed a suspicious radar echo with his type 268 REL radar. It appeared and disappeared and was never visually detected; it could be seen only on radar during his watch from 0000 to 0400. The target size and echo indicated a large iron-hull vessel 300 feet long or more. Every morning before dawn, the signal disappeared.[41]

The lengthy delay in reporting this incident precluded any investigation by the navy. The next report of a suspicious object received at Esquimalt caused more alarm. Late on May 22, 1951, a Department of Transport agent reported that a native woman in Clo-oose, a small community on the west coast of Vancouver Island, had reported seeing a submarine. HMCS *Crusader*, at sea on a training cruise, was ordered to race to the scene. The ship arrived on the morning of May 23 and sent a Lieutenant Derosenroll ashore to interview the women. The captain's report left little doubt that he believed it was a false alarm:

> Thompson a poor witness says object was about six inches in diameter and projected from 15 to 0 feet from surface. Object approached close to Nitinat Bar and then retreated being in site for 23 hours. Thompson's four year old child only other witness. Woman herself had no idea what it was but reported incident to other members of her tribe including chief who in late afternoon Tuesday decided it was a submarine and reported to another Indian in Cloose [*sic*] who then informed Dept. of Transport agent. Chief and other Indians seemed impressed

> with the results of their report. Movement of object may be explained by tides here yesterday. Do not consider that this could be a submarine. Am abandoning search and heading for Royal Roads.[42]

Threats of lurking submarines were not the only security concerns on the West Coast. As we have seen, the navy was deeply worried about both internal and external agents smuggling weapons of mass destruction into ports. The navy saw itself as having the central role in securing Canada and its allies against all potential maritime threats. The navy tried to keep close watch on and liaison with shipping and ship repair companies and harbour authorities. In the 1950s, the navy maintained a system of Merchant Navy Liaison Officers (MNLOs) at all major sea ports, including Victoria and Vancouver. The MNLOs were to operate out of reserve divisions and were to report on a monthly basis to the Staff Officers (Intelligence) at the closest naval base.[43]

In March 1951, the MNLO at Vancouver reported to Naval Headquarters that it was not the only government agency involved in maritime security. He informed headquarters that he had been briefed by Vancouver port authorities about a request originating with the Department of External Affairs. On January 10, External Affairs, acting on an informal request from the US Embassy, had asked the Department of Transport and the RCMP for assistance in defending American ports "against various unconventional weapons which might be carried secretly in merchant ships." The Canadian official was asked to provide the US Coast Guard with advance warning of any merchant ships from Eastern Europe and of "any vessels owned or operated by other countries suspected of carrying such weapons."[44]

The Department of Transport passed on the request to its local marine agents, instructing them to pass on to the RCMP any information about suspicious merchant ships that might be heading to the United States after visiting a Canadian port. The Vancouver harbour authorities, uncertain as to how to identify suspicious vessels, contacted the MNLO in Vancouver for assistance. He in turn passed on the request to NSHQ.

Naval Headquarters staff officers were deeply concerned about being left out of the loop. One headquarters staff officer commented:

> This is a subject in which the Navy is vitally interested and in which a considerable amount of research has recently been done. Had it not been for the close and friendly liaison which exists between ourselves and the Harbour Authorities, we might not have known of this directive, which includes only the Dept. of Transport and the RCMP. Although the co-operation of these two bodies may be most desirable, it is felt that the Navy should at least be the co-ordinating authority.[45]

The staff officer further complained that while the navy had treated the matter of unconventional weapons as secret, the Department of Transport instructions to its agents "has now had fairly wide circulation."

The RCN may not have been kept abreast by External Affairs of threats to North American security. However, it was keeping close watch over possible internal threats – specifically, on Communists and Communist sympathizers who might disrupt Canadian society. The Staff Officer (Intelligence) at Esquimalt issued regular reports on possible Communist activities and kept close watch on labour unions. On June 20, 1951, he issued a three-page briefing note outlining the history and current organizational structure of Canadian labour unions. Of chief concern was Communist influence on the trade union movement. He concluded his report on a hopeful note:

> The main Communist-line unions are the Canadian Seamen's Union, the United Electrical Workers, the Union of Mine and Smelter Workers, and the Woodworkers International Union. Although all of these unions were once influential, the Reds are gradually being eliminated by the union congresses themselves. The labour organizations have found that the existence of Red-dominated unions has proven a handicap to them in labour–management negotiations, and so they are systematically conducting a purge of their own. The CCL has been particularly active in "raiding" Red-led unions to decrease the membership in those particular organizations. The Communist and Labour Progressive Party influence on labour unions is waning fast, but the small core of Communists remaining are well organized and are still capable of a good deal of mischief in times of emergency.[46]

Concerns over union activity were not simply academic, for by this time the Korean War had started and the RCN had begun to expand. West Coast shipyards were being pressed into service to refit and modernize warships needed for the war and for training the enlarged fleet. Any potential labour disruption was carefully monitored, especially if it threatened to slow work on RCN vessels or might spill over to civilian workers in the dockyard.

On September 26, 1951, boilermakers employed by Victoria-area shipyards went on strike and began picketing the Yarrows and Victoria Machinery Depot shipyards as well as the government dry dock. The navy was immediately affected by the strike: a RCN minesweeper and gate ship were under construction at VMD, and the destroyer *Algonquin* was being refitted at Yarrows. Most important was that both companies were helping dockyard workers refit HMCS *Quebec*. The cruiser was in the first section of the government dry dock, with the Canadian Pacific steamship *Kathleen* astern. While most dockyard workers reported for work, the dockyard's boilermakers and welders refused to work on

Quebec, since this would involve crossing the picket line of their privately employed colleagues. The dockyard superintendent ordered them to work there or go home. The entire force of seventy-eight boilermakers refused, and all were sent home without pay. The situation continued for the next three days, even though VMD, Yarrows, and the dockyard employees in other trades crossed the boilermakers' picket lines to continue to work on the cruiser. When other dockyard workers began to show some sympathy for the boilermakers, they were informed that any sympathy stoppage of work would result in their immediate dismissal. All returned to work with "apparent enthusiasm." Even so, the dockyard superintendent thought it prudent to have all men working on *Quebec* clock in at the dockyard and then be transported by water to the dry dock, in order to avoid possible picket line incidents.[47]

The refit continued on the cruiser. However, all progress ceased on October 2 without the boilermakers. The dockyard staff would have preferred leaving the workers to their own resources; however, the cumulative effect of a delay in completing the *Quebec*'s refit would have resulted in delays in refitting the *Ontario* and *Crusader*. So on September 27, the superintendent asked Naval Headquarters for permission to have the work declared emergency in nature, given that union officials had indicated they would not oppose an end to the work stoppage if it were found to be jeopardizing national security.

On September 29, Naval Headquarters refused permission for the work on the *Quebec* to be labelled emergency work; it did, however, authorize the superintendent to issue the following ultimatum to the striking workers: "It is not considered under the circumstances there is any justification for the action of the dockyard boilermakers concerned and they are to be instructed to return to work or be liable to dismissal."[48]

The superintendent met with union officials that same day and passed on to them the ultimatum, as suggested by headquarters. The workers were ordered to return to work by the morning of October 2 or face dismissal. Despite this, the meeting remained "amicable and fruitful." The superintendent pressed the union executive to remove the pickets from around the dry dock because of its close proximity to the entrance to HMCS *Naden*. After the meeting, the ultimatum to the boilermakers was widely reported in the press, and the superintendent was pleased to note that it received no negative comments from the media or the public.[49]

On October 2, the dockyard boilermakers dutifully returned to work on the *Quebec*, although the strike by the shipyard's boilermakers continued. The superintendent was pleased with how the ultimatum had been received. The superintendent's heavy-handed approach might appear one-sided, but he had made it clear that his purpose was not to support either the union or the shipyard owners, but to stick to his agenda of ensuring that the refit to the cruiser was finished on schedule. As much as possible, he wished to keep the labour turmoil outside the dockyard. On September 29, to appease union concerns that striking workers would join the dockyard staff and to win assurances that picket lines would be removed from the graving dock, the superintendent agreed "that no man employed at Yarrows or VMD in last 6 months to be hired by dockyard." At the same time, the superintendent "politely refused" a suggestion by private yards management that all dockyard boilermakers be sent home for the duration of the strike. The superintendent understood that this request was intended to force the Dominion government to intervene in the labour dispute. On October 10, with the strike at the shipyards continuing, the superintendent turned down a request by Yarrows to dock a merchant ship in the dockyard dry dock because it was considered that the "action [was a] manoeuver to realize management's stated desire that Dominion government become involved in strike." He feared that picketing of the dockyard would result.[50]

The strike ended on October 20, with the boilermakers winning an increase in base pay of 30 cents an hour, bringing their pay up to $1.90 per hour. According to Rear Admiral Creery, as far as the navy was concerned, "the Boilermakers strike was conducted in an orderly manner with no incidents of violence and amicable relations was maintained." The refit on *Quebec* was completed on schedule, which had been the whole point of the confrontation with the dockyard workers.[51]

Conclusion

The re-establishment of US–Canadian maritime defence cooperation in the late 1940s led to the first of the ALCANUS agreements for West Coast maritime defence. ALCANUS clearly defined Pacific Command's area of defence responsibility, yet the RCN, which was fully committed to NATO in the Atlantic, would not even commit minimal resources to West Coast security until long after the start of a conflict. Lacking warships, Admiral Creery tried to cobble together an effective defence using minefields and other passive measures. He also turned to the army to provide guns at Yorke Island – perhaps the last time in Canada that efforts were made to incorporate coastal artillery in a defensive scheme. Ultimately, technical problems and the army's refusal to return to its traditional role in coastal artillery doomed Creery's efforts and left the West Coast without an effective defence plan. The lack of Canadian resources devoted to the Pacific did not go unnoticed by the American military.

Fortunately for Pacific Command, there were no reliable submarine sightings off the West Coast and the navy's principal concern was internal security. The navy's careful handling of the boilermakers' strike shows that the service's main concern was that labour unrest not interfere with important new repair and refit work.

4

Cold War Expansion

In the 1950s the RCN went through a major expansion and rebuilding in order to address the growing security threats posed by the Soviet Union and its allies during the Cold War. Given the state of the RCN in the years immediately after the Second World War, the navy suffered from tremendous difficulties in managing this expansion. The unexpected commitment to the Korean War exacerbated the manpower and training crisis that had gripped the service. But as this examination of the Pacific fleet reveals, the navy came through the difficulties of expansion and by mid-decade had laid the groundwork for a first-class ASW force.

West Coast Naval Operations and the Manpower Crisis during the Korean War

While the navy on the West Coast planned for a world war that would never happen, it had to deal with the real conflict that broke out in Korea on June 25, 1950. Just ten days later, on July 5, all three operational West Coast destroyers – *Cayuga*, *Sioux*, and *Athabaskan* – set sail for Pearl Harbor. They were accompanied for the first two days by the *Ontario*, which topped off the destroyers' fuel tanks on July 7 before returning to the West Coast for a training exercise. The destroyers arrived at Pearl Harbor on July 12. Two days later they left for the Korean area of operations, now transferred to the operational control of the Commander United Nations Force Korea. For the next three years, naval activity on the West Coast would be confined to training cruises and the teaching of basic seamanship and combat skills to reserve, UNTD, and *Royal Roads* naval college cadets. In effect, the entire operational force in the Pacific had been sent to Korea.[1]

Few ships would be available to train new personnel for the navy, despite the increased demand. The navy was faced with the dual problem of providing full wartime complements for the ships operating off Korea and training crews for the additional ships that were gradually being recommissioned from the reserve fleet or were being built to meet the already-agreed-to Cold War expansion of the service. The organization of the Korean War–era fleet was determined by the naval staff in the late summer of 1950. The government had authorized the navy to grow to 13,440 personnel, from a complement of only 9,500 at the time.

That summer the RCN brought five destroyers up to wartime manning levels. These included the three West Coast vessels dispatched to the conflict in July and two of the East Coast–based ships that were then working up to relieve them. This increased manning of the destroyers required three hundred personnel, and in addition to this, the navy was required to provide additional instructors for *Cornwallis*, to handle the intake of new recruits, and to provide more men for seaward defence. Recruitment between January and September 1950 was only sufficient to maintain the current complement; any real increase in the number of naval personnel would take at least fifteen months.[2]

As a result, there were few ships left in Pacific Command. Between July 1950 and December 1953, the FOPC usually had under his command the light cruiser *Ontario* and the frigates *Antigonish* and *Beacon Hill*. Supplementing these were the two West Coast naval reserve tenders, the minesweeper *Sault Ste. Marie* and *ML 124*, assigned to HMCS *Malahat* and *Discovery* respectively. The only significant addition to this occurred in April 1951, when the destroyer HMCS *Crusader* was recommissioned and joined the West Coast Training Squadron. *Crusader* remained until her dispatch to Korea in the summer of 1952, at which time *Sioux* replaced her.

The destroyer and frigates were formed into the Pacific Training Force, designated Task Group 214.6 in May 1952. The primary mission of the force was to provide basic training to UNTD cadets; and this task dominated the summer cruising schedule from mid-May to early September each year. Usually three groups of UNTD cadets were trained. The program generally involved an extensive period in Bedwell Harbour, where basic seamanship was taught, and a longer cruise, usually to an American West Coast port or to Pearl Harbor. The frigates usually embarked thirty-eight cadets, with the destroyer accommodating around seventy-five. When not employed in UNTD training, the ships of the Pacific Training Force were used by classes of the Torpedo and Antisubmarine School (TAS) and by other training centres at *Naden*, as well as to train ordinary seamen. The *Sault Ste. Marie* and *ML 124* were usually employed in training naval reservists but were often used by TAS for day training cruises.[3]

The *Ontario* provided seaborne training for officer cadets from *Royal Roads*, for short-service commissions, and for the reserves, as well as for sea training for new-entry ordinary seamen. At least one lengthy training cruise, either across the Pacific or to South America, was undertaken by the cruiser each year. From October 1950 to February 1951 the cruiser underwent a $300,000 conversion to an officers' training ship. The conversion took place at the graving dock in Esquimalt. Alterations included increased accommodations for cadets, electrification of the galleys, and the fitting of four 40mm Bofor quadruple mountings as well as a number of new single 40mm Bofor mountings.[4]

The ships were worked hard, now that training had become the principal occupation of Pacific Command's ships and shore establishments. The only other major activity at Esquimalt was the refitting and resupplying of destroyers as they rotated to and from Korea. The total scope of training activities is difficult to measure, but in the summer of 1950 more than five hundred UNTD cadets undertook summer training programs at *Naden* and on Esquimalt-based ships.

In 1952, for instance, the *Ontario* spent 168 days away from Esquimalt, this despite the fact that in January and February the ship was in the finishing stages of its conversion to an officer training vessel; it then spent most of March in a post-refit work-up. The frigates started the year with a forty-nine-day South American training cruise. On this cruise, the ships were fully involved in training three different groups of personnel. The *Antigonish* carried nine subordinate officers, who learned basic watch-keeping and navigational skills; eleven able and ordinary seamen for advanced training; and twenty-nine new ordinary seamen who were completing their basic sea training. On such a small ship, this meant that almost the entire crew was involved in instructing the trainees.[5] From May 16 until September 5, the frigates, joined by the *Sioux*, were almost fully employed in UNTD training. There can be little doubt that the navy was pushing the operational capacities of its ships well beyond any peacetime norm.

Commander H.V.W. Groos, captain of the *Crusader* when the destroyer was recommissioned on April 2, 1951, provides some fascinating insights into the state of the Pacific Training Force – and the navy in general – during the Korean War. The navy had hoped to bring the *Crusader* back into service in late 1950, as part of the first round of Cold War expansion. The outbreak of war meant that no personnel were available to man her, and in the late summer of 1950 the naval staff determined that her recommissioning would be delayed for "at least one year."[6] However, in February 1951 the need to provide additional training capacity on the West Coast during the summer season forced the navy to proceed with refitting the destroyer despite the desperate shortage of trained personnel. Captain B.R. Spencer, the dockyard superintendent, reported to the FOPC that the "outstanding event of the Month from a Ship Repair point of view was completion of refit and commissioning of HMCS *Crusader* early in April. After trials and minor adjustments *Crusader* is now fully prepared to take part in the forthcoming summer training schedule."[7]

Commander Groos was far less sanguine about the state of his newly commissioned ship and about its prospects for carrying out its forthcoming assignments. Groos's immediate complaint was that on his arrival on the *Crusader*, he had found the ship filthy to the point of being unfit for human habitation. He reported to the FOPC that "as an example of what we have experienced, this ship's heads were in a revolting condition prior to re-commissioning." When he complained to the dockyard's deputy superintendent about the mess, he was informed "that if Dockyard labour was ordered to clean them 'they would strike.'" Groos felt it was imperative to have the ship's entire advance party of crewmen spend their last weekend prior to the commissioning of the ship cleaning heads and wash places. Once they were done, Groos ordered all the toilets locked shut, to prevent dockyard hands from soiling them again prior to the ship's being officially turned over to his command. Groos warned the FOPC:

> If, in the event of mobilization, it is necessary to bring forward in a hurry other ships from longtime reserve using mainly re-entered personnel to man them at a high pressured Dockyard, I predict it is going to immeasurably complicate the problem of making them operational units with high moral unless more is done to clean the ships before re-commission. Canadians have grown to expect a high standard in their living accommodation.[8]

Groos was not being anal-retentive when he ordered the cleanup: he believed that a slovenly ship would prevent him from fulfilling his primary mission. He argued that it was "essential that this ship be clean and smart to impress UNTD cadets from whom it is hoped to obtain many RCN officers."

Groos also realized that a happy and well-trained ship's company was necessary, since "bright youths [were] unlikely to be impressed by any organization that is not as efficient as it can be made." He knew that maintaining high morale was going to be difficult in a ship that was both understaffed and fully committed to training young officer cadets. Immediately after the *Crusader* was recommissioned, he outlined to his crew its training assignment, telling them that "while not as glamorous as going to KOREA,[it] was an essential part of the plan to expand the navy." Efficiency was also needed, he told them, because "the pace of world events could carry us into war at any time when we would have to become operational immediately." He urged his men "to strive harder than might otherwise be expected to produce a smart ship."

There was no question that personnel problems bedevilled Groos's efforts to produce an efficient and highly motivated crew by mid-May. The obstacles included all of the manning issues that beset the navy in the early 1950s. One dilemma faced by Groos related to the structural imbalance that resulted when the defence minister compelled the RCN to make its rank structure conform to those of the other services; this created a whole new group of petty officers.[9] Morale on the stoker mechanics' mess deck was adversely affected because of the high proportion of Petty Officer Second Class and Leading Seamen Stoker Mechanics relative to Able and Ordinary Seaman Stoker Mechanics. The result was too many "*bandmasters*, and the junior rating resented it." Groos solved the problem by reducing the number of senior ratings permitted to give orders on the mess deck.

Groos also felt that his crew should have been brought together for at least a month prior to commissioning for "special instructions in the excellent school facilities available in both RCN barracks." As it was, officers who arrived on the ship prior to commissioning were fully occupied with getting it ready for sea. "As for the men," Groos lamented, "RCN Depot had great difficulty in assembling them until the last minute because of the continuing *tight* manning situation [with] which I am well acquainted." Even Groos was fully employed with duties at *Naden* until just days before the destroyer was brought back into service.[10]

Groos soon overcame these difficulties and was quickly able to bring morale up to a high standard in all departments, something he attributed to the excellence of his Chief Petty Officers and Petty Officers First Class. Yet the ship's small complement made it impossible for the *Crusader* to fulfill any duties beyond providing basic training to officer cadets. Groos recounted his efforts to exercise his ship's armaments in early May:

> Unfortunately though the very small number of men borne in the Seaman Branch makes it impossible to man more than two mountings at one time and even these cannot be manned at the same time as the Bofors guns or the TAS armament. The ship therefore is not able to produce a satisfactory action organization and any exercise of the armament requires considerable ingenuity to provide personnel to do it. [*sic*][11]

The personnel crisis of the early 1950s would continue throughout the Korean conflict. The primary responsibility for solving the situation rested with Naval Headquarters in Ottawa. Still, it is surprising that little was done in Pacific Command until the spring of 1953 to alleviate the manning and training problems faced by the navy. The replacement as FOPC of Rear Admiral W.B. Creery by Rear Admiral J.C. Hibbard led to a more direct action in Pacific Command to improve the situation with regard to manpower and training. Creery had seemed content to allow Ottawa to solve the manpower crisis; Hibbard brought an entirely different, more professional, and more activist management philosophy to the command. One of Hibbard's first acts was to hold weekly meetings between the FOPC and the Superintendent of the Dockyard (SUPYARD), the Commander of *Naden* (COMBRAX), and the Admiral's Chief of Staff. These meetings allowed Hibbard to coordinate the problems facing the navy on the West Coast.[12]

One of the first issues Hibbard tackled was the manpower and training crisis. In late January and mid-February, the naval staff issued two directives

FIGURE 11 Naval dockyard at Esquimalt, May 24, 1953. Foreground left, five minesweepers in reserve. Center left is the minesweeper HMCS *Sault Ste. Marie* (176), and on the far side of the jetty the destroyer HMCS *Cayuga* (218). (Courtesy DND)

concerning the severity of the manpower and nonsubstantive training crisis.[13] In response, in late April Hibbard created two new staff positions, Assistant Chief of Staff (Training and Personnel), and Assistant Chief of Staff (Plans and Operations). The new staff officers were assigned to coordinate operations, training, and planning between the operational command and *Naden* training establishments, ensuring that manpower was used as efficiently as possible.[14]

In May, Hibbard ordered the establishment of a Command Complement Committee to deal with manpower policy. He also established two subcommittees to deal with civilian and service personnel respectively. The subcommittees would vet any new requests for personnel or personnel reclassification and examine the existing organizations and complements within the command. Hibbard explained to his staff that these new committees were a direct response to Naval Headquarters' creation of a Travelling Complement Committee. That committee would have the power to determine both current and future civilian and service manning levels for all shore establishments. Hibbard warned his staff they "must be in a position at all times not only to justify new requirements but also existing complements."[15]

The setting up of these new committees and staff positions did little to assist Hibbard in managing manpower, at least in the short term. By mid-June it was apparent that one of the biggest problems facing the command was that it had no accurate data indicating whether the command was meeting its authorized commitments, or to forecast trends in time in order to eliminate problems before they occurred. As a result, there was no way "to keep the Flag accurately informed of all aspects of the general personnel and training situation in the Command in order that he may be fully informed when making policy decisions and recommendations."

Pacific Command finally began to come to grips with extent of the manning crisis in the summer of 1953, and began to take steps to improve the situation. There was a sense of urgency about bringing some order to the chaos, particularly since it was unclear whether enough trained personnel would be available to man the first new-construction minesweepers, which were due to be commissioned early in 1954, let alone the Prestonian-class frigates and St. Laurent-class destroyer escorts that would soon follow. Pacific Command tackled various personnel issues. One problem was the large number of able-bodied seamen who were not yet qualified to assume their duties because they had not finished their nonsubstantive training at shore-based training establishments. Hibbard recommended to Naval Headquarters that no unqualified able-bodied seamen be drafted to ships and that those already at sea be transferred ashore for the necessary courses. He also ordered that all ships and establishments "keep nominal lists for all men showing qualifications lacking for promotion, reasons for the deficiencies and the action being taken to complete qualification or obtain courses."[16]

Another major issue was finding enough qualified personnel to man the vessels being used for training; a related issue was finding enough berths for trainees. Various fixes were proposed, but few of these could be implemented, which further illustrates the depth of the crisis that gripped the navy. Commodore K.L. Dyer, COMBRAX Esquimalt, suggested that some training might be carried out on ships serving in Korea.[17] When this proposal went nowhere, Hibbard suggested that "the RCN had been generous in the manning of destroyers in Korean waters."[18] He directed his Chief of Staff to investigate whether their complements could be reduced without reducing their combat efficiency. It remains unclear whether anything came of this suggestion. Yet Pacific Command did find some trained personnel by carefully analyzing its own manning levels. Some twenty officers were found surplus to requirements at *Naden*.[19]

Pacific Command's efforts to improve manning and training mirrored the work being done by Naval Headquarters staff. While the crisis was not over, by the time ships finally began to come home from Korea and the first new-construction ships were completed in 1954, much had been done to alleviate manpower shortfalls. Personnel were available to man new ships, primarily at first from retiring older frigates and minesweepers. The summer of 1953 was the last training season for the *Antigonish* and *Beacon Hill* before their removal from service for conversion to Prestonian-class frigates. The work begun in 1953 would enable the navy to grow and to man the new ships, but personnel shortages would continue to bedevil the navy for years to come.

The Cold War Expansion and the 2nd Canadian Escort Squadron

The year 1954 marked a transitional period for the RCN on the West Coast. For three-and-a-half years, Pacific Command had struggled to provide destroyers for Canada's commitment to the UN forces in the Korean conflict and to build up a nucleus of trained personnel for the soon to be expanded Cold War fleet. Almost completely sacrificed in the process was operational training. While ships continued to be rotated to Asia in 1954, the end of active hostilities with the signing of the armistice in July 1953 allowed for the gradual winding down of the RCN's commitments there. The end of the conflict could not have come at a better time, for the first of a flood of new or rebuilt ships were beginning to enter service. On April 1, 1954, HMCS *New Glasgow* and *Stettler* arrived at Esquimalt after a three-week journey from the East Coast. These were the first of the Prestonian-class (converted from Second World War–vintage River-class frigates) to join Pacific Command. That same month, HMCS *Comox* and *James Bay*, new Bay-class minesweepers, were commissioned at Esquimalt. In May the minesweepers formed the 2nd Minesweeping Squadron (CANMINRON TWO). In November, HMCS *Fortune* was commissioned and joined her sister ships in the minesweeper squadron. That same month, the Prestonian-class frigate *Jonquiere* and the Bangor-class minesweepers *Brockville* and *Digby* arrived at Esquimalt from Halifax.

By the spring of 1954, Naval Headquarters had decided to create permanent squadrons for almost all major RCN warships. Squadrons were organized with consideration of both operational and mission assignments. Thus, the minesweepers formed a minesweeping and reserve training squadron. The *Bangors* were organized into the 2nd Training Squadron (soon redesignated the 12th Escort Squadron), which handled much of the Regular Officer Training Plan (ROTP) as well as nonsubstantive or trades training. In January 1955 the destroyers and *Prestonians* were grouped together as the 2nd Escort Squadron (also known by its USN designation CANCORTRON TWO), the sole Canadian operational escort group in the Pacific. The light cruiser *Ontario* was alone in remaining outside any formal squadron organization. This reflected the cruiser's lack of a wartime operational role; her sole purpose was to serve as a basic training platform for young officer cadets and recently joined seamen.

A detailed examination of the activities of CANCORTRON TWO from 1955 to 1958 illustrates the rapid transformation of the RCN during this period. The navy was finally coming to grips with its commitments to NATO and ALCANUS and with the revolution in technology that was radically transforming naval tactics and strategy. A striking feature of the navy at this time was that for the first time since the Second World War, it had sizeable and well-trained groups of ships ready for immediate combat deployment. Between March 1955 and October 1957, CANCORTRON TWO took part in twenty-five major operational training exercises. The nature of these exercises reflected the navy's rapid development and growing professionalism.

For the first nine months, the squadron existed only on paper; just two or three ships were available, and there was no group training. The rest of the vessels were either still in Korea, completing refits, being converted to destroyer escorts, or involved individual ship work-ups. Three of the first four exercises undertaken by the squadron show the navy reverting back to its pre–Korean War routine. On March 11–12, 1955, Operation Jack Pine simulated the navy's then current defensive plan of sealing off the Strait of Juan de Fuca from enemy submarines. The USS *Redfish* pretended to be a Soviet submarine attempting to penetrate the strait defences at the start of hostilities. Early in the morning of March 11, USN and RCN warships were alerted to the presence of the "enemy" submarine; they then attempted to establish, as rapidly as possible, a defensive barrier to thwart it. From Esquimalt, *Athabaskan* and *Jonquiere* raised steam and headed towards the scene of the last sighting. Also sortieing was CANMINRON TWO, comprising *James Bay*, *Comox*, and *Fortune*. All of these ships simulated the realities of modern war; after leaving harbour they assumed an Atomic-Bacteriological-Chemical Defence (ABCD) state of readiness, closing up the ships from possible atomic, biological, or chemical attack. The minesweepers were assigned to keep a channel through the straits clear of any mines laid by the submarine. The *Athabaskan* and *Jonquiere* attempted to quickly establish a defensive barrier to prevent the submarine from entering further into the strait. They were joined by the destroyer escort USS *Charles E. Brannon*. Overhead, maritime patrol aircraft searched for the submarine. The three ships began an extensive, but futile, search. One probable sonar contact was made by the American destroyer escort, but the submarine apparently escaped by diving below a thermal layer before an attack could be launched. The exercise demonstrated the near impossibility of sinking a submarine operating in the confused acoustical environment of inshore waters. Still, the captain of the *Jonquiere* reported, "much valuable experience was gained, attacking a rock pinnacle, patrolling and searching under adverse weather conditions, until *Redfish* surfaced" the next morning.[20]

That summer the squadron engaged in a variety of training and work-up cruises. Only in early autumn were most of the ships assigned to the unit able to exercise together. On September 22–23, the *Cayuga, Athabaskan, New Glasgow, Ste. Therese, Stettler,* and *Jonquiere* engaged in advanced squadron ASW training, using the submarine USS *Queenfish* as a target. Only the Prestonian-class frigate *Sussexvale* was unavailable. The ships were supported by Lancaster maritime patrol aircraft of 407 Squadron, based at Comox. It was the beginning of a long association between the RCN and RCAF squadrons.

Squadron training was then interrupted for two amphibious assault exercises, Sea Serpent I and Sea Serpent II. These involved invading beaches just a few miles from Esquimalt as well as Jericho Beach in Vancouver. The ships carried the troops to the beach for transfer to army Landing Craft Assault landing craft. The main purpose of both exercises seems to have been publicity, since both operations were deliberately staged in full view of the public. There would be no further such exercises in Pacific Command.

Instead, operations increasingly focused on the two key pillars of the navy in the Pacific during the Cold War – ASW warfare and a close working relationship with the USN's Pacific Fleet. From October 3 to 15, all available maritime forces on the West Coast except *Ontario* were mobilized for Operation Fullhouse. This exercise provided the ships of CANCORTRON 2 with their first opportunity to work together for an extended time. CANMINRON 2, CANCORTRON 12, and 407 Squadron supported the operations. "Practically every type of exercise was carried out, the emphasis being placed on Screening and ASW exercises."[21] During the first week of Fullhouse, *Digby* and *Brockville* acted as ships requiring screening from attack. Ships practised individual and group evolutions, gunnery tracking, blind and visual full-calibre shoots, night encounters, and many exercises in communications. In the second week of the exercise, the pace of operations quickened. On October 14 the minesweepers acted as the main body of an outbound convoy, protected by the ships of both escort squadrons as well as RCAF Lancasters. On October 15, all ships were subjected to air attack by Lancaster aircraft as they passed up the strait, acting this time as an inbound convoy.[22]

Captain P.D. Taylor, the commanding officer of 2nd Escort Squadron, believed that Operation Fullhouse demonstrated the great value of the group working together "in a fully operational role." He reported to Rear Admiral Hugh Pullen, the FOPC, that "the progress achieved has been noticeable and the morale of the ship's [*sic*] companies involved has increased visibly." Taylor argued that it was desirable that the group be kept together for the whole of the next year, rather than being broken up into small groups for other types of training. Taylor's proposal was warmly endorsed by Pullen. Over the next several years the squadron was usually kept together as an operational group.[23]

The RCN vessels would soon be given a much more difficult challenge: full integration into a major exercise of the USN's Pacific Fleet. The inclusion of RCN units into Pacific Fleet exercises was the outgrowth of discussions held in Hawaii in February 1955 between Rear Admiral Hibbard, then FOPC, the Commander-in-Chief Pacific Fleet (CINCPACFLT), and other senior USN officers. The Americans agreed to integrate the RCN into future "joint exercises," and Canadian officers would be given opportunities to take tactical command (OTC) of some of the units involved. Exercises were to be planned with the Commander First Fleet, who would be responsible for training USN forces in the Pacific.[24] The first opportunity to participate in a Pacific Fleet exercise arose at the end of July. *Cayuga* and *Athabaskan* were incorporated into Destroyer Division 152 during the first two days of REX 56A, a convoy defence exercise.[25]

PACTRAEX 56L, held from November 7 to 18, was a much bigger affair, involving all ships of CANCORTRON 2 and CANMINRON 2 as well as aircraft

FIGURE 12 The destroyer *Cayuga* in 1955 after conversion to an ASW destroyer escort. (CFB Esquimalt Museum)

from 407 Squadron. The Canadian forces were incorporated into a huge simulation of an opposed amphibious assault by the First Marine Division. USN forces involved in the exercise included two aircraft carriers (one operating as a helicopter amphibious assault ship), two heavy cruisers, fifteen destroyers, and dozens of other ships and aircraft. The RCN was warmly welcomed into the final planning stages of the exercise. Between September 19 and 30, Lieutenant-Commander R.K. Niven (RCN) acted as the Canadian liaison officer with the First Fleet. Niven ensured that the RCN was kept aware of the Pacific Fleet's communications and tactical doctrine. As well, he provided the Americans with details of the capabilities of Canadian warships. An appendix showing the operational capabilities of RCN warships was attached to the briefing notes for the exercise sent to all senior USN personnel.[26]

For the ships of Pacific Command, PACTRAEX 56L provided an unparalleled opportunity to engage in a major fleet training exercise at close to wartime conditions. "The purpose of the exercise, as well as improving the state of readiness of participating units, was to develop new tactics, doctrines and techniques. Particular emphasis was placed on amphibious–mine–A/S warfare, air defence, ECM and sneak attacks (underwater swimmers)." Most of the ships of CANCOMCORTRON 2 began the exercise by joining the screen of a slow group of amphibious assault ships. They then took part in a series of hunter-killer exercises to thwart the efforts of submarines to attack the invasion fleet. This was followed by a live firing exercise, simulating a pre-invasion bombardment. The final phase of the exercise involved the simulated ocean passage of the amphibious assault force and the assault on the beaches of Camp Pendleton.

The RCN personnel realized they had a lot to learn from the USN. Lieutenant-Commander W.F. Potter, captain of the *Ste. Therese*, reported that like Fullhouse, the experience was invaluable, and that "the added experience of working with a large number of various types of US Naval ships has done much to broaden the tactical knowledge and experience of the ship's command/control teams."[27]

The Canadian warships seem to have more than held their own, particularly the minesweepers of CANMINRON 2. The three ships swept half of all the mines cleared by the amphibious attack force, leading the USN to make special mention of their "ability and efficiency."[28] This was a good start to the very close working relationship that would swiftly develop between the USN and the RCN in the Pacific.

Although few of the subsequent USN–RCN exercises were as large or elaborate as PACTRAEX 56L, the ships of Canada's Pacific Fleet became far more comfortable in working with their American counterparts than with other elements of the RCN. This is understandable, given that only once during the decade – during Operation Springtide in April 1956 – did the Esquimalt-based ships have an opportunity to exercise with their Halifax-based counterparts. The USN welcomed the RCN with open arms, providing access not only to training exercises but also to fleet training facilities, such as the air defence simulator in San Diego. In March 1957, Captain Taylor informed the FOPC that the "cooperation and generosity" of the USN had been "almost overwhelming." Taylor continued: "Nothing we have asked for in the way of training facilities has been denied if its provision was possible. The understanding and liaison between the two navies has, I think, reached a very high order indeed."[29] One year later, Taylor's successor in command of the escort squadron, Captain M.G. Stirling, reported on the results of exercise REX 58J: "The integration of Canadian–US units was accomplished smoothly and successfully. Common doctrines were employed and understood by all units."[30]

Differences in doctrine, tactics, and communication procedures all were noted by RCN officers. The Canadians often found the USN's techniques and technology superior. Some USN procedures were adapted by Pacific Command. For instance, there were distinct differences in the approaches taken by the two navies in the deployment of naval aircraft. Captain Taylor reported after the REGSUBEX exercise of July 1956: "It was interesting to note the far greater degree of flexibility and 'self' control under which the United States Navy antisubmarine [*sic*] helicopters and fixed wing aircraft operated in contrast to the far more rigid control of aircraft by the Royal Canadian Ship MAGNIFICENT during the spring exercise."[31] RCN officers regularly commented on the value of operating with aircraft that had all of the latest submarine detection gear. After PACTRAEX 56L, Commander G.H. Davidson, captain of the *Cayuga*, reported on his experiences of working with USN antisubmarine aircraft: "I found the US Naval Aircraft operating with us in the Hunter Killer role to be particularly efficient and a pleasure to work with. They were equipped with MAD gear, which proved to function in a dependable, accurate manner under the conditions existing at this time and place."[32]

It is not surprising that commanders of RCN warships often commented on the need for their own navy to have similar air support. While the Esquimalt-based ships worked regularly with 407 Squadron, the air force's Lancasters were not equipped with Magnetic Anomaly Detectors (MAD), nor were they always available for naval exercises. The only RCN aircraft on the West Coast after 1954 were from VU-33, a utility squadron based at Pat Bay, now Victoria International Airport. The squadron consisted of just three Avenger aircraft. No Canadian ASW helicopters were assigned to the Pacific during the decade.

At the same time, the Canadians felt they had much to teach the Americans in return, especially in the field of shipboard ASW. A convoy protection exercise in February 1957 revealed serious weaknesses in the abilities of two divisions of

US destroyers. In the previous twelve months, the American ships had had only one opportunity to practise tracking and attacking a submerged submarine. Captain Taylor reported that as a result of this "pathetically small" number of opportunities to practise, the American destroyers' conduct during antisubmarine exercises was "not of a particularly high standard." The captain of the *Athabaskan* was more charitable, proudly reporting that "the RCN's standard of ASW training was equal to if not higher than that of the USN." Taylor explained that the cause of low standards of the US ships had been the lack of emphasis placed on ASW by the Pacific Fleet, a situation that was gradually being rectified.[33]

The Canadian warships were warmly received by the Pacific Fleet, largely because they provided a welcome addition to the ASW resources on the West Coast. After PACTRAEX 56L, almost all of the major exercises undertaken by CANCOMCORTRON 2 focused on antisubmarine warfare. Interestingly, one of the few exceptions to this was Operation Springtide, which placed a heavy emphasis on surface attacks.

The REGSUBEX and subsequent hunter-killer operational exercises of July 1956 were an important turning point in the transformation of the Canadian escort squadron into a force that specialized in ASW. Commander Philip Booth, captain of *Athabaskan*, praised the exercises as "a most welcome change on the emphasis that has previously been placed on Gunnery and Torpedo firings in the 2nd Canadian Escort Squadron." This emphasis had been wrong, Booth argued, since the primary wartime mission for all Canadian operational warships, including the Tribal-class destroyers, was ASW. "Therefore the Command must be trained to carry out all phases of A/S Warfare, whether it be close A/S attacks, searches or joint Sea Air Co-operation Exercises." Booth also pointed out that in the not too distant future, the personnel of the command would find themselves manning St. Laurent-class destroyer escorts (DEs), "where they will find their knowledge of fighting a surface Gunnery or Torpedo action will be of little value to them in their new A/S roles."[34]

The captain of the *Sioux* agreed with Booth's assessment but went even further regarding the value of such operations. He reported that REGSUBEX and the subsequent CASEX exercises off Pearl Harbor had generated more intensive and up-to-date ASW training than a normal year of submarine availability. He strongly recommended that every opportunity to take part in such RCN/USN operations on such a high training level be exploited, even at the expense of other training and "goodwill" cruising. Only through such exercises would the required standards of efficiency in war be achieved. The RCN's desire to prove itself to USN forces would contribute much to the standard achieved and partly nullify the impact of outdated equipment and control arrangements.[35]

This REGSUBEX exercise was the first opportunity for Canadian warships on the West Coast to train against submarines deploying the new long-range missile technology. Very rapidly in the second half of the decade, the notion of close defence of local waters gave way to new strategies and tactics to defend against submarines mounting surface-launched nuclear-tipped guided missiles with ranges of more than 100 miles. In REGSUBEX the defending forces succeeded in detecting and destroying three guided-missile submarines. Canadian officers, however, realized that the exercise was unrealistic. The defender had a substantial force, including an ASW aircraft carrier, a large number of destroyers and destroyer escorts, and two full squadrons of shore-based antisubmarine aircraft. As well, the attackers had been forced by the parameters of the exercise to operate in a very restricted area of ocean, making the defenders' task that much easier.[36]

The Regulus antisubmarine exercise of March 1957 provided a more realistic assessment of the ability of Allied forces to defend the approaches to the Strait of Juan de Fuca from a submarine-launched guided missile attack. The defending forces were mainly Canadian, including three destroyers from the 2nd and three frigates from the 4th Escort Squadron, supplemented by an American destroyer and a Coast Guard cutter. Air support was provided by 407 and VU-33 Squadrons, joined by a squadron of USN aircraft based at Whidbey Island. The defending forces were unable to stop four American submarines from successfully reaching positions to strike Puget Sound and the Strait of Georgia. Captain Taylor believed that a lack of resources had prevented the defending forces from detecting and intercepting the attacking submarines in time.[37]

The 2nd Escort Squadron participated in two further REGSUBEX exercises in 1957, in July off Pearl Harbor and in September off the southern coast of California. In both exercises, the attacking submarines were able get into their firing positions, although not without sustaining casualties. Canadian ships played a disproportionately strong role in the successful attacks. In the first exercise, the new St. Laurent-class destroyer escort HMCS *Skeena* shared the destruction of one of the attackers with a USN destroyer. In the second exercise, the *Fraser*, another new DE, and the *Crescent* destroyed the USS *Caiman*, although the submarine disputed the Canadians' claim that it had sunk her before she fired her missiles.[38] In other ASW exercises the Canadian vessels acquitted themselves equally well, although on at least one occasion, the effectiveness of a Canadian attack was disputed because USN umpires did not take into account the superiority of the RCN's trainable limbo mortar system.

The RCN was forced to confront the growing threat of submarines, a threat that went well beyond the deployment of guided missiles. In several convoy defence operations, American submarines were able to use their long-range sonar to track a carefully screened convoy up to 100 miles away. In June 1957, the 2nd Escort Squadron just missed its first opportunity to tackle the most revolutionary new addition to naval warfare when the USS *Nautilus* made its first appearance in the Pacific.

Canadian warships were exposed to many other technological advances in naval warfare. Electronic counter-measures (ECM), including the simple but risky expedient of shutting off ship's radar, were regularly practised during convoy exercises. Simulated fighting in atomic, chemical, and bacteriological weapons environments became the norm during most operations. In several air defence exercises, the RCN was forced to confront the complete inadequacies of its radar, Identify-Friend or Foe (IFF), gunnery, and command and control systems to detect, track, and shoot down jet aircraft.[39]

Within two years of its formation, the 2nd Escort Squadron had developed into an effective operational ASW force; however, there were problems endemic to the RCN that hampered the unit. The navy of the mid-1950s consisted of a rather odd collection of ships. The aircraft carrier, based at Halifax, remained the main fleet unit. The two light cruisers, the other large ships, played no clearly defined role other than as training platforms. The cruisers would be decommissioned between 1956 and 1958. Escort vessels included Second World War Tribal- and C-class destroyers, converted to varying degrees to reasonably modern escort vessels. Supplementing them were the Prestonian-class frigates. The new, small Bay-class minesweepers were the only ships capable of sweeping mines and served as training platforms for naval reservists. Until 1957, the navy relied for training purposes on a hodgepodge collection of wartime *Bangor*, *Algerine*, and ex-USN minesweepers. Throughout this period, the navy awaited the arrival of the new St. Laurent-class destroyer escorts, which would provide the service with the cutting-edge ASW platform it needed to fulfill its NATO and ALCANUS commitments.

However, the efficacy of the navy's rapid expansion from 1954 onwards can be doubted. Until January 1957, the 2nd Escort Squadron was a rather heterogeneous collection of two distinctly different types of warships. The Prestonian-class frigates were simply not suitable for modern ASW work, mainly because their maximum speed was a mere 19 knots. Captain Taylor reported during Operation Springtide: "Perhaps the most satisfactory experience for the two Pacific Command Destroyer Escorts was that of working at high speed with a sufficient number of similar ships to shake off the fifteen knot mentality that is the almost inevitable result of always steaming in company with frigates."[40] During several exercises with the USN, the Canadian squadron was broken up so that the destroyers could be matched with their American counterparts, while the frigates joined American destroyer escorts.

Figure 13 The Prestonian-class frigate HMCS *Beacon Hill*, circa 1967. The *Prestonians* began to enter service in 1954. The seven ships in MARPAC were formed into the 4th Escort Squadron after the fleet reorganization of 1959 and were relegated primarily to training duties. (CFB Esquimalt Museum)

The RCN recognized that the *Prestonians* were, at best, a stopgap measure. On August 14, 1956, a Pacific Command staff officer commented on the problems of "obsolescent equipment and control arrangements" raised by the captain of the *Sioux* in his report on the REGSUBEX of the previous month (see above). The staff officer placed the blame squarely on the frigates: "I feel the USN will welcome our participation a good deal more when we can produce homogenous squadrons."[41] In January 1957, as soon as enough destroyers were available, the frigates were removed from the 2nd Escort Squadron. The *Prestonians* were formed into the 4th Escort Squadron, a formation that existed in name only, since the ships mainly conducted individual basic training cruises for both substantive and nonsubstantive courses.[42] Taylor remarked on the departure of the frigates from his unit: "It is with mixed feelings that I saw them go. In spite of their limitations of equipment and speed, they have for the last 18 months fitted in well, and accomplished a great deal by their enthusiasm and hard work."[43]

The other major component of the squadron, the Tribal-class destroyers, while far more capable ships than the frigates, suffered from one major defect that limited their operational utility, especially in the vast expanse of the Pacific. Three different destroyer captains complained that the endurance of these ships was insufficient for Pacific Ocean operations. According to statistics provided by Pacific Command to the USN in 1955, the maximum range of a Tribal at an economical speed of 12 knots was a mere 1,896 miles. Other figures state the range of the ships as 2,200 miles. Whatever the figure, the range was inadequate. In comparison, the *Prestonians* had a maximum economical range of 5,049 miles, and even at their maximum speed they could travel 2,430 miles before refuelling. The distance between Esquimalt and Pearl Harbor is 2,321 nautical miles. Not surprisingly, the Canadian destroyers usually travelled to Hawaii either in company with the *Ontario,* from which they could refuel, or via San Francisco, which is 300 nautical miles closer to Oahu. On several occasions, the Tribals could not refuel at sea and were forced to return to port in the middle of an exercise. In April 1956, Captain Taylor proposed that the number one boilers be removed from the Tribals for additional fuel tanks; this would increase the ships' range by 1,000 miles while only reducing the maximum speed by a few knots. Taylor's proposal was rejected by Pacific Command, who doubted that it was economically feasible to conduct such a large alteration of these older warships. As well, in the advent of a nuclear war, the ships would be patrolling no more than 300 miles off the coast, which meant that speed was likely a more crucial factor than endurance.[44] Still, the lack of "legs" was a principal reason why all of the wartime destroyers were transferred to Halifax during the fleet reorganization in 1958.

In May 1957, with the arrival of the *Skeena*, the first of the new St. Laurent-class DEs to serve in Pacific Command, the 2nd Escort Squadron finally had a cutting-edge ASW platform. These new ships were the product of one of the most successful and innovative industrial design and construction programs in Canadian history. The design, which stemmed from the late 1940s, was a response to the threat of high-underwater-speed conventional submarines. Designed with a mix of a British-inspired hull design, RN Limbo ASW mortars, sonars, and propulsion systems, and American guns, radar, and other sensors, the class represented the RCN's embrace of its role as a modern antisubmarine force. The ships were built to the highest standard, with a futuristic streamlined design, included a rounded bow and a squat, rounded superstructure. Part of the rationale for the program was to support Canada's shipbuilding industry; yards in Quebec and Halifax and Burrard's in Vancouver had undertaken the work. Extremely complex, the first three ships took three times longer than expected to build, and each ship cost a then staggering $22 million – nearly three times more than first estimated. Dubbed the "Cadillacs," by their crews, the *St. Laurents* would form the backbone of the RCN for almost the next forty years.[45]

The *Skeena* was closely examined by both the USN and the general public. In May 1957, Captain Stirling reported: "*Skeena* caused a sensation wherever she went, and great interest amongst the public on the jetty at Long Beach when one of *Skeena*'s men was heard to assure a friend that she was submersible and nuclear powered." Canadian officers were proud of the ship's ASW capabilities but less sanguine about her sea-keeping qualities. Compared to the Tribals, the *Skeena* had some difficulty in rough seas, especially with maintaining speed when heading directly into the wind. Stirling commented that "her flared bow cushions her against a sea and slows her up perceptibly, conventional destroyers slice through wetly under these conditions." As well, the ship had an unusual motion in rough seas that made even seasoned sailors feel the pang of seasickness for the first time in years.[46] But whatever the new ship's sea-keeping qualities, there would be no criticism of the ship's endurance.

Manning, drafting out, and training also vexed the operational performance of the 2nd Escort Squadron, at least until the formation of the 4th Escort Squadron in January 1957. While the navy dramatically improved the manning and training situation after 1954, thereby maintaining some stability in crew complements, finding the right balance between operational and basic training remained a serious issue. Pacific Command made a concerted effort to relieve the 2nd Escort Squadron of many basic training duties. Until the end of 1956, in

FIGURE 14 *Crescent* refuelling from the cruiser HMCS *Ontario* in 1949. The British-designed destroyers' short legs hampered their operational usefulness in the Pacific. (CFB Esquimalt Museum)

addition to *Ontario*, the four old minesweepers of the 12th Escort Squadron, *Oshawa*, *Cordova*, *Brockville*, and *Digby*, and the ships of the 2nd Minesweeper Squadron did much of the substantive and almost all of the nonsubstantive training required. Yet there remained the need to utilize the operational squadron for ROTP cadet training. To ensure there were berths available for cadets, the *Prestonians* had only a full training complement. And even on the destroyers, there was concern that providing basic training to cadets interfered with the operational readiness of the squadron.

In August 1956, Captain Taylor informed the FOPC that he believed that cadet training was interfering with the operational readiness of his squadron. During the previous year, the squadron had been forged into a reasonably effective operational unit, steaming over a quarter of a million miles, firing over 1,500 rounds of practice ammunition, and engaging in just under 1,500 hours of antisubmarine practice. Unfortunately, in that same period, almost 1,100 personnel had been drafted from his ships, representing over 65 percent of the squadron's complement. This huge turnover necessitated constant retraining of the squadron; in addition, the obligation to conduct cadet training interfered with its efficacy. Taylor suggested that the FOPC carefully weigh "the relative values of the two types of training."[47]

Admiral Pullen, the FOPC, while sympathetic to Taylor's complaints, rejected any notion of altering the situation. On September 18, 1956, Pullen informed Naval Headquarters that "the principle of keeping the Squadron together, minimizing drafting, and dispersing the Cadets amongst as many ships as possible, appears to be the best solution to providing the standard of ROTP training required, and also maintaining an operational Squadron of reasonable proportions."[48]

Cadet training on ships of the squadron continued. Interestingly, after the removal of the frigates from the 2nd Escort Squadron in January 1957, there were no more complaints from captains of the ships of the unit about either manning or the need to mix operational and basic training. The issue of crew stability remained, but only on the frigates of the 4th Escort Squadron.

The overall improvement in the manning situation can be clearly seen by contrasting the commissioning of *Crusader* in 1951 with that of *Skeena* in 1957. As discussed previously, when *Crusader* re-entered service, she was handed over by the dockyard in a disgusting state, unfit for human habitation. Her officers and crew arrived only upon commissioning and were given no opportunity to train together or to learn necessary skills before coming on board. After re-entering service, the crew was so small that the ship remained incapable of performing anything more than training duties until just before her first Korean tour, more than a year later. By contrast, all of *Skeena*'s officers and most of her crew arrived at HMCS *Naden* in January 1957, more than two months before commissioning on March 30. Officers and men were enrolled in courses at *Naden*. As many men as possible were given the opportunity to qualify for promotion. Training was hampered only by the lack of suitable facilities to familiarize personnel with the equipment found on this radically new type of warship. Most of the officers and a large number of warrant officers spent time with the advanced party in North Vancouver, where the ship was being completed and put through her builder's trials. The members of the advanced party were given the opportunity to observe and even use much of the ship's equipment. So thorough were the precommissioning preparations that *Skeena* was able to give a good account of herself in the 2nd Escort Squadron's exercises with the Pacific Fleet in early May, little more than five weeks after she entered service.[49]

Conclusion

By the time the decade came to a close, the RCN had transformed itself from the dark days of the late 1940s and early 1950s. While the problems of ensuring crew stability and finding enough adequate training platforms remained, a large proportion of the service was available for immediate operational deployment. By early 1958, the 2nd Escort Squadron had five destroyer escorts, including three of the new St. Laurent-class, ready to defend the West Coast of North America. As we shall see, this transformation came at an opportune time, for in the Pacific, as in the Atlantic, the Soviet Navy and its supporting merchant marine had begun to seriously challenge the security of the continent.

5

Reorganization of Pacific Command and West Coast Defence Planning, 1958–61

In the late 1950s, almost every aspect of Canadian West Coast naval organization and defence planning was dramatically transformed. The revolutionary changes that took place in a little less than four years were not the result of any one factor, but of a multitude of issues that were reshaping Canadian defence policy in the late 1950s. The increased emphasis on continental defence, usually seen in the context of the formation of NORAD in 1958 with the emergence of a Soviet nuclear threat to the continent, also influenced the reshaping of West Coast naval defence plans. While much attention has been paid to NORAD and the Diefenbaker government's acceptance of an American being in charge of Canadian air defence, a similar integration of American and Canadian naval forces was already well under way in the Pacific. MARPAC's defence planners had to contend with the growing security threat posed by the Soviet Navy, the reorganization of the RCN, technological change, and the navy's evolving relationship with the RCAF. The entire RCN was reorganized to maximize operational and training efficiency, and one result was the reduction of operational squadrons on the West Coast to only the 2nd Escort Squadron. The 4th Squadron took over most training duties after the retirement of the *Ontario*. The development of new ALCANUS defence plans further integrated the new Canadian Maritime Command Pacific (MARPAC) with the US Pacific Fleet; it also led to Canadian naval officers exerting their independence from American command, especially prior to the outbreak of hostilities.

West Coast Defence Organization and the Creation of Maritime Command Pacific (MARPAC)

In October 1955, the Chiefs of Staff agreed to a proposal by the RCN that Maritime Commands be established on the Atlantic and Pacific coasts; these commands "would exercise operational control of forces allocated to the Maritime Theatres by the Chiefs of Staff Committee." Yet the Chiefs of Staff also determined that they would take no action at this time to appoint maritime commanders. The Chiefs of Staff understood the need for unified coastal commands but also realized that more work needed to be done to lay the groundwork before the new commands could be established.[1]

On the West Coast, the issue of a unified interservice Maritime Command structure was initially confined mainly to determining whether such a joint command headquarters was necessary and, if it was, where a headquarters should be located. Prior to December 1957, except for the minimal RCN contributions to local defence, no other military units were committed to remain on the West Coast in the advent of war. Canada's commitments to SACLANT and NATO took precedence over any concerns in the Pacific. Ever since the navy had moved its West Coast headquarters back to Esquimalt in 1946, DND had maintained the wartime joint service headquarters at Jericho Beach in Vancouver. The facility was rarely activated for exercises, and a series of FOPCs had judged it impractical to relocate to the mainland in times of emergency.[2] Still, Jericho Beach was maintained throughout the decade because of its close proximity to land lines of communications and the unwillingness of the Chiefs of Staff to spend money on a new headquarters in "view of the limited operations which were expected on the west coast."[3] A variety of alternative locations for a new interservice Maritime Command Headquarters were proposed by naval officers between 1954 and 1959. The issue was considered a critical one, especially as the Soviet nuclear threat to North America grew. In 1956 the navy recognized that Vancouver would likely be an "A" priority target and that, therefore, Jericho Beach was unsuitable for wartime Maritime Headquarters. While the Victoria–Esquimalt area was the best location for a headquarters in peacetime, since it was unlikely to be a priority target of Soviet forces in an initial attack, the area was considered by the navy to be vulnerable as a target of opportunity. Logically, a new Maritime Headquarters outside either Vancouver or Victoria needed to be established, but the expense of building and manning such a facility deterred the RCN from taking any action. Admiral Pullen, the FOPC in 1956, preferred another option – a headquarters ship. He argued that "the advantages to be gained in establishing a Maritime Headquarters in a ship, for reasons of mobility, dispersal, security, and versatility, far outweigh any possible advantages which may be found in having an establishment ashore." Pullen realized that the cost of building such a vessel would be prohibitive but suggested that the USN might have a suitable one or that an existing RCN ship could be converted.[4] Naval Headquarters refused to take any action concerning this proposal.

In December 1957, the Chiefs of Staff approved a major restructuring of Canadian defence commitments in the Pacific, authorizing 407 Maritime Patrol Squadron, based at Comox, to remain on the West Coast in the event of a war. For the first time since the Second World War, the RCN was forced to take action on establishing a proper joint service Maritime Headquarters. By February 1958 an interim headquarters had been established in Building 77 of the Esquimalt dockyard. Owing to the vulnerability of the dockyard in times of war, an alternative Maritime Headquarters was established at the RCAF base in Comox.[5]

Establishing a location for a Maritime Headquarters was only the first stage in creating a unified Maritime Command Pacific. The issue of how to coordinate RCN and RCAF coastal defence activities was more contentious and illustrates the difficulties with interservice cooperation in the years leading up to unification. The Chiefs of Staff recognized that maritime defence remained primarily a naval responsibility, and on each coast, the flag officer was given the dual appointment of Maritime Commander. The question of how air force officers were to be incorporated into the new command structure was subject to some debate. Originally, the Chiefs of Staff had approved a Canadian Maritime Headquarters Manual that called for "a joint headquarters," with naval and air force officers "working *side by side*, and only the intelligence staff *integrated*." Rear Admiral H.S. Rayner, the FOPC, strongly supported a joint headquarters structure:

> It is considered that integration or interchangeability cannot be carried out at the working level, at the same time preserving economy and efficiency, (i.e., one cannot expect an Air Operations Officer to be able to conduct surface operations effectively any more than one can expect a Naval Officer to conduct fighter operations in support of NORAD). Each service has its separate problems and modus operandi. It is considered that harmony, efficiency and effectiveness can best be preserved when parallel staffs get on with the duties for which they have been trained, at the same time of course, preserving liaison so that each knows what the other is doing. Integration should come at the command level; joint staffs are more effective than an integrated staff.[6]

On February 11, 1959, Air Marshal Hugh Campbell, the Chief of Air Staff, expressed his strong disagreement with Rayner's position on staff organization, insisting that the RCAF wanted an integrated staff and that 407 Squadron would only be put under the control of the Maritime Commander when the staff was established. Campbell cited as his authority Chief of Staff directives, which superseded the original Maritime Headquarters manual when the Atlantic Coast headquarters had been established. Campbell proposed that an Air Commodore be appointed as Deputy Commander and that four other senior air force officers form the RCAF's contribution to the integrated headquarters.[7] Captain J.A. Charles, the Director of Plans and Operations, agreed with Campbell's assessment of the Chiefs of Staff policy regarding the organization of Maritime Command Pacific.[8] By the end of 1959 an integrated Maritime Headquarters was in operation, marking the establishment of MARPAC. The first test of the new organization took place during the Emergency Defence Exercise (EDPEX-59), held in October.

The Fleet Reorganization of 1959

Before considering EDPEX-59, two other developments that transformed the navy on the West Coast must first be examined. In early 1959 the RCN undertook a major reorganization of the fleets on both coasts. The *Crescent*, *Cayuga*, and *Athabaskan* – that is, all of the older wartime destroyers converted to destroyer escorts based at Esquimalt – were removed from the West Coast and sent to the Atlantic. As well, there was some shifting of Prestonian-class frigates. In turn, three newer St. Laurent-class destroyer escorts, the *Assiniboine*, *Saguenay*, and *Ottawa*, moved from the Atlantic to the Pacific. The transfer was made for a variety of reasons, including the need to form homogeneous squadrons on both coasts. The driving force for the reorganization, however, was the requirement to provide enough training berths for cadet training while maintaining as many fully operational squadrons as possible to fulfill the RCN's commitments to SACLANT.

The West Coast had been undertaking most of the cadet training for some time, so the decision to retire *Ontario* after the end of the 1958 training season would cause serious shortages in berths for cadets. *Ontario*, along with *Quebec*, the Halifax-based cruiser, no longer had any wartime function, having been removed from any NATO role in 1955. *Ontario*'s conversion to a training ship in 1954, capable

FIGURE 15 *St. Laurent* and two sister ships at dockside before her transfer to the Pacific in 1959. Two American destroyers are tied up behind them. (CFB Esquimalt Museum)

of carrying eighty cadets, had given her a new role, but just three years later the navy was faced with the prospect of having to pay for a major refit to extend the ship's useful life. By 1957, the navy had significantly increased the number of destroyer escorts and frigates in commission, and as we have seen, much of the cadet training still took place on these vessels. There was evidence that "those cadets embarked on the smaller ships appeared to have received better training than those in *Ontario*."[9] The destroyers and frigates gave cadets experience on the types of ships on which they would be serving, but the navy had to balance the value of training on ASW vessels with the corresponding decrease in operational readiness that would result. During 1959, the RCN had to find berths for around eight hundred cadets on training cruises, and through 1957 and 1958 a great deal of discussion went into how to accommodate them without the cruiser.[10]

The navy finally decided that the most economical solution, and the one that would do the least harm to the RCN's NATO commitments, was to convert the Pacific-based frigates into a training squadron. Each frigate would carry between twenty-four and thirty cadets per training cruise. The training squadron would consist of eight frigates – an increase in three originally scheduled to be based at Esquimalt. At least five of the frigates would have a reduced complement to accommodate the cadets; this would cause a corresponding reduction in their operational effectiveness. There would be no change in designation of the frigate squadron, which would still be called the 4th Escort Squadron (CORTRON 4), although the formation was to be noted as having "reduced operational complements." The decision to not give the squadron a training designation was originally made in August 1957, on the recommendations of the flag officers on both coasts, in order to improve morale among the crews of training squadrons, but in fact, it resulted in the 4th Escort Squadron continuing to have an operational role to play in times of war. Additional training billets could be found on St. Laurent-class ships without impeding their operational capabilities. The older wartime destroyers had limited space for additional accommodation, and this appears to have been one of the factors that led to these ships' removal from Pacific Command.

The exchange of destroyer escorts and their crews took place in early 1959. Pacific Command operational ships would include the 2nd Escort Squadron (CORTRON 2), consisting of seven St. Laurent-class destroyer escorts; the 4th Escort Squadron (CORTRON 4), consisting of eight Prestonian-class frigates (reduced to seven in 1960), and the 2nd Minesweeper Squadron (MINRON 2) of four Bay-class minesweepers. Air support was to be provided by the aircraft and helicopters of VU-33.[11]

While this force was significantly smaller than the naval forces based in the Atlantic, it marked a considerable increase in the RCN's commitments to the Pacific.

FIGURE 16 Rear Admiral Herbert Sharples Rayner, FOPC, 1957–59. (CFB Esquimalt Museum)

Revamping Strategic Defence Planning in the Pacific

The reorganization of the fleet occurred at almost the same time there was a radical revamping of the defence plans for the West Coast. As we have seen, in the early part of the decade, in times of war, most Esquimalt-based operational ships were slated to be transferred to the Atlantic. Defence of the West Coast would be confined to trying to control the local approaches to Vancouver,

TABLE 1

RCN operational and training forces in the Pacific, 1959

2nd Escort Squadron (CORTRON 2) St. Laurent-class DE	*Skeena, Fraser, Margaree, Assiniboine, Ottawa, St. Laurent, Saguenay*
4th Escort Squadron (CORTRON 4) Prestonian-class Frigates (FFEs)	*Sussexvale, Stettler, Jonquiere, New Waterford,* Antigonish, Beacon Hill, New Glasgow, Ste. Therese*
2nd Minesweeper Squadron (MINRON 2) Bay-class	*Fortune, James Bay, Miramichi, Cowichan*
VU-33	2 Avengers, 2 HUP2 helicopters, and 1 T33

* Ship transferred to Atlantic at the end of 1959

Victoria, and Seattle by blocking the entrances to the Strait of Juan de Fuca and the Johnstone Strait. By the middle of the decade the navy had begun to realize that these plans were both absurd and obsolete. The notion that in a rapidly developing international crisis, or in a nuclear war – which might be over in just a few hours – the RCN would have the time to transfer its ships through the Panama Canal was, to say the least, unrealistic. As well, Canadian defence planners were beginning to realize that there was a growing Soviet submarine threat in the Pacific and that these submarines were deploying a new generation of weapons that made all existing West Coast defence plans redundant. In earlier plans the navy had hoped to use the geographical advantages of the restricted approaches to major ports to institute a low-cost defensive strategy, but as Soviet submarines could now strike from hundreds of miles off the coast, a much greater commitment was needed to provide even minimal security.[12] On March 7, 1958, Admiral Rayner, while visiting Pearl Harbor, was given an opportunity to learn about the new threat posed by surface-launched cruise missiles. He was given a detailed briefing about the American equivalent of the new generation of Soviet missiles, the Regulus I, and witnessed a demonstration of a "Ram Out" or preparation-to-fire exercise.[13]

Just a few weeks later, Rayner, as Maritime Commander Pacific, issued Operational Emergency Defence Plan Pacific – 1958 (MAROPEDPAC). This document provides a detailed account of the threat facing the West Coast of North America and of the strategy for addressing it in the Canadian Pacific zone of operations.[14] This plan was designed to fit into the latest strategic thinking as contained in the most recent RCN Emergency Plan and in the ALCANUS agreement.[15] MAROPEDPAC envisioned an attack by Soviet submarines firing surface-launched guided missiles, with very little warning, at targets on the West Coast. The Soviets would "first strike at any strategic nuclear targets; this would be followed by attacks on centres of industry, government, and population." Secondary activities by the Soviet navy would include mining, torpedo attacks on shipping, reconnaissance activities, and the landing of small raiding parties, saboteurs, and agents. The focus of the defensive efforts would be on protecting the Vancouver–Spokane–Portland area, with particular emphasis on the approaches to the Strait of Juan de Fuca.

The far greater range of submarine-launched cruise missiles necessitated the establishment of a defensive zone 500 miles from any potential target. This huge increase in the defended areas was predetermined by the need to detect submarines before they submerged for a run into firing locations. The depth of the defensive zone was determined by the cruise missiles' maximum range of 200 miles and by the fact that a submarine could travel 300 miles fully submerged without using its snorkel. The key to establishing a defensive barrier was the deployment of maritime patrol aircraft, supported by a picket line of ASW vessels. The aircraft should be able to detect "at least 90%" of snorting [snorkelling] submarines and to hold contact with them for at least four hours. Two ASW vessels would be vectored onto the target and would arrive no later than six hours after the initial detection by the aircraft. Once the ships had established contact, their job was either to sink the submarine or to exhaust its ability to get within missile range of its target.

Rayner envisioned a second, inner line of defence, if the forces were available, located at least 20 miles offshore on a line running from Cape Cook to the Swiftsure Light Vessel. This line was to be located approximately 200 miles from priority targets but close enough to the coast that submarines would be using radar to get an accurate navigational fix before firing their missiles. This line would be patrolled by ASW vessels and aircraft carrying ECM equipment, designed to home in on a submarine's radar signal. Additional forces provided for in the plan included a mine counter-measures force and a mobile logistics and repair support force.[16]

An appendix to MAROPEDPAC outlines the forces to be assigned to carrying out the plan. Unfortunately, it does not specifically link these forces to actual units, but it is possible from later documents to piece together what Rayner envisioned. The outer picket line, ASW Group Alpha (Task Group 38.0), would be made up of the destroyer escorts of the 2nd Escort Squadron; the outer patrol of maritime aircraft, ASW Group Bravo (TG 38.1), would consist of Neptune aircraft of 407 Squadron. The inner patrol ships, ASW Group Charlie (TG 38.2), would be made up of the frigates of the 4th Escort Squadron. It remains unclear where the ECM aircraft, designated as ASW Group Delta (TG 38.3), envisioned to operate in the inner patrol area, would come from, since no such aircraft were available on the West Coast. It is possible that Rayner hoped for an upgrading of the capabilities of VU-33 to fulfill this task.[17] The mine countermeasures forces would be made up of the 2nd Minesweeper Squadron.[18]

MAROPEDPAC marked a radical recasting of security planning for the West Coast and was the blueprint for future defensive schemes until at least 1965. Almost immediately after the plan was completed, however, Rayner realized that the navy's pending fleet reorganization, other demands placed on his squadrons, and the geographic reality of operating in the Pacific made his defensive strategy, at best, a chimera. During 1958, Rayner attempted to alter headquarters' planned changes to the Pacific fleet's composition. Rayner argued, correctly, that changes to his fleet made it impossible for it to achieve the naval staff's own priorities for the fleet in 1959. Naval Headquarters had mandated that the service's primary concern was "the formation and training of operational squadrons and the maintenance of these squadrons in a high state [of] operational efficiency and readiness." This was because "the policy of the RCN [was] to have the maximum number of ships available on D Day to meet NATO and national commitments." Sea training was judged a secondary task. Fleet commanders were ordered not to send their ships for extended cruises "with no particular aim or operational requirement" and were required to maintain sufficient forces on hand to meet probable operational requirements, even during major NATO or joint RCN–USN exercises. The commanders were also instructed to regularly test their defensive plans.[19] In September, Rayner complained about the decision to retire the *Ontario* and convert the 4th Escort Squadron to a training role, since it effectively reduced his operational forces by 50 percent, leaving him with only one operational squadron. He recommended that the transfer of two of the Tribal-class destroyers to the Atlantic be deferred so as to give him more operational ships. When this suggestion fell on deaf ears, all he could do was point out the detrimental impact of fleet reorganization on the operational readiness of his command. He explained that in the case of the 2nd Escort Squadron:

> In order to achieve squadron operational training, other than that facilitated by very limited local submarine allocation, it is necessary for the squadron to proceed out of local waters. In order to maintain operational ships in the local areas to deal with emergencies as required ... operational training can now be carried out only by divisions. Therefore, the squadron will very seldom if ever have an opportunity to exercise together.[20] These difficulties were exacerbated by the geography of the Pacific. The nearest American operational ASW units were based in San Diego and Pearl Harbor, and this forced lengthy trips by ships to engage in

joint RCN–USN exercises. Moreover, the sheer size of the area that Pacific Command was required to patrol made it extremely difficult to keep the squadron together either for group training or to implement the defensive plan. From an operational perspective, the situation of the 4th Escort Squadron was even worse. The frigates would have a reduced crew complement to accommodate cadets, and furthermore, from January to September, the ships were fully committed to cadet training cruises. With refits and leave time, the squadron was only available for individual ship and group operational training, and to participate in national defence exercises, for a few weeks in the autumn. There was so little time available for training the crews of the frigates that Rayner believed that all non-substantive training for ratings would have to be undertaken on the destroyer escorts of the 2nd Escort Squadron.[21]

Rayner failed in his efforts to change headquarters' policy towards the Pacific Fleet. While the RCN had committed significantly more resources to West Coast security than earlier in the decade, it remained strongly focused on the Atlantic. Esquimalt would be the centre of officer cadet training. There is some evidence that the 2nd Escort Squadron remained in the Pacific because Halifax was unable to absorb so many additional personnel and because of the social consequences and expense of moving a large number of families across the country. The complexity of such a move can be seen in the difficulties caused when the navy tried to correct a small imbalance in personnel between the two coasts, by temporarily transferring ninety-seven petty officers and seamen from Esquimalt to Halifax.[22]

Once naval headquarters made the decision to base the 2nd Escort Squadron on the West Coast, however, it committed itself to a policy of having a separate fleet in the Pacific, dedicated to West Coast defence. In June 1959, Rayner suggested that in 1960 one division of the 2nd Escort Squadron take part in a combined exercise in the Western Atlantic or Caribbean with Halifax-based destroyers. This would give his ships an opportunity to compare "operational effectiveness with other than USN forces," as well as "an opportunity for Atlantic and Pacific Command forces to work together, thus avoiding the 'two-ocean Navy concept.'"[23] Headquarters turned down Rayner's proposal for a joint exercise involving the Atlantic and Pacific Commands, citing the need to keep RCN ships as close as possible to the wartime areas of operations during a time of "international stress," as well as the requirement to conserve money by avoiding Panama Canal toll charges. "Moreover," headquarters added, "HMC Ships of the Pacific Fleet are firmly committed to wartime co-operation with the USN through the medium of CUSRPG [Canada–US Regional Planning Group], should exercise with US ships at every opportunity."[24]

The new defensive scheme for West Coast defence was first tested during EDPEX-59, held from October 19 to 30. All aspects of the Maritime Commander Pacific's defence plans were implemented, as much as possible to simulate war conditions. The frigates *Ste. Therese* and *Stettler* were chosen to act as approaching Soviet submarines; the naval auxiliary vessels *Whitethroat* and *Laymore* laid mines in the approaches to Prince Rupert and Nootka Sound. To respond to this threat, a general recall of personnel ashore was issued and the *Naden* defence battalion, designated to secure the naval base, was activated. Rayner, as the maritime commander, manned his headquarters and made token efforts to activate the alternative command centre at Comox as well as his control of shipping organization. Ships were brought up to as close to war complement as possible. The available vessels of the 2nd Escort Squadron – *Assiniboine, Fraser, Ottawa, St. Laurent*, and *Margaree* – sailed for their defensive stations to the west of Vancouver Island; the remaining ships of the 4th Escort Squadron – *Sussexvale, Antigonish*, and *New Glasgow* – took up positions near the entrance to the Strait of Juan de Fuca. Meanwhile, all four ships of the 2nd Minesweeper Squadron – *Fortune, Miramichi, Cowichan*, and *James Bay* – swept channels clear of mines. The operation well demonstrated the new defence scheme for the West Coast, although the use of frigates to simulate submarines greatly limited the military value of the exercise.[25]

ALCANUS Planning and Threat Assessment, 1958–61

The defensive plans tested during EDPEX-59 were strictly national in scope, but they were to form a part of broader discussions concerning the recasting of US–Canadian joint planning for the defence of the West Coast of North America that begin in mid-1958. The origins of the new defensive scheme for the Pacific are found in "Instructions for the Coordination of Canada–United States ASW Operations in the Defence of North America," developed in August 1958 "to provide agreed Canada–United States measures for the coordinated defence of North America against attack by submarine." The instructions were approved by the Canadian Chiefs of Staff and the American Joint Chiefs of Staff to provide guidance to regional planners in developing local defence arrangements against the large numbers of submarines being deployed in the Atlantic and the North Pacific. The regional commanders were told that the surveillance and control of the ocean approaches to North America required that three general goals be accomplished:

1) The acquisition, evaluation and exchange of information concerning the patterns of action by non-friendly submarines with the setting of the international situation as it may exist at any time.

2) Prior to the outbreak of war, the detection, tracking, surfacing and identification of non-friendly submarines in North American waters, and the prevention of hostile action by such submarines, or the destruction of a submarine which commits a hostile act.
3) After the outbreak of war, the detection and destruction of enemy submarines.

Overall responsibility for coordinating the development of ASW plans was assigned to the Commanders in Chief of the USN's Atlantic and Pacific Fleets. These plans were to include provision for mutual training exercises and the sharing of ASW intelligence. Also, both countries were to be kept aware of the location of friendly forces.[26] On August 7, Vice Admiral H.G. DeWolf, the Chief of Naval Staff, informed the Maritime Commanders on both coasts of these instructions and ordered them to develop new plans for defence against submarines in cooperation with designated USN commanders.[27]

Many of DeWolf's instructions simply reinforced what was already part of ALCANUS planning on the West Coast. Rayner's MAROPEDPAC plan incorporated a clear understanding of his command relationships and responsibilities, which were defined both in his role as Maritime Commander, responsible to the Chiefs of Staff for "the conduct of Maritime Warfare on the Pacific Coast," and as an ALCANUS commander, responsible to CINCPACFLT for the operational control of Canadian Maritime forces and the US forces assigned to the Canadian Maritime Area Pacific. The national and ALCANUS responsibilities were analogous, but there were some important differences, the major one being that ALCANUS only came into effect during a war. The biggest single stumbling block to developing a new workable West Coast defence agreement had to do with developing an understanding and translating it into wording acceptable to all parties regarding how Canadian and American forces would cooperate before hostilities commenced. This should have been a simple task; instead, discussions on establishing a Canadian–US ASW Emergency Defence Operational Order (OPORDER) took four years to conclude. There were several reasons why these negotiations were protracted, in particular, the desire of the Canadian Chiefs of Staff not to have Canadian forces placed under the direct operational control of CINCPACFLT during peacetime. The COS had grave concerns about being dragged into situations outside the ALCANUS area, since CINCPACFLT's responsibilities extended throughout the Asia–Pacific. As well, the COS wanted to ensure that Canadian forces operated under their own national rules of engagement against submarines even when there was a joint American–Canadian operation under the tactical command of a USN officer. Admiral Herbert G. Hopwood, CINCPACFLT from February 1958 to

August 1960, wished to be in clear command over the entire northeastern Pacific to defend against any potential deployment of Soviet forces prior to an attack. Hopwood believed he was authorized to exercise command over this region under the terms of the current US–Canada Emergency Defence Plan (MCC 300/1). In the middle of this conflict was the Canadian Maritime Commander in the Pacific – at the time, Rayner, who was succeeded after August 1960 by Rear Admiral E.W. Finch-Noyes.

In May 1958, negotiations to revise the terms of the Naval Operations Annex of the ALCANUS plan began at the ALCANUS planners' conference. A working draft of the annex stated that CINCPACFLT had "overall operational control" of ASW forces, but the COS disagreed with giving the USN officer direct control over Canadian forces. Instead the COS suggested that CINCPACFLT be designated the "Co-ordinating Authority." In December, the proposed amendment was discussed at the ALCANUS Planners and Commanders Conference at Pearl Harbor. Hopwood felt that the term "co-ordinating authority" was "adequate for planning purposes but not acceptable from an operational aspect." As a result, a new draft of the ASW annex was proposed in which CINCPAC was specifically listed as having overall responsibility throughout the Pacific Ocean and the eastern portion of the Indian Ocean. To appease the Canadian service chiefs, however, a new section was added in which the three ALCANUS operational commanders – COMWESTSEAFRON (Commander Western Sea Frontier), COMALSEAFRON (Commander Alaskan Sea Frontier), and CANCOMPARPAC (Canadian Maritime Commander Pacific) – would "exercise operational control within their respective areas of responsibility of all ASW forces assigned."[28]

This rewording did not end the dispute. Throughout 1959, planners continued to try to finalize the naval annex to the ALCANUS plan. In May, Hopwood requested that a phrase be inserted into the OPORDER giving him operational control of ASW units "under special circumstances" in preconflict situations. Hopwood wanted to ensure that he had the power to exercise overall control of an operation or to assign an OTC (Officer in Tactical Command). Hopwood was concerned that he be able to impose his authority in a situation where a USN ASW carrier group might cross into the MARPAC area or in a prewar joint US–Canadian operation, where one nation's units were withdrawn "due to a lack of jointly accepted rules of engagement." On June 24, Rayner wrote to Naval Headquarters supporting Hopwood's proposal, explaining that it in no way interfered with his control of Canadian forces:

> During the planning and prior to the assignment of forces to an ASW task, CINCPACFLT is the "co-ordinator." However, once the forces have been assigned,

and it is a national prerogative whether they are or not [emphasis provided], it would seem reasonable and in accordance with ATP's 1 and 2 [Allied Manoeuvring Instructions], that there should be a common superior. This is logically CINC-PACFLT. It is considered that the national interests are protected in both AL-CANUS and the proposed ASW OPORD.[29]

Despite Rayner's explanation, on June 30, the Chairman of the COS rejected Hopwood's proposal, stating that "Canadian forces will not be placed under the command of US authorities" prior the commencement of hostilities.[30] During the summer, Rayner apparently suggested several compromises, including the inclusion of both American and Canadian rules of engagement with submarines into the OPORDER, which would mitigate against any risk of CINCPACFLT ordering Canadian forces into actions not approved by Canadian authorities. On August 17, Naval Headquarters emphasized to Rayner the need to heed the COS's concerns in new rounds of talks with the Americans, including the need to alter or drop Hopwood's amendments to the draft plan. Rayner was informed by headquarters that it was "agreed that a common superior should be responsible for coordinating the operations of combined forces"; however, they wished to emphasize that "the Canadian Maritime Commander Pacific and those forces assigned to him have no direct operational responsibility to the Commander-in-Chief US Pacific Fleet." Headquarters did, at least, agree to Rayner's suggestion to include the respective rules of engagement in the plans.[31] Rayner realized that Hopwood would not accept the Canadian position. On September 11, he reiterated to the Chairman of the Chiefs of Staff Hopwood's arguments and proposed a compromise. Hopwood's wording, Rayner suggested, would remain, but CINCFLT authority could only be exercised in a specific situation outlined in the overall plan for North American defence, MCC 300/10. Rayner believed he could win the support of the COS, since this plan had already been approved by the service chiefs of both countries. The situation outlined by MCC 300/10 allowed for prewar "detection, tracking, and identification of non-friendly submarines in North American waters" and authorized action to prevent a submarine from committing a hostile act, and the submarine's destruction if it committed such an act.[32]

Unfortunately the documents here fail us, but it is certain that despite Rayner's best efforts a compromise could not be brokered between the Canadian service chiefs and Hopwood. It would be more than a year before new negotiations apparently led to an agreement on a Canadian–US operational order covering prewar ASW in the ALCANUS area. This delay occurred even though there was a perception that the security threat to the West Coast was growing. In March 1959, Canadian officers, including Admiral Rayner, attended a major

Pacific Fleet conference at San Diego regarding the ASW situation in the Pacific. One senior Canadian officer informed headquarters: "I came away with the knowledge that there is a growing awareness, *bordering on alarm*, held by cognizant USN Pacific Authorities in the deficiencies of the existing organization, training, and readiness of the forces assigned to anti-submarine defence [emphasis added]."[33]

Despite this sense of alarm, it took a change of the Commander-in Chief of the Pacific Fleet to restart talks with the Canadians. On March 14, 1961, Admiral Finch-Noyes, then the Canadian Maritime Commander Pacific, received an extensively revised draft of the OPORDER from Admiral John H. Sides, the new CINCPACFLT. Sides and Finch-Noyes agreed that, with rising international tensions and a growing Soviet threat in the Pacific, it was imperative to expedite the approval of the draft document. Finch-Noyes and his staff carefully went over CINCPACFLT's proposal, marking on the document areas that needed revision to make it acceptable to the COS. A copy of this marked draft survives in the files of the RCAF and provides a fascinating insight into American–Canadian defence cooperation during the height of the Cold War. The document also provides a great deal of detail on how the two countries intended to defend the approaches to the West Coast of North America from a Soviet submarine offensive.

Gone from this draft of the OPORDER were any references to "special circumstances" that might allow CINCPACFLT to circumvent Canadian control over its forces or area of responsibility. Instead CINCPACFLT created a new subsidiary commander, COMNASDEFFORPAC (Commander A/S Force Pacific), who was designated the "coordinating authority" for all antisubmarine operations in the ALCANUS area. Moreover, the order was written to be a bilateral defence agreement between CINCPACFLT and the Canadian Maritime Commander Pacific, acting as equals. The mission of these forces was "to conduct combined AS operations and training, including surveillance in the North Pacific Ocean, prior to the outbreak of hostilities, *to develop the maximum capability* to protect allied shipping, and to defend North America against attack by submarines [emphasis added]."

The OPORDER stipulated that nothing in it would "abrogate or supersede the responsibilities of the principals in the agreement insofar as their national policy or their national military planning is concerned." The Canadian rules of engagement with submarines were incorporated into the plan as an appendix. These rules stipulated that if a surfaced, non-US or Allied submarine was located in Canadian territorial waters, the vessel was to be escorted to the nearest protected anchorage that was not in the vicinity of a major port. If a submerged submarine of unknown origin was detected, every effort was to be made to

FIGURE 17 Rear Admiral Edward W. Finch-Noyes, FOPC, 1960–62. (CFB Esquimalt Museum)

signal the vessel to surface; that, or Canadian forces would remain in contact either until the submarine was forced to surface or until it escaped. The rules of engagement for detecting an unknown submerged submarine outside of territorial waters were to remain in contact until the submarine was forced to surface. To further guarantee Canada's authority over its own military forces, the OPORDER unequivocally stated that "any action, other than in self-defence, prior to the beginning of general hostilities will be taken only under the National Authority." Each country's officers were given the right to withdraw their forces from any joint operation if any "apparent or proposed" act violated their government's policies.

The basic objectives of ASW operations indicate that there was a broader security concern than just the Soviet Union; for the first time, China was mentioned as a potential adversary. ASW forces were

1) To determine Sino-Soviet submarine operational and tactical abilities.
2) To determine patterns of Sino-Soviet submarine operations so that departure from normal patterns can be detected and analysed.
3) To create doubts in the Sino-Soviet minds as to the effectiveness of their submarine operations.
4) To counter the threat to North America of a submarine attack through the successful accomplishment of (1), (2) and (3) above.[34]

The forces available for this mission were outlined (see Table 2). American forces included one ASW aircraft carrier with a squadron of maritime patrol aircraft and one helicopter squadron on board, two destroyer squadrons, and four shore-based ASW aircraft squadrons. Canada's contribution consisted of the two West Coast escort squadrons and 407 Squadron. Canadian forces were, therefore, a major part of the resources available, providing the only escort groups based north of San Diego, and were given primary responsibility for protecting not just Canada but also the approaches to Seattle and a large part of Alaska (see Figure 1). Admiral Sides recognized that there was an "overall shortage of US Pacific Fleet ASW capable forces" and appreciated the need to coordinate efforts with Canada. The OPORDER emphasized the requirement to continue joint Canada–US antisubmarine patrols, to control and protect shipping, to conduct exercises, "to exchange and review tactical methods and doctrines, and to share shore-based ASW training facilities."

One aspect of the draft OPORDER was heavily edited by Finch-Noyes: he deleted every reference to the broader geographic responsibilities of CINCPACFLT, making it unambiguous that Canada would strictly limit itself to providing for North American security. Interestingly, though, the map outlining the responsibilities of the various American task groups assigned ALCANUS responsibility for waters as far south as South America and as far west as the Soviet Union. The OPORDER also included methods for coordinating intelligence and operational information. MARCOMPAC was made privy to CINCPACFLT's intelligence sources on submarine activities throughout the

Table 2

Forces available for ASW defence of ALCANUS areas, 1961

Task Force #	ALCANUS title	Unit	Forces
30	Anti-Submarine Defence Force Pacific	COMASDEFORPAC (Commander A/S Force Pacific)	1 CVS (ASW carrier) VS (ASW aircraft) 1 RON (squadron) with 20 S2F trackers 1 RON with 14 HSS Sea King Helicopters 2 DD (destroyer) RONs with 14–16 DDs
31	Naval Defence Forces Eastern Pacific	COMNAVDEFEAST-PAC	
31.4	San Diego ASW Group	COMFAIRWING 14	1VP Maritime RON with 12 aircraft
31.5	San Francisco ASW Group	COMFAIR Alameda	1 VP RON with 12 aircraft
31.6	Seattle ASW Group	COMFAIR Whidbey	1 VP RON with 12 aircraft
33	Alaska Sea Frontier	COMALSEAFRON	
33.1	Patrol Squadron Assigned		1 VP RON with 12 aircraft
38	Commander Maritime Forces Pacific	CANCOMMARPAC	
38.0	Canadian AS Group Alpha	CANCOMCORTRON 2	7 DDE
38.1	Canadian AS Group Bravo	407th Sqd RCAF	12 PSV-7 Neptune aircraft
38.2	Canadian AS Group Charlie	CANCOMCORTRON 4	7 FFE (frigates)

Asia–Pacific. CINCPACFLT did not object to Canada's involvement in these wider responsibilities.[35]

There is no documentary evidence indicating whether the OPORDER was finally approved, but it does appear likely that in the end, the revised draft received the blessing of the COS. No further discussions concerning the

OPORDER have been recorded, and in 1960 Rayner became the Chief of Naval Staff. Rayner was well acquainted with both the worsening security situation in the Pacific and the need to formalize MARCOMPAC's close working relationship with CINPACFLT. By 1960, Maritime Command Pacific was aware of the rise of Soviet naval power in the region. A unique Canadian analysis of Pacific security from 1960 has survived in a document prepared by the Joint Maritime Warfare School (JMWS). The JMWS brought RCN and RCAF operational officers together for annual courses, including shore-based instruction, followed by joint sea and air ASW exercises.

According the JMWS paper, the best intelligence estimates indicated that the Soviet Pacific Fleet had five "Z-class" and fifty-seven "W-class" submarines available. The primary mission of this large fleet would have been to "reduce the retaliatory power of SAC by striking their bases with submarine-launched guided missiles at H-Hour." Intelligence could not confirm that any of these submarines had missiles, but it was assumed that at least some of them did. The Soviets would not require many missile-equipped submarines, since the deployment of a large number of these vessels off the coast of North America would give warning of an impending attack. The JMWS estimated that the ideal number of missile-equipped submarines would be fourteen, since any more operating close to North America would raise suspicions of an impending attack. Larson Air Force Base, five miles from Moses Lake, Washington, was the one SAC target that would be threatened by submarines operating in the Canadian maritime area. Larson was home to a wing of B-52 strategic bombers, a Semi-Automatic Ground Environment (SAGE) air defence radar site, and some of the first Titan ballistic missile silos, which were under construction in 1960. Only two hours after the initial assault, the submarines would turn to secondary targets, primarily major port and industrial cities. In the Canadian maritime area, secondary targets included Vancouver, Victoria, Seattle, and Portland. Only after all missiles were expended would the Soviet submarines begin to attack shipping, either with torpedo attacks or by laying mines.

The JMWS paper examined various methods the Soviets might use to determine their firing positions. Two types of missiles were assumed to be in service, the first similar to an American Regulus I, the other a longer-range and much faster missile that would approximate the performance of the recently cancelled Regulus II. No mention was made of submarine-launched ballistic missiles or nuclear-powered vessels. Various factors were considered in determining the likely firing positions of these submarines, including the following:

- The need to achieve the greatest possible accuracy when attacking an SAC installation.

- The desirability of reducing the missile's flight time to reduce warning time.
- The avoidance of interference with other submarines and the desirability of dispersing ASW forces.

Ideal firing positions could include Barkley or Nootka Sound, since in both, comparative isolation would make detection from shore-based radar unlikely while giving the submarine an opportunity to make an extremely accurate navigational fix before firing. In any case, the JMWS estimated that a submarine firing a Regulus II–type missile would not fire on a primary target while more than 100 miles from shore.

The JMWS recognized that defeating a Soviet submarine-launched missile attack would not be easy, particularly since there could be "no guarantee" that ALCANUS forces would be "fortunate enough to enjoy any warning." The JMWS believed, however, "that a major assault would be attended by statistical raid indication," which could be achieved through normal peacetime surveillance by shore installations and sea and air forces. If an enemy attack seemed likely, the JMWS suggested that "prompt and effective action" be taken before a submarine could launch its missiles.

> When there is evidence that a missile assault is imminent, the principal concern should be to hit every enemy submarine which may surface to launch weapons. This means that every object which comes to the surface should be brought under fire within ten minutes. To do this we must pack our forces into an area from which the enemy was most likely to launch, and take a calculated risk in less likely regions.[36]

This ten-minute window of opportunity could be achieved by deploying maritime aircraft in small, fixed areas; these aircraft would make full and continuous use of radar. Each aircraft would be able to patrol an area of 6,000 square miles. Surface escorts would be employed to deny access to headlands where submarines might attempt to establish navigational fixes before launching. The JMWS document was one of the earliest to suggest using a comparatively new and top secret submarine detection system, SOSUS (sound surveillance system). SOSUS used a chain of underwater listening posts for the long-range detection of submerged submarines. Surface escorts could be used to track down SOSUS indications and other contacts with potential submerged submarines. Having acquired the target, the escorts could use hold-down tactics to prevent a submarine from surfacing and "take under gunfire any surfaced submarine within range."

The suggestion that a surfaced submarine be sunk with gunfire before hostilities commenced flew in the face of Canadian rules of engagement. While doing so might meet a military requirement, the authors of the JMWS report were revealing themselves as politically naive, besides showing that the COS had reason to be concerned about allowing tactical commanders free reign when cooperating with USN forces. One last recommendation made in the report also would have concerned the COS. The JMWS argued that since the area to be covered crossed international boundaries, and because SOSUS coverage was increasing, it was "essential" that the command of all of these forces be established in one Joint American–Canadian Headquarters. One RCAF officer found this suggestion so bizarre that he wondered whether such a command centre would be "staffed by Scotsmen."[37] Still, despite these limitations, the report provided an excellent summary of the threat faced by ASW forces on the West Coast as well as the challenges they would face in preventing a missile attack by Soviet submarines.

Conclusion

The creation of MARPAC and the interservice headquarters at Esquimalt in 1959, and the near simultaneous fleet reorganization, provided Admiral Rayner with resources to implement a comprehensive defensive scheme for Pacific maritime defence. Rayner's MAROPEDPAC plan incorporated all available elements of the naval and air forces. This marked a significant improvement over earlier schemes; even so, Rayner realized that he lacked sufficient resources to make his plans truly effective, particularly when his ships spent so much time conducting basic training,

The struggle between Rayner and Admiral Hopper to negotiate a bilateral operational agreement between the RCN and the USN's antisubmarine forces in the Pacific is a remarkable example of Canadians exerting their national interests over the demands of their more powerful American allies. By preserving the far less combative Canadian rules for prewar engagements with Soviet submarines, the Canadian Chiefs of Staffs ensured that Canadian warships, and USN vessels operating in MARPAC's area of responsibility, would not accidentally provoke a nuclear war. The demands to maintain Canadian sovereignty took place against the backdrop of the increasing power of the Soviet Navy and the growing threat of submarines equipped with cruise missiles with nuclear warheads.

6
The Golden Age

THE FLEET REORGANIZATION of 1959 marked the beginning of Pacific Command's brief golden age. At the start of the fiftieth anniversary of the RCN in 1961, Canada's Pacific Fleet consisted of just under one-third of the RCN's ships – some 20 vessels out of a total of 64 in commission. This number hides the fact that a much larger proportion of the navy's resources were devoted to the Atlantic, as a result of the huge cost of maintaining at Halifax the HMCS *Bonaventure*, the navy's only aircraft carrier and major fleet unit. Still, Pacific Command was far stronger and more capable than it had been at any time since 1911, when HMCS *Rainbow* became the first Canadian warship based at Esquimalt. Naval officers who had lived through the hard times the RCN faced in the years immediately after the Second World War were mindful that the navy was in a golden age, one that had seen the force flower quickly since the Korean conflict. Commander Cocks, captain of the *Antigonish*, wrote in his report of proceedings for January 1959:

> The year 1959 opened with our solar system peering myopically at its newest but microscopic planet, the North Atlantic Treaty Organization plagued by duplicated effort and the disunity of nationalism, Canada spending her way to prosperity and the RCN looking forward to a year that would see more operational units in commission than at any time since the second world war [*sic*]. We in *Antigonish*, unable to influence events other than by being ready, are undismayed by any forebodings and believe, with Dr. Pangloss, that all shall be for the best in 1959.[1]

The navy's golden age was much more than a measure of the number of vessels in commission. Gone were the days when captains faced massive crew turnovers and shortages. The reports of proceedings of ships are almost devoid of complaints about personnel. In February 1958 the commanding officer of the *Skeena* reported that his ship had enjoyed a highly successful first year in commission, in which the ship had steamed 40,112.3 miles, spending 167 days at sea, and, while under way, had replenished and transferred supplies fifty-two times. He concluded: "A very satisfactory and highly commendable feature is that drafting changes during the year amount to only 32. This has contributed greatly to the well-being of the ship."[2] When in September 1959 the captain of the *Antigonish* reported that

75 percent of his crew had been replaced during a recent refit period, he expressed little concern since the "new group seems very satisfactory."[3]

The Commissioning of HMCS *Cape Breton* and Acquisition of HMCS *Grilse*

On November 16, 1959, at Esquimalt, HMCS *Cape Breton* was recommissioned as a mobile repair ship. *Cape Breton* was built in 1944–45 at Burrard Dry Dock Company in Vancouver as a maintenance and accommodation ship, provided under the Mutual Aid Agreement to the Royal Navy. Originally commissioned as HMS *Flamborough Head*, the ship was returned to Canada in 1950 and renamed *Cape Breton*. From 1953 to 1958, *Cape Breton* was at Halifax serving as a floating naval trades school. By the late 1950s, permanent shore facilities for the Naval Technical School had been completed at *Naden*, and the *Cape Breton* was transferred to the West Coast for conversion to a repair ship, later redubbed an escort maintenance ship: "When completed she was fitted out with engineering and electrical workshops and possessed such facilities as a blacksmith shop, sheet metal shop, welding shop, a pipe and coppersmith's shop, and a plate shop." A large proportion of the ship's company consisted of technical personnel, and the ship was capable of "carrying out repairs on all manner of electrical and electronic equipment, diesel engines, communications equipment, and indeed all the equipment in a modern ship-of-war." She could also carry out hull repairs and had limited logistical support capabilities. She was equipped with a helicopter landing platform. The *Cape Breton* was ready for duty on February 1, 1960.[4]

The *Cape Breton* fulfilled three roles for the Pacific Fleet. Her primary function was to provide a mobile base facility that could be deployed away from the vulnerable Esquimalt dockyard in times of emergency. When paired with a naval auxiliary tanker, *Cape Breton* could maintain escort ships for an extended period from any convenient anchorage, something that fitted well into the navy's vision of any future conflict in the Pacific.[5] Her secondary role was to accompany escort ships on distant training exercises to places like Pearl Harbor or San Diego, supplying maintenance and logistical support services that otherwise would have to be provided by USN facilities. The *Cape Breton* could provide spare parts as well as the expertise to maintain Canadian warships – expertise that was unavailable in American dockyards.[6] When not engaged in either of these roles, *Cape Breton* provided additional ship repair facilities at Esquimalt. The repair ship was particularly appreciated by captains used to dealing with the overly bureaucratic dockyard. For instance, in January 1962, the captain of HMCS *Grilse*, the RCN's new West Coast–based submarine, commented that ten days alongside *Cape Breton* had been the most productive in harbour since the ship arrived in Esquimalt in July of the previous year. He reported: "Of particular note were the willing workers, the minimum of paper work and the lack of countless supervisors and examiners before a job was commenced. It was a refreshing and exhilarating experience, a new look forward to the day *Cape Breton* also has a few men qualified to submarine welding standards."[7]

The addition of the *Grilse* to the Pacific Fleet in the summer of 1961 came about because of major shortfalls that had existed since the Korean War in submarine training time available to ships of the command. Submarines were provided to Atlantic Command by arranging for the Royal Navy to provide suitable numbers of vessels, and, in 1955, the Sixth [RN] Submarine Squadron was formed and based in Halifax. The RCN paid for the operations of these vessels, usually two per year, at an average cost of $1,000,000 per annum, and provided volunteer personnel to serve in the RN's submarine service. In 1956, with additional time available from USN submarines, the Atlantic Fleet could count on 510 operating days on which a submarine would be available for ASW training. That was more than enough to meet Atlantic Command's training requirements. In the Pacific, the situation was much bleaker. The only submarines available for local training were the few USN boats operating in the Pacific Northwest, which were able to provide only 43 operating days per year to the Canadians. In 1956, the RCN estimated that by the 1950s Pacific Command would need at least 200 days per year to meet its basic training and operational requirements; there were concerns that the amount of time USN submarines would be available would actually decline. The only immediately available alternative was to have Pacific Command's ships spend as much time as possible participating in USN ASW exercises. This option reduced the number of operational ships available for West Coast defence and was not always suitable for training vessels responsible for teaching the basics of submarine detection.[8]

As a result, throughout the late 1950s and into the early 1960s, the FOPC and Pacific Command ship's captains made regular complaints about the lack of realistic ASW training opportunities. In July 1959, Admiral Rayner observed that a four-day exercise between ships of the 2nd Escort Squadron and the USS *Menhaden* would be the last opportunity for ships of the command to train with a submarine until early 1960.[9] In October 1959, because of the lack of submarines, Pacific Command was forced to use two frigates to simulate submarines during the Emergency Defence Exercise (EDPEX-59).[10] In February 1960, the consequences of the lack of submarine time were outlined by Commander E.M. Chadwick, captain of the *Saguenay:*

> As this was the first time since May 1959 that *Saguenay* had actually pinged on a live submarine there was considerable rustiness, but as the exercise progressed, improvements could be observed. Such long periods without training in the aim for which they have been expressly created renders these ships virtually non-operational.[11]

FIGURE 18 The submarine HMCS *Grilse* docked in Esquimalt, June 29, 1961. In the background, *St. Laurent* is entering harbour. (CFB Esquimalt Museum)

Captains cherished any opportunity to track a submarine. In November 1960, Commander Chadwick did not complain that the *Saguenay* was forced to operate at slow speeds, in very rough weather. He explained that "the value of these ASW exercise[s] is inestimable; especially in consideration of the fact that, except for the stolen moments with [USS] *Rock* on the surface this was the first opportunity *Saguenay* had had to ping on a live submarine since the hour or so organized with an 'enemy' submarine on completion of exercise Uppercut in July."[12] Ships' commanding officers bewailed any missed opportunities for realistic ASW experience. Engaged in a major USN exercise in February 1959, the captain of the *Margaree* should have been proud to have been incorporated into the screen defending and providing plane guards for the aircraft carrier USS *Hornet.* Instead, the *Margaree*'s skipper lamented that he was stuck with the carrier and not given an opportunity to track down attacking submarines. He reported: "I could not help but feel this valuable submarine time slipping through my fingers. We get so little ordinary contact time which my sonar operators need so badly."[13] Similarly, in March 1961, Commander Chadwick, after a particularly successful exercise between *Saguenay* and a USN hunter-killer group, expressed his strong opinion that the destroyers of the 2nd Escort

Squadron should spend as much time as possible serving alongside their American colleagues. Admiral Rayner, the FOPC, reported to Naval headquarters that while he agreed with the remarks of the commanding officer about the advantages of constant training with the USN, it was impracticable, since "ships cannot be away from Canadian waters all the time."[14]

Beginning in 1956, the RCN explored a variety of options for providing additional submarine training time in the Pacific. Talks with the RN to provide a submarine to be based at Esquimalt failed. Discussions with the USN to increase the number of hours available to Pacific Command were no more successful; in fact, the RCN was informed that the USN would likely have to reduce its commitments in the years ahead. Finally, in June 1959, the RCN reluctantly realized that it would have to acquire its own submarine and that the best available option was to obtain one from the USN. That month, naval headquarters made an exploratory inquiry to the USN about acquiring a submarine on loan. Between November 9 and 13, after the US Navy indicated its support for the Canadian proposal, Naval Headquarters sent a group of RCN officers to Washington, DC, and the New London submarine base to select the most suitable vessel and to work out arrangements for the transfer of the submarine. The USS *Burrfish* was chosen as the best available submarine, since she had undergone a complete overhaul just before being placed in reserve in 1956.

The *Burrfish* had been launched in Philadelphia on June 18, 1943. Originally she had served as a fleet submarine. In 1949, she was converted into a submarine radar picket. The submarine displaced just over 2,000 tons, could travel on the surface at 19 knots, and had a maximum underwater battery endurance of just thirty minutes at 8.2 knots, or twenty-four hours at 2 knots. She was equipped with a snorkel, which allowed her to travel just below the surface at 7 knots using her diesel engines. Armament consisted of 4–21 torpedo tubes and she was capable of carrying eight torpedoes. Most of her electronic sensors – radar and sonar – dated back to the Second World War; the RCN did not believe it needed to modernize a vessel whose primary purpose was to provide training opportunities for its surface fleet.

The loan agreement called for the USN to supply the RCN with the *Burrfish* for five years. The RCN would be responsible for the full cost of activating the submarine, providing it with spares and handbooks, outfitting it with torpedoes, and training the crew. The total cost of the activation was estimated at $877,000. In large measure because it was necessary to secure US Congressional approval before the transfer could take place, the official approval of the loan agreement only took place on September 15, 1960. Work on activating the submarine commenced in Philadelphia in December 1960. This work was completed in the spring of 1961, and the new RCN submarine, renamed HMCS *Grilse*, was commissioned in New London on May 11, 1961.[15]

After commissioning, the crew spent more than a month at New London completing advanced tactical training courses and passing a series of exercises under the watchful eyes of USN instructors. The exercises included an attack on two American destroyer squadrons in conjunction with another submarine, the USS *Angler*. The destroyers were supported by a squadron of ASW helicopters. Both submarines were able to penetrate the screen of the destroyers undetected, in large measure because of unusually poor acoustical conditions that hampered the destroyers' sonars. However, neither submarine was able to get into firing position, in part because of the constant harassment of the helicopters. The *Grilse* also was involved in four separate sub versus sub exercises, which showed the new emphasis the USN was placing on submarines as ASW vessels. Twice, the crew of the *Grilse* had opportunities to learn first-hand of the limited military value of their newly commissioned vessel. In one of the sub versus sub exercises, *Grilse* found herself completely outclassed by the USS *Grenadier*, which was equipped with more modern sonar systems. The *Grenadier's* "long ears" enabled her to detect and fire on *Grilse* long before the Canadians located the American boat. As well, just before leaving New London, the *Grilse*'s officers were invited onboard the USS *Tullibee*, the prototype for all future nuclear-powered ASW hunter-killer submarines. The Canadian officers were given a detailed briefing on the *Tullibee*'s capabilities and intended role. Some of the discussion included information to which RCN personnel had hitherto been denied access at New London. One can only wonder what the Canadians thought of the possibility of facing such a formidable submarine in combat.[16]

The *Grilse* finally arrived at Esquimalt in July 1961. Preparations to receive the submarine had been under way at the base for the previous year. Dockyard workers and technical personnel from *Cape Breton* had been sent to San Diego to learn the special skills necessary to maintain such a complex vessel. Shore facilities provided crew accommodations, since unlike with the frigates and destroyers, personnel could not be expected to live onboard the cramped quarters of the submarine. A workshop was built to help maintain the vessel.[17] The *Grilse*'s arrival on the West Coast was cause for great optimism among the members of Pacific Command, which finally would have a submarine regularly available for ASW training and exercises.[18]

Operations Exercises on the West Coast, 1958–65

The two Esquimalt-based escort squadrons followed two very different patterns of service, as one might expect from their dissimilar primary roles. The 2nd Escort Squadron devoted most of its time to operational training and missions;

the 4th Escort Squadron, to training cadets. Once or twice a year, generally in the autumn, ships of the two squadrons came together for a major command exercise.

Between January 1958 and March 1963, Canadian warships took part in nineteen major exercises with elements of the USN. This number does not include the regular exercises in which the 2nd Minesweeper Squadron took part, mainly in waters off Long Beach, California, the main USN West Coast base for this type of vessel. Most of these exercises involved elements of the 2nd Escort Squadron; rarely were the frigates of the 4th Escort Squadron allowed to divert themselves from cadet training duties. These joint exercises were of three basic types: ASW exercises, mainly of the hunter-killer (HUK) type; convoy screening exercises; and West Coast continental defence exercises. Except for continental defence exercises, the ships of the 2nd Escort Squadron were generally required to travel to waters off San Diego or Pearl Harbor to join USN vessels' ASW training. Twice the exercises took place, in part, in waters off Japan, and included elements of the Japanese Maritime Defence Force. Most of these operations involved being integrated into larger American naval formations. The RCN's DEs were regularly incorporated into USN carrier ASW groups, working with six different aircraft carriers in seven exercises during this period. On one occasion, Pacific Command's warships had the opportunity to form the screen around the USS *Ranger*, a fleet carrier. After the fleet reorganization in 1959, normally only one division of the 2nd Escort Squadron – three or four St. Laurent-class vessels – was involved in any exercise. As Admiral Rayner had predicted in 1958, it was impossible, with just one operational group on the West Coast, for more than a division to participate in a distance exercise; some operational capacity in home waters had to be maintained.

The exercises with the Americans were highly valued by the officers and men of Pacific Command, for they provided opportunities to learn skills impossible to acquire elsewhere. The RCN crews gained experience in such things as working in a carrier screen, cooperating with helicopters and ship-borne maritime patrol aircraft, and hunting down the latest high-speed GUPPY-type submarines. Important combat skills were gained, and Canadian sailors were able to practise handling their ships in large formations, communicating with American sea and air units, and refuelling at sea. On at least four occasions through 1965, ships of the 2nd Escort Squadron were given an opportunity to track nuclear-powered submersibles. In November 1959, *Assiniboine*, *Fraser*, and *Margaree* conducted ASW exercises with USS *Swordfish*. During February 1960, the same submarine worked with *Margaree*. In July 1961, the *Fraser* and *Saguenay* had thirty-six hours to exercise with USS *Scamp*. Finally, in March 1965, the frigate *Beacon Hill* and the destroyer escort *Saskatchewan* had a day-long session working with *Swordfish*.

The RCN ships were almost seamlessly integrated into all the USN formations during the exercises, an example of the very close relationship between MARPAC and the American Pacific Fleet. Canadian officers often commented on the close bonds they felt with their American counterparts, and the respect was mutual. At a major USN conference on the ASW situation in the Pacific held at San Diego in March 1959, Admiral Rayner and several other Canadian officers joined some two hundred American officers for full and frank briefings and discussions. Rayner felt that the Canadians were treated like "old pros."[19] Meetings like this reinforced the notion that Canada was a partner in maintaining continental security on the Pacific Coast. Yet neither in these meetings nor in the exercises did Canadian sailors ever lose sight of their unique identity. Canadian officers were proud of their men, ships, and equipment and believed they were at least as good, if not better, at hunting submarines than their allies. Typical are the comments made by the captain of the *Skeena* after an exercise with a USN carrier division in November 1963:

> After a somewhat diffident start, the Ship's Company emerged from the HUKEX period with a hard-earned and well deserved feeling of confidence in themselves and their ship. Skeena had worked and operated hand-in-hand with some of the most sophisticated and modern ASW ships of the USN and at no time did she take a back seat to them.[20]

The Americans often agreed with their Canadian counterparts.[21]

It is not necessary to go through each of these exercises in detail, but a close examination of several will illustrate the nature of ASW training and cooperation in the Pacific during these years. From January to March 1958, *Crescent*, *Cayuga*, *Fraser*, *Margaree*, and *Skeena* took part in REX 58, one of the largest ASW exercises yet attempted in the Pacific. The ASW forces were charged with escorting a nonmercantile convoy from Long Beach, California, to Yokosuka, Japan, via Pearl Harbor. The exercise involved a series of active and inactive phases. The active phases occurred as the convoy approached each port and entailed submarine and air opposition to the convoy, with surface and air augmentation to the convoy escort. "The inactive phase consisted of a series of day and night exercises that made the active phase seem restful." The operation was designed to test various new doctrines and tactics as they related to the passage of this type of convoy in the face of submarine and air threats, with the goal of maximizing the chances of achieving "the safe and timely arrival of the convoy." The Canadian destroyers formed the through escort, responsible for protecting the convoy, which consisted of six USN high-speed transports for the entire passage. Commanding the escorts was Captain M.G. Stirling, commander of the 2nd Escort Squadron. In each active phase, additional USN forces augmented the escorts. For example, in active phase "Alpha," off Long Beach, the Canadian destroyers were supported by maritime patrol aircraft and by the destroyers USS *Erben*, *Shields*, and *Colahan* from COMDESDIV 172.

In each active phase, the convoy was subjected to either submarine or air attack. The convoy sailed from Long Beach on January 21. During the first active phase, which began that evening, the escorts thought they had detected a number of submarines, which they kept down while the convoy passed by. Subsequent analysis, however, found that none of these contacts were actual subs and that no attacks were made on the convoy. Active phase "Bravo" began on the afternoon of the January 27 and ended on the morning of January 28, as the convoy approached Hawaii. The escorts were told to expect air attacks, but they found it difficult to distinguish between commercial aircraft and any approaching bandits. Only one attack actually developed, carried out by US marine jet fighters. The Canadians were able to detect them with their ships' air warning radar, which gave exceptionably good results, and were able to lock on to their three "mounts on target at the maximum effective range of the guns." As the convoy approached Pearl Harbor, it was attacked by three USN submarines, *Pickerel*, *Blackfin*, and *Tang*. *Pickerel* attacked first, penetrating the convoy and managing to sink two of the transports, before she in turn was attacked by *Fraser*. *Blackfin* attacked next and was penetrating the convoy screen when she was detected by *Margaree*. *Margaree* attacked, and *Blackfin* retaliated by firing a torpedo at the destroyer escort. *Blackfin* then carried along the port side of the convoy, where she was detected by *Skeena*. *Skeena's* captain recounted what followed:

> A number of attacks were carried out during which *Blackfin* fired a circling torpedo, sounding like an express train on the sonar, which was judged to have obtained a hit. It was believed that in order to do this she had come to periscope depth to sight the ship visually. This is considered to be an unlikely wartime gambit in the face of exploding mortar salvoes and the fact that it brought the submarine above layer depth thus presenting a much more easily detectable target. Nevertheless, it was agreed in underwater telephone discussions at the time to call the engagement a draw.

The exercise continued through much of February as the convoy headed for Japan. On arrival there, the crews had an opportunity to visit Tokyo. The ships then toured Southeast Asia, with stops at Hong Kong and Saigon. On March 10, the 2nd Escort Squadron arrived in Okinawa to prepare for the final phase of REX 58, the escorting of another convoy from that Japanese island to Hawaii.

Again the Canadian ships formed the convoy's through escort, joined by the USS *Cook*, a high-speed transport converted from a wartime destroyer escort. The convoy consisted of six USN amphibious assault ships and fast transports. As the ships left Okinawa on March 12, the escorts and convoy were augmented by six USN destroyers, two destroyer escorts, another high-speed transport, and the Japanese Maritime Defence Force (JMDF) ships *Hatsuki* and *Asahi*. The group was divided into fast and slow convoys and had to traverse an area patrolled by three enemy submarines and aircraft from the USS *Hornet*. The Canadian ships ran into little opposition during this phase of the exercise, but learned a great deal from their close cooperation with the USN and Japanese warships. It was the first time that RCN vessels had exercised with ships from the JMDF.

On March 14 this active phase ended; the augmentation force returned to Okinawa while the convoy and its escorts proceeded to Hawaii. Eight days later, the next active phase of the exercise commenced. The escorts sailed ahead of the transports, forming a dummy convoy to draw off any opposing forces. Meanwhile, the transports were ordered to sail independently, well behind the escorts and at least ten miles apart from one another. A squadron of USN P2V Neptune aircraft from Hawaii reinforced the six surface escorts. Three USN submarines, *Pickerel*, *Blackfin*, and *Sabalo*, and a group of US Marine aircraft formed the attacking forces. The first sign of the opposing force was a green flare sighted some 7½ miles from the dummy convoy. A Neptune aircraft, *Skeena*, and *Crescent* were sent to investigate. *Skeena* gained firm sonar contact on a submarine, later identified as *Sabalo*, and conducted five attacks before a bubble decoy allowed the submarine to break sonar contact. *Crescent* carried out one further attack before *Sabalo* made good her escape. At one point in the fracas, *Sabalo* simulated firing a torpedo equipped with an atomic warhead, believing she had destroyed both Canadian vessels. Post-exercise investigations concluded that, given the capabilities of the RCN's antisubmarine mortar Mark 10, *Skeena* likely sank *Sabalo* before she could fire her torpedo.

As the two destroyer escorts returned to the dummy convoy, the other two submarines launched a coordinated attack. A wild nighttime fight ensued, the results of which were hotly debated in the post-exercise conference between the escort and submarine commanding officers. *Skeena*'s captain concluded that the whole thing turned into a "debacle." *Cayuga* started out by sinking *Pickerel*. In the next thirty minutes *Fraser* and *Skeena* both claimed successful attacks on *Blackfin*, but the American submarine believed she had torpedoed four of the escorts before she herself was destroyed. It was difficult to determine immediately the exact sequence of events, so initially it was decided to declare the attack a draw. Later analysis, however, tended to support *Blackfin*'s claim that she had struck first at the escorts. When this was announced, the captain of *Skeena* observed that *Blackfin*'s "use of periscope in such close proximity to four gyrating A/S vessels did appear more courageous than realistic in war, when mortar salvoes would be landing all around him." Whatever the outcome of the battle, by focusing on the escorts, the submarines had allowed the merchant ships to escape unscathed. This was caused by the failure of the attackers to detect the ruse of the false convoy, in large measure because the Marine aircraft assigned to the attacking force never appeared.

The final phase of REX 58 commenced on March 25, after a two-day sojourn in Pearl Harbor. The Canadian ships and *Cook* were joined by four USN DEs of CONTRON 11. The American DEs were equipped with new SQS-4 long-range sonar. The convoy left Pearl Harbor in an extended atomic formation, leaving at least 3,500 metres between each ship. Again three submarines were assigned to the opposing forces, and they launched a coordinated attack on the convoy just a few hours after it left port. The presence of the submarines was announced by the passing of two torpedo tracks just in front of one of the transports. *Skeena* and the destroyer escort USS *Silverstein* were assigned to hunt down the attacker. *Skeena* achieved firm sonar contact within ten minutes and launched a series of three attacks. The submarine fired a circling torpedo at her; even so, *Skeena*'s persistence paid off, and she was rewarded with *Sabalo* surfacing and reporting herself destroyed. Soon after this victory, *Margaree* detected a second submarine penetrating the convoy, but the attacker escaped before she herself could be attacked. *Silverstein* and *Skeena*, returning to the convoy after their successful hunt, picked up where *Margaree* left off. The American DE gained firm sonar contact and launched two attacks on the submarine before allowing *Skeena* to take over. The Canadian ship made three further attacks, and the USS *Blackfin* declared herself out of action and surfaced. *Skeena*'s skipper concluded: "It had been a brief and engaging hour and a quarter. With two submarines 'in the bag' it was a satisfactory forenoon's hunting." Only one further attack developed, later in the afternoon, when the third submarine attempted to attack the convoy. The submarine was thwarted by *Crescent* and *Fraser*, which detected it and attacked it until the convoy had passed by. The overall results for this phase of the exercise were two confirmed sub sinkings, while only one convoy vessel was destroyed – "a very favourable ASW attrition rate."

With that, REX 58 came to an end. The 2nd Escort Squadron headed back to Esquimalt, taking time to conduct close air support exercises with 407 Squadron, and arrived home on April 2. It had been an extraordinary cruise for the escort squadron: they had been away from home for seventy-eight days, and at sea for sixty-five of them, steaming just under 20,000 miles and engaging in operations almost constantly. This included eight attacks on the convoy that simulated wartime conditions as closely as possible. All captains agreed that it had been a remarkable learning experience. The captain of *Margaree*, whose ship had joined the fleet only the previous October, believed the cruise was a transforming experience for his crew: "The tense and enquiring air of a green crew is no longer prevalent as when the cruise began, but was replaced with a more knowing and relaxed air of a team who knows how to act on the plays."[22]

No future exercise would match the length and intensity of REX 58, but there were other opportunities to work with the USN. In March and April 1960, *St. Laurent*, *Ottawa*, and *Saguenay* exercised with elements of the US 7th Fleet in waters off Japan. The vessels had left Esquimalt in February, starting their cruise with a convoy escort exercise from Long Beach to Hawaii. This exercise closely mirrored the opening phases of REX 58 and need not be examined in detail. However, some new elements were involved. For at least part of the convoy operations, the escort ships operated without any active sensors, radar or sonar, on the theory that using these devices revealed their position to enemy air and submarine units. The importance of air support for the escorts was emphasized, since ships would only activate their sensors when an aircraft had detected a nearby threat to the convoy. After leaving Hawaii, the ships travelled around Southeast Asia before arriving at Okinawa in late March, ready to begin a series of complex tests with the 7th Fleet. The operation was divided into five separate phases:

1) Unopposed sorties, followed by independent A/S exercises with assigned submarines.
2) Opposed underway replenishment.
3) Submarine transit exercise.
4) Opposed underway replenishment.
5) Special exercises and tactical evaluation.[23]

On the morning of April 2, all forces involved in the exercise formed a screen around the aircraft carrier USS *Yorktown* and proceeded out to sea. Late in the afternoon the formation broke up, and the three Canadian warships proceeded for a submarine tracking exercise with USS *Medregal*, assisted by aircraft from *Yorktown*. The DEs conducted a "three-ship lock-on procedure," holding contact with *Medregal* despite her efforts to escape. Experience was gained in control of antisubmarine aircraft. The next day the RCN DEs worked with airborne early warning (AEW) aircraft from the American carrier. This was the first opportunity they had had to test the ships' AEW receiving equipment, which allowed them to use the aircraft's radar information without activating their own radar sets. The RCAF's ASW aircraft on the West Coast were not fitted with AEW radar. On Monday, April 4, the Canadian vessels rendezvoused with the USS *Platte*, a fleet tanker, and refuelled, while submarines attempted to ambush the ships. Supported by four helicopters, the division was able to complete its mission and prevent the submarines from launching a single attack. Later that day, the Canadian ships engaged in experimental tracking exercises with a GUPPY II–type submarine, the USS *Pomfret*. Details of these experiments are sketchy, but they appear to have involved using passive listening to locate and follow a submarine.

On April 5, the three RCN vessels joined the two USN destroyer divisions to form a barrier to prevent two submarines, *Pomfret* and *Medregal*, from entering the Philippine Sea. Surface attack units (SAUs) of two ships each were formed. Each SAU was assisted by one VP and three VS aircraft, and later by helicopters from *Yorktown*. *Ottawa* and *Saguenay* formed the northernmost SAU; *St. Laurent* paired with the USS *Walker* to form a unit just to the south of them. Late in the afternoon, a helicopter supporting *St. Laurent* and *Walker* made an underwater contact, and "a very short time after a copy book close action, *Medregal* surfaced out of action."[24] The other submarine was brought to the surface by a USN SAU. Another "opposed refueling exercise" followed the next day. This time a submarine was able to penetrate the screen and fire her torpedoes before she was detected. Thirty minutes later, a helicopter and *Saguenay* almost simultaneously detected a submarine at very short range. Unfortunately, the helicopter was operating far too close to *Saguenay*, and the ship was unable to get into attack position without fouling the helicopter; as a result, the submarine was able to get between the screen and the tanker. Still, *Saguenay* maintained contact and eventually forced *Medregal* to surface. The captain of *Saguenay* explained that the sub had been detected at such short range because the screen commander had made far too many changes in formation, which compelled the ship to operate at speeds higher than was ideal for sonar use in order to maintain position. He recommended that formations be changed infrequently; he also advised that helicopters be required to maintain at least one mile between themselves and the ships.

The final stage of the exercise took place that afternoon, when the SAUs worked with aircraft equipped with magnetic anomaly detection (MAD) to hunt submarines. Unfortunately, the MAD equipment malfunctioned on most of the aircraft; even so, *Ottawa* was able to detect *Pomfret* and force it to surface.[25]

Usually, exercises were held with elements of the US Pacific Fleet off San Diego or Pearl Harbor. On occasion the RCN vessels were joined by 407 Squadron. In June 1960, for example, the DEs carried RCAF ground crew personnel, tools, and spare parts to Hawaii, where they were joined by 407 Squadron's Neptune aircraft. Typical of such exercises is the one held from March 7 to 23, 1961, in Hawaiian waters. On March 2, *St. Laurent, Ottawa*, and *Saguenay*, under the command of Captain J.A. Charles, commander of the 2nd Escort Squadron, left Esquimalt and headed south. Five days later the ships rendezvoused with Carrier Division 17, consisting of the USS *Kearsarge*, three destroyers of DESDIV 72, and four destroyer escorts of CORTRON 3. The USN warships were heading for Hawaii to undertake work-up exercises prior to deployment to Southeast Asia. The ships of the 2nd Escort Squadron were incorporated into the screen around the carrier. The formal exercises began with an opposed entry into Pearl Harbor, starting at midnight on March 9. Three submarines attempted to sink the carrier, and the USN surface units were sent out ahead of the carrier to find them. The Canadian vessels provided close escort to the carrier, zigzagging at 25 knots as they approached the harbour. The defences were extremely effective, no attacks were launched at the carrier, only one submarine even sighted the main force, and one of the attackers was sunk by the USN surface ships.

FIGURE 19 HMCS *St. Laurent*, first of her class, arriving at Esquimalt, June 29, 1961. The introduction of these cutting-edge Canadian-designed ships in the mid-1950s significantly improved ASW defences in the Pacific. (CFB Esquimalt Museum)

After a stopover at Pearl Harbor, on March 13 the three DEs joined *Kearsarge* and other USN ships for two weeks of manoeuvres in Hawaiian waters. The first week focused on Cold War–type exercises, in which enemy submarines were to be located, then tracked until they had exhausted their batteries and been forced to the surface, where they could be identified. Initially the submarines were allowed to operate anywhere north of Hawaii, and none were detected. The DEs rushed from one possible submarine sighting by aircraft to another, but at no time did they make contact with their elusive prey. In the next part of the exercise, the submarines were required to transit a particular area. *St. Laurent* and the destroyer USS *Taussig*, which formed an SAU, made contact with a submarine. With the assistance of aircraft, helicopters, and other USN ships, their sonars held the contact despite violent manoeuvres by the submarine trying to escape. Finally, the USS *Sabalo* was forced to surface.

After a long weekend in Pearl Harbor, the exercise recommenced with a series of "hot" or wartime simulations against three enemy submarines. Scenarios included the following: having a HUK group provide A/S protection to an amphibious group transiting through a submarine probability area; refuelling at sea; maintaining A/S coverage of an area together with VP aircraft; and providing A/S protection for a fleet aircraft carrier. The Canadian ships were assigned to a variety of tasks. *Ottawa* and *Saguenay* spent most of the week paired with USN ships in SAUs, while *St. Laurent* was mainly occupied as part of the screen around *Kearsarge*. All of the ships had ample opportunity to practise their ASW skills. Despite being mainly tied to the carrier, *St. Laurent* participated in bringing two submarines to the surface and detecting several others. *Saguenay* had the most successful exercise. As it commenced, Captain Alford, USN, Chief of Staff to Admiral Jimmy Thach, in charge of ASW operations for the Pacific Fleet, joined the ship to observe. *Saguenay* was able to demonstrate its abilities by taking over a contact from *St. Laurent* and, after a few quick attacks, forcing USS *Blackfin* out of action. Over the next three days, *Saguenay* carried out three more successful "kills" on submarines, two of which were on the unfortunate *Blackfin*. In the last attack, however, the American submarine was able to achieve a measure of revenge when she was judged by "the unfortunate roll of an umpire's dice" to have torpedoed her adversary at the same time *Blackfin* herself was destroyed by Canadian A/S mortars. Senior Canadian officers were enthusiastic about the effect the exercise had on their crews. Stronger ASW skills had greatly improved the sailors' morale, as well as their health.[26] Commander J.B. Fartheringham, captain of *St. Laurent*, reported that

> the lessons learned and the experience gained during this month of operations with the USN can only be described as invaluable. Operating in ideal sonar

> conditions with a large number of ships, aircraft and submarines is undoubtedly the only way in which ASW capabilities of RCN ships can be tested and improved. It is considered therefore that every opportunity should be taken by the RCN to work with USN task forces under similar circumstances.[27]

These major exercises with the USN were considered the best opportunity for the 2nd Escort Squadron to practise combat skills, but they were only part of the squadron's training regime. Plans for West Coast defence did not call for RCN ships to be incorporated into hunter-killer carrier groups; instead, they were to work closely with maritime patrol aircraft of 407 Squadron and USN squadrons based in the Northwest Pacific. The ships of the 4th Escort Squadron were also called upon to play an important role in the defensive scheme. The annual emergency defence preparation exercises, such as EDPEX-59 (see above), provided Pacific Command's warships with an opportunity to practise their wartime mission. These exercises brought all available Canadian units and nearby American forces into an exercise that as closely as possible followed the established defence scheme for the west coast of Canada. Occasionally these Canadian exercises were subsumed into larger ones involving all of the ASW defences on the Pacific coast of North America, such as Operation Uppercut (July 1960) and Operation Seashell (October 1961). All of these exercises were designed to approximate as close to wartime conditions as the budget allowed. During EDPEX-59, for instance, two ships were manned, fuelled, provisioned, and munitioned to war standards.[28] To start EDPEX 1–61, no advanced warning was given of the exercise, which began at 1300 on Saturday, September 30, with an emergency order for ships to recall their crews and sail as soon as possible. "This was arranged," wrote Admiral Finch-Noyes to naval headquarters, "with malice aforethought, this being considered to be the most difficult time and day of the week in which to stage a sudden recall and bring ships up to war complement." There were limits to how realistic these exercises could be. Finch-Noyes informed Ottawa that he had tried to simulate wartime conditions; "as usual, however, the limitations imposed on the expenditure of funds introduced a sense of unrealism, it being impossible to create a sense of real emergency when action is got under way with all dispatch but no extra funds can be expended. Costs and emergency action are incompatible."[29]

Despite these limitations, there were many advantages to these exercises over those conducted with the USN in the comparatively calm waters off San Diego or Hawaii. Usually conducted in autumn or winter, these exercises exposed the ships and aircraft of MARPAC to the far more demanding conditions of the Northeast Pacific. Even during Operation Uppercut, which was unusual because it took place in July, ships were forced to contend with the typical finicky weather conditions off the west coast of Vancouver Island. Commander Chadwick of *Saguenay* reported that from the start of Uppercut on July 21, 1960, until July 27, the exercise involved "rather trying days of keeping unproductive patrols in the damp murk of the waters to the west of Vancouver Island." The only break from this dismal weather occurred when the ship "burst through the curtain of fog into the sunshine to secure along *Cape Breton* at Quatsino Sound and to fuel from CNAV *Dundurn*." As soon as *Saguenay* refuelled she returned to the fog for a further three days of fruitless patrolling with *Ottawa*. Chadwick concluded:

> Upper Cut was a valuable exercise despite absence of sub contacts, demonstrating actual war conditions at sea, testing the endurance and vigilance of the escort destroyer and the feasibility of our war plans. The *Saguenay* was still well up on her toes at FINEX, and could have carried on for at least another equal period of time. The Sonarmen [*sic*] in particular, including OJT's, continued to report with alacrity and classified correctly whales, porpoises, and fishing boat hydrophone effect.[30]

Admiral Finch-Noyes agreed with Chadwick's assessment. He informed Naval Headquarters that Operation Seashell "was of great value as the Maritime Command, Operations, and most of the ships in the command were given a thorough workout under very adverse conditions at sea."[31]

These major defence exercises demonstrated that MARPAC was prepared to defend the west coast of Canada and that it had all but two of the major assets needed for this purpose. *Cape Breton*, when paired with a naval auxiliary tanker, could provide a forward base for Pacific Command's warships. The RCN, however, lacked the ability to support its ships while at sea; instead it was entirely reliant on USN fleet tankers. For instance, during Operation Seashell, the USS *Talluga* fuelled twelve ships of the 2nd and 4th Escort Squadrons. No logistical support was available at sea. This capability gap explains the navy's major investment in the 1960s in developing operational support ships. Also lacking were any helicopter ASW capabilities. Although VU-33 provided a few helicopters for personnel transfer and small-scale logistical support, and 407 Squadron provided fixed-wing antisubmarine support, Pacific Command warships had learned in their exercises with the USN that ASW helicopters were a very tangible force multiplier when hunting down submarines. Yet at no time during this period were ASW helicopters allotted to Pacific Command.

Of all the major exercises undertaken by MARPAC between 1958 and 1965, only four did not focus on ASW. In March 1962 and March 1964, Esquimalt-based ships took part in two JET exercises in the Indian Ocean with vessels and aircraft of the British, New Zealand, Australian, Indian, and Malaysian navies. This was the first time the RCN had worked with the Indian and Malaysian forces. The exercises were the highlights of extensive cruises through Asia. The ships visited places rarely if ever encountered by the RCN, such as Ceylon (now Sri Lanka), Burma (now Myanmar), Thailand, and Indonesia. The crews had many encounters with cultures they thought were exotic if not outright bizarre. For example, Commander L.A. MacPherson, captain of *Ottawa*, reported with great enthusiasm about his 30-mile trip upriver to the port of Bangkok. They were guided by a local pilot, whose competency came into question because he answered "yes" to every query. MacPherson was amazed to see local children playing in the river like Canadian children played in a park, and he claimed that people simplified their cleaning chores by jumping in the river with their clothes on. MacPherson was particularly amused by the water buffalo that worked in the paddy fields that lined the riverbanks. He gleefully reported: "I'm sure *Ottawa* is the only ship in the Royal Canadian Navy which has slowed down to allow a herd of the beasts to cross her bows, and that from port to starboard."

The JET exercises gave Pacific Command warships their first opportunity in many years to train with their Commonwealth partners. While the Canadian warships may have been fully integrated into the doctrines of the US Pacific Fleet, they had much to gain from the JET exercises. The Canadian warships were given opportunities to practise skills seldom called for in antisubmarine warfare. *Assiniboine*, *Margaree*, and *Ottawa* participated in the first of the JET exercises. Other ships involved included two aircraft carriers, HMS *Centaur* and the Indian Navy's *Vikrant*, two cruisers, including HMS *Belfast*, sixteen destroyers and frigates, and eight vessels of the Royal Fleet Auxiliary. The RCN vessels began the exercise by forming part of the screen around *Centaur*, a task they found very different from supporting an American carrier. Commander MacPherson reported:

> Having been used to operating with the United States Navy carriers, it took a few watches before my Officers of the Watch accustomed themselves to screening *Centaur*. A very few tactical signals were used, a flying programme was not normally issued, and a sector-type screen was used. Officers had to watch closely, interpret tactical signals very freely, and act quickly. There was no "My rudder is left" from *Centaur*.[32]

After two days of escorting the carrier, the Canadians were detached from the main body to take on the unaccustomed role of villains, simulating an attacking force of missile-armed ships trying to get into launch position to strike the fleet. The Canadians were subjected to fierce air attacks. *Assiniboine* and *Ottawa* were judged to have been sunk, but *Margaree* was able to get in firing position. After this exercise, the fleet practised resupply while under way, something the RCN had not attempted with USN vessels. While a one-ton load was being transferred from RFA *Fort Langley* to *Ottawa*, a pole collapsed when the ships rolled unexpectedly, resulting in injuries to six Canadian sailors. The Canadian officers were impressed with the speed with which Commonwealth ships could take on supplies and fuel. HMAS *Vampire*, for example, commenced refuelling within four minutes after it positioned itself 300 yards astern of an RFA oiler. The exercises concluded with some ASW practice, during which the RCN vessels were able to demonstrate their expertise, as well as simulated air attacks and a final stint screening *Centaur*.[33]

The 1964 JET exercise involved *Fraser*, *St. Laurent*, and *Mackenzie*, a new DE that had been commissioned on the East Coast in October 1962 and that had recently joined Pacific Command. Highlights of this exercise included assignments screening *Vikrant*. This was the first time that Canadian warships had worked so closely with the Indian Navy. Frequent air attacks gave the DEs an opportunity to practise their anti-aircraft defences, "a notable soft spot in the RCN."[34]

As well, Pacific Command engaged in two amphibious warfare exercises, CANLEX 64 in November 1964 and Operation Sockeye in November 1965. These were the first such exercises held on the coast since the Sea Serpent series in 1955. This operation had become possible because, for the first time in a decade, the Commanding Officer of Western Command, Major-General J.M. Rockingham, had managed to have a regular force battalion allocated for regional defence operations.[35] CANLEX 64 simulated a small-scale landing by an enemy raiding party near the RCAF radar station at Holberg on the northern tip of Vancouver Island. *Antigonish* and *Sussexvale* landed a force of four officers and fifty men of the First Queen's Own Rifles to deal with the raiders; meanwhile, the ships tracked down the trawler, played by *Stettler*, that had delivered them.[36] Operation Sockeye was a more ambitious affair, designed to test amphibious warfare landing capabilities in the Queen Charlotte Islands. HMCS *St. Croix*, *Stettler*, and *Antigonish* landed elements of the 2nd Battalion of the Princess Patricia's Canadian Light Infantry (PPCLI), the 2nd Battalion of the Queen's Own Rifles, the 3rd Field Squadron Royal Canadian Engineers, and the BC area signal squadron. They were joined there by air support troops from the Canadian Joint Transport Centre in Manitoba and units of Air Transport Command.[37]

The JET and amphibious assault exercises were useful but did not prepare the ships of Pacific Command for their intended operational role; they also seemed out of character with the focus of the command since 1955. There is no definitive explanation for this change of direction, but it might tie into the increasing demands placed on the US Pacific Fleet as the commitment to the Vietnam War expanded. Certainly at least one RCN–USN exercise was disrupted – the HUK exercises with *Kearsarge* in March 1961, when the carrier was rushed to Southeast Asia to deal with growing tensions there. It is likely not a coincidence that Pacific Command involved itself in nontraditional exercises just as the frequency of opportunities to work with the US fleet began to diminish. Still, there may have been other factors at work, including a political desire to show the Canadian flag more widely and a desire to test capabilities other than ASW.

Before ending this discussion of major exercises, one other type of operational testing must be briefly discussed. While the furthering of the operational readiness of its ships was Pacific Command's first priority, it was also responsible for being ready to instigate a regime to control shipping on the West Coast if war should break out. Detailed plans were developed in the 1950s for the navy to take control of merchant traffic; this would be an extremely complex operation involving a number of government and nongovernment agencies such as the Vancouver Board of Trade, shipping companies, and merchant captains. To practise implementing these plans, an annual control-of-shipping exercise was undertaken by the command and cooperating agencies. The exercises, such as REPEX 1–61 in September 1961, Exercise Prairie Wolf in March 1962, Operation Windmill in March 1963, and Operation Long Pine in June 1965, included the simulated movement of ships to dispersal anchorages and the activation of the control-of-shipping organization, which consisted of port directors, customs officers, and fisheries personnel. Just one example of the complexity is that the navy prepared sets of instructions for ships' captains, which in times of crisis or war would be distributed to every merchant ship in BC waters or approaching the coast from the Pacific. Sealed envelopes would be given out under naval supervision by the harbour masters of Victoria, Vancouver, and Prince Rupert, as well as by the pilots in Victoria who guided ships through the Strait of Juan de Fuca.[38] These annual tests, along with the EDPEX exercises, were a constant reminder to the command that war was a very real possibility in the late 1950s and early 1960s, at the height of the Cold War.

Conclusion

MARPAC's forces during the golden age reached their zenith in operational readiness. By working as an integral part of the USN's Pacific Fleet, by participating in major Asia–Pacific exercises with the naval forces of Japan and of the Commonwealth, and by taking part in national defence training drills, the 2nd

Escort Squadron made itself ready for wartime, if and when the Cold War became hot.

The commissioning of the repair vessel HMCS *Cape Breton* and the acquisition of HMCS *Grilse* further enhanced the capabilities of Pacific Command. In particular, *Grilse* provided MARPAC with a dedicated submarine that greatly enhanced the operational training of the 2nd Escort Squadron and the basic training mission of the 4th Escort Squadron.

7

The Cold War on the Pacific Coast, 1958–65

In the envelopes that MARPAC's control-of-shipping organization planned to distribute to merchant captains if war became imminent was information on what to do to avoid destruction in a nuclear attack. On opening the envelope, the first thing the captain would read was a document that warned in bold letters: "A State of Emergency Exists." There then followed these instructions: "Minutes Count. Start to get your ship underway now while you are reading the following orders. Do not delay sailing to await a pilot." The envelope included further information on how the merchantman could reach safe dispersal areas, along with instructions to batten down all hatches and to use fire hoses to wash off any radioactive fallout to reduce the risk of nuclear contamination.[1] The existence of these envelopes and of the organization developed to distribute them illustrates that in the late 1950s and early 1960s, nuclear war was viewed as a very real possibility.

The personnel of Pacific Command were well aware that all of the training was being conducted because the Cold War could at any moment become hot. As Operation Uppercut started in July 1960, Commander Chadwick of the *Saguenay* wrote: "With the actual world crisis becoming so loud and shrill, it was difficult to ascertain which was worse: the exercise or the actual situation."[2] Chadwick was referring to the growing tensions sparked by the shooting down of Gary Powers's U-2 in May, but also to the downing of a USAF RB-47 aircraft off the Pacific Coast of the Soviet Union on July 1, just a few days before Uppercut commenced. Canadian and American forces treated every possible detection of a submarine as a potential threat to North American security. In April 1962, *Grilse* experienced first-hand just how seriously the submarine threat to the continent was being taken. The Canadian submarine was travelling submerged during an exercise with *Antigonish*, *Beacon Hill*, and USN aircraft when she had a chance encounter with the USS *Pivot* (MSO 463) and USS *Energy* (MSO 436) while still 10 miles from the exercise area. The USN minesweepers had not been briefed on the exercise; assuming that their sonars had detected a Soviet submarine, they "made a deliberate run" on *Grilse* before being contacted by the aircraft and frigates that their target was a friendly submarine. *Grilse*'s captain played down the incident; even so, inaccurate press reports indicated that the Canadian submarine had almost been attacked by the American vessels.[3]

Real or Imagined Encounters with Soviet Submarines

In the late 1950s, the intelligence that there was a growing Soviet submarine presence in the Pacific led to a major reorganization of the defensive scheme on the West Coast. Confirmed sightings of Soviet submarines remained rare, however, and were confined to the Task Force 33 area, under the commander of the Alaskan Sea Frontier. The submarine threat remained mainly theoretical; the risk posed by a growing Soviet merchant marine and fishing fleet presence off the northwest coast of North America was more concrete. One of the biggest problems facing the Maritime Commander Pacific (MARCOMPAC), after that command was formed in the late 1950s, related to its inability to ascertain whether Soviet vessels were operating either off the coast or in the numerous inlets, bays, and other hiding places along the sparsely populated coast of British Columbia. By the summer of 1958, the command had initiated a regular series of patrols from the west coast of Vancouver Island as far north as the Queen Charlottes. These patrols became the main operational mission of MARPAC from this point onward. The justification for these patrols was "the known fact that Soviet submarines are capable of and do carry out operations in the North East Pacific Ocean Area." In September 1959, for the captains of ships carrying out these patrols, Maritime Command outlined nine possible aims of Soviet operations in the MARPAC area:

1) Gaining Navigational Experience.
2) Improving knowledge of weather condition.
3) Hydrographic, oceanographic and bathymetric survey.
4) Study of sound propagation.
5) Landing or picking up of Soviet or Satellite agents
6) Surveying and/or establishing missile guidance stations on remote and inaccessible places on the Coast.
7) Establishing mobile fuelling stations (submersible fuel tanks which could be raised by submarines).
8) Gaining knowledge of our defences.
9) Collecting intelligence; particularly in the electronics field.[4]

The captains were informed of one indication of suspicious activity in the area: "Objects such as cylindrical tanks about 4 feet by 2 feet with a head secured by wing nuts, rafts and floats, balloon gear and parachutes have been recovered along the coast of Alaska and British Columbia. Some of these were marked 'Made in USA,' but closer investigation revealed they were not."

Patrols were, if possible, to consist of an SAU of at least two ships and were to be given distant support by aircraft from 407 Squadron. Since Soviet vessels in Canadian waters could be engaging in clandestine operations, it was necessary that "wiliness and extreme security must be used by forces attempting to achieve detection." Ships were authorized to use the "*ruse de guerre*" of disguising themselves as commercial vessels by shutting off most radar and active sonar systems and were instructed to maintain radio silence. Only navigational radar that had an electronic signature indistinguishable from civilian sets was to be used. Passive sonar listening only was to be maintained, and the ships were to use their electronic search equipment to detect any unusual radar signals. Ships were to operate at night at their "best silent speed and anchor in protected anchorages during the daylight hours."[5]

A number of accounts of these MARCOMPAC patrols have survived, and they reveal the RCN's serious concern that Soviet vessels were operating both inside and just outside Canadian territorial waters. One such patrol was undertaken by *St. Laurent* and *Saguenay* from November 28 to December 5, 1960. The patrol began on the evening of November 28 as the ships left the Strait of Juan de Fuca and proceeded up the west coast of Vancouver Island in a loose line abreast formation, travelling at 7 knots. At 0100 hours on November 29, "complete radio silence was imposed, all radar reverted to stand-by, and ships were darkened with navigational lights off." Only as the ships approached Sydney Inlet at 0900 did they switch on their Sperry radar for navigational purposes; this was the set that most closely emulated civilian radar equipment. At 1040, *Saguenay* was detached to patrol Shelter Inlet while *St. Laurent* continued to investigate Sydney and then Stewardson Inlet. At the same time, both vessels lowered their sonar domes and turned on their active sonars. "Look-outs were briefed to keep a constant vigil for submarines and evidence along the shore line of any untoward activity." Ships' boats were used to examine more inaccessible bays and inlets. No sign of Soviet activity was detected, and at 1530, the two ships rendezvoused and left the inlet.

The ships then assumed night patrol positions off the coast. "All-around passive sonar and ECM [electronic counter-measures] watches were kept. Ships were completely darkened, and a maximum speed of 7 knots was used to maintain stations." Radar sets were only periodically switched on to ensure safe navigation, and radio silence was maintained. The ships rejoined at 0740 on November 30 as they entered Nootka Sound. With both active sonar and radar, the ships then proceeded to investigate the various inlets and islands in the sound. Again their ships' boats were launched to enter areas that the DEs could not enter. That night they again assumed patrol positions off the coast, maintaining electronic silence and shutting off navigational lights. On the morning of December 1, they repeated their inshore investigations, this time of Kyuquot Sound. Again there was no trace of any untoward activities.

This completed the inshore patrol, and *Saguenay* proceeded back to Esquimalt. *St. Laurent*, however, sailed off the coast to a position 50° 54′ North 14° West to effect a rendezvous with a P2V Neptune aircraft of 407 Squadron. The ship spent much of December 2 investigating possible submarine contacts made by the aircraft. On further investigation, *St. Laurent* found all of these contacts to be nonsubmarine in origin. *St. Laurent* continued her offshore patrol for two more days, each evening turning off active detection systems and navigation lights. No submarines or any other suspicious vessels were detected. The DE returned to Esquimalt on the morning of December 5.[6] Patrols such as this continued to be carried out into the mid-1960s, if not beyond. One interesting feature of the MARPAC patrols was that ships of the 2nd and 4th Escort Squadrons were equally involved in carrying them out.

By 1960, another tool had become available for detecting submarines. On May 14, 1958, the USN, in cooperation with the RCN, opened two SOSUS bases in the Pacific Northwest – one at Pacific Beach, Washington, the other at Coos Head, Oregon. The Pacific Beach facility was connected to two widely spaced subsurface listening arrays; Coos Head monitored a single array. Each array was capable of giving a single bearing of a low-frequency underwater sound source with a bearing accuracy of plus or minus 2 degrees. This did not provide the most accurate information; numerous exercises involving accurately positioned sound sources demonstrated that errors of 8 miles for each 100 miles from the array could be expected. Information from the station's array was evaluated by an Oceanographic Unit, which correlated information from other stations and transmitted results to the Commander Navy Defenses Eastern Pacific (COMNAVDEFEASTPAC) and from there to various operational commands, including MARPAC. During operations, the Oceanographic Unit could transmit information directly to ASW units.

The SOSUS stations were integrated into the defensive scheme for the coast, especially for the approaches to the Strait of Juan de Fuca. SOSUS was most effective when the submarine was snorkelling, so it had to be forced to submerge before reaching the area covered by the underwater arrays. Thus, the distance of the inner limit of the initial defensive barrier of maritime patrol aircraft, whose radar would force Soviet submarines to submerge, was based on the seasonal maximum effective SOSUS operating range. In May 1960, this range was estimated as varying from 140 miles in mid-summer to 190 miles in mid-winter from Cape Flattery, on the northwesternmost tip of the state of Washington.[7]

It is unclear how useful SOSUS was to West Coast security, although Canadian warships demonstrated its effectiveness in two patrols in September 1960. From September 4 to 8, *Ottawa* conducted an inshore patrol and demonstrated that the ship could use SOSUS lines of bearing to detect targets. Several merchant ships and a fishing vessel were located using bearings from SOSUS. Between September 12 and 16, *Saguenay* conducted a similar patrol and also succeeded in confirming the presence of ships detected by SOSUS. *Saguenay*'s technique was to sail to the closest point of the SOSUS line of bearing and then turn seaward along the bearing line until the target was located.[8]

Regular patrols by the ships and aircraft of Maritime Command Pacific, supported by SOSUS and by American forces, kept as close an eye as possible on the sea approaches to the west coast of Canada. Despite these measures, there was a sense that the security situation was deteriorating as international tensions and the Soviet maritime presence in the Eastern Pacific continued to increase. A number of incidents along the coast in the late 1950s and early 1960s – both real and imagined – illustrate the serious nature of the Cold War. There continued to be a number of unsubstantiated sightings of submarines in the MARPAC area – at least six between 1957 and 1965. None of these sightings were confirmed, but every report was treated with the utmost seriousness by the command. While reports of submarine sightings in the early 1950s had been made mainly by amateur civilian observers, a number of the later sightings were made by more experienced personnel and could not easily be discounted. A number of reports were received from lighthouse keepers. Late in the evening of May 15, 1958, the keeper at San Miguel Lighthouse in Nootka Sound reported to the navy that he had observed a submarine flying a US flag. Quick checks with the USN by MARPAC revealed that it had no submarines in the area. At 0055 hours, MARPAC ordered *Athabaskan* and *Skeena* to immediately proceed to the area to investigate. The former ship was conducting torpedo trials in Patricia Bay, at the mouth of the Saanich Inlet, and was able to immediately raise steam and sail for Nootka Sound. *Skeena* had just returned to Esquimalt that afternoon, after three days of ASW exercises in the Strait of Juan de Fuca with *Athabaskan* and the submarine USS *Redfish*. On arrival, the ship was placed on eight hours' notice for steam and the off-duty crew dispersed to their homes or to the bars of Victoria. On receiving the order to proceed to sea immediately, *Skeena* instigated emergency recall procedures for the crew; meanwhile, duty personnel refuelled the ship and made sure she was provisioned. With the help of the Victoria City Police, who rounded up sailors (and also forgave the captain for speeding after he was caught red-handed rushing back to the ship), all but twenty-eight of crew were on board when the ship set sail just 2½ hours later. Personnel from *Fraser*, *Margaree*, and the naval barracks replaced the missing crewmen.

Skeena arrived off Nootka Sound at 1145 and rendezvoused with *Athabaskan*. The latter had arrived several hours earlier and had managed to exchange radio messages with the lighthouse keeper. The keeper reported that the submarine, despite flying an American ensign, was clearly Russian, and that it had been sighted at 2100 the previous evening moving out to sea at 20 knots. The two destroyer escorts took up a patrol 20 miles off the coast. They were joined by aircraft from VU-33, which scoured the shoreline, and from 407 Squadron, which attempted to find the submarine offshore. The military forces were augmented by two RCMP patrol boats, *Victoria* and *ML 16*, which searched the coastline for signs of intruders. Despite several false alarms, there was no sign of the submarine, and the search was terminated by MARCOMPAC at 0900 on May 17. Commander J.P.T. Dawson, captain of *Skeena*, felt the operation was "an excellent peacetime exercise" and was pleased to report that his ship's company had "responded well to the emergency, were in a fighting fettle and game for anything." Dawson also informed MARCOMPAC that there was a need to develop methods to expedite the sending, receiving, and coding of encrypted messages. He also reported that the ships were hampered in their search for the submarine by the presence of fog and by a large number of fishing vessels. This made it impossible to investigate every small radar contact, since the radar profile of a fishing vessel looked very much like that of a snorkelling submarine. Still, Dawson concluded "that apart from these two factors the operation ran smoothly and all participating forces worked well together in harmony."[9]

There was no way to verify or deny the existence of the submarine in Nootka Sound, but the sighting of a possible submarine periscope by the US Coast Guard lighthouse keepers at Turn Point, Stuart Island, just across the border from Sidney, BC, could be more readily explained. Just past midnight on December 11, 1961, BM1 Horace W. Corlett, the officer in charge of the lighthouse, and seaman Garry S. Hawkins, observed an object similar to a submarine periscope approximately one nautical mile west of their station. "Both observers described the object as being vertical, black in colour, cylindrical in shape, approximately 3 to 4 feet in height, having a base diameter of at least 8 inches, and a top diameter of approximately 6 inches." They saw a log approximately six feet in length roughly 100 yards behind the cylindrical object. Both the object and the log were travelling on a similar course at a speed of 3 or 4 knots. At 0015, they changed course, heading towards Swanson's Channel, but gradually the log veered away towards Moresby Island while the object proceeded up the channel. This divergence of course seemed suspicious to Corlett, who had initially assumed that the object was simply a deadhead. Corlett alerted the Coast Guard Station at Port Angeles, which promptly notified MARCOM.

Saguenay was immediately dispatched from Esquimalt, but the ship could find no sign of anything except deadheads. Further investigation by MARCOM officers concluded that the strange movements observed by the lighthouse keepers were in keeping with tidal conditions. That is, a boundary area between currents caused by rips had led to the separate movements of the object and the log. The sighting was firmly classified as nonsubmarine.[10]

Lighthouse keepers were not the only ones to make mistakes in identifying submarines. Naval vessels and aircraft also made a number of unconfirmed sightings of submarines off the West Coast. Between October 19 and 27, 1960, *Ottawa*, *St. Laurent*, *New Glasgow*, *Antigonish*, and *Beacon Hill* joined USN Task Group 31.8, consisting of the aircraft carrier USS *Kearsarge* and four destroyers, in an attempt to confirm a submarine sighting made just outside the MARCOM area of responsibility. Despite extensive searches over eight days by aircraft and ships, the submarine sighting could not be verified, and the Canadian vessels returned to normal duties.[11]

In June 1962, frustrations with determining a submarine's presence led Naval Headquarters to propose Canadian "submarine classification criteria" titled "The Submarine Contact Evaluation Instructions." Headquarters ordered ships and commands to use the criteria when pursuing possible contacts. Officers were instructed to assess and comment on the criteria in order to improve the documents. The criteria were developed "using probability ratings derived statistically from contacts with exercise submarines, from operational evaluations of detection equipment and from available intelligence on Soviet submarines." All aspects of ASW warfare were considered, the only exception being SOSUS and LOFAR (low-frequency analysis and recording) sonobuoys, new technologies that had not as yet provided enough statistical evidence to be included in the criteria. Headquarters felt that the development of an effective, statistically derived method of assessing a contact would be "a most valuable contribution to Western anti-submarine fighting efficiency."[12]

"The Submarine Contact Evaluation Instructions" were designed to be a simple system in which points were given under twelve different categories. If the cumulative score of all applicable categories added up to 100 or more, a submarine sighting was positive; from 90 to 99 points, the sighting was probable; from 30 to 90, possible. From 10 to 30, evidence was insufficient, and below 10, the contact was not a submarine. The categories included a confirmed visual sighting of a submarine or any part of it, which gave an immediate score of 100, to detection from MAD-equipped aircraft, valued at from 70 to 90 points, to sonar contacts, which could be assessed 5 to 50 points depending on the strength of the submarine characteristics as assessed by the operator and the ship's captain. Other criteria included different types of radar reflections, ECM intercepts, and the sighting of submarine pyrotechnics. Headquarters asked ships' captains to help improve the evaluation criteria by carefully assessing and reporting on all types of sonar contacts. The captains were urged to follow up on any contact showing submarine characteristics "until the cause of the contact can be established beyond reasonable doubt." The captains were informed: "It is an important peace-time task to locate permanent non-sub echoes accurately, and also to gain extensive knowledge on the classification of sonar echoes caused by marine life and other natural phenomena."

The document also revealed the state of knowledge in 1962 of Soviet submarine characteristics and techniques. Captains were told it was a "confirmed fact" that Soviet submarines had an automatic depth-keeping device that allowed them to hover stationary at a chosen depth. This device helped shield the submarine from sonar detection, since it eliminated the Doppler effect that indicated the presence of a moving underwater object. As well, headquarters reported that "Soviet submarines are expert in locating and using thermal layers to avoid detection." Finally, the document discussed the possibility that the Soviets were introducing antisonar coatings to reduce the strength of a sonar echo, although as of yet no photograph of Soviet submarines had revealed any sign of these coatings. Passive or LOFAR listening for the distinct sounds of Soviet submarines was encouraged, although headquarters warned that a lack of knowledge about the sound characteristics of these vessels limited the usefulness of this technique. So far, there was limited knowledge of Soviet propulsion systems and a lack of LOFAR signatures for specific types of submarines; there were also indications that some Soviet submarines were equipped with variable pitch propellers that could enable them to alter their sound signature. Captains were cautioned: "Until more good recordings of Soviet submarine noise are obtained and identified, it cannot be categorically stated that underwater noise did not come from a Soviet submarine unless the source of the noise is positively identified." Still, captains were provided with a list of possible sounds made by Soviet submarines that might be useful in confirming their detection.[13]

In the year after the "The Submarine Contact Evaluation Instructions" were issued, Esquimalt-based ships had only one opportunity to assess their effectiveness. This reflects the rarity of submarine contacts in the MARPAC area; in fact, the one possible submarine sighting in 1962 occurred south of the Canadian zone. On October 24, 1962, *Fraser*, *Skeena*, and *Saguenay* were on their way to an exercise in Hawaii when they were ordered to aid USN aircraft and warships that were pursuing a possible submarine. The contact was treated very seriously by MARCOM because initial detection had been made by aircraft using MAD. USN surface units reported a sound contact with mechanical noise, as well as sonar contact with strong submarine characteristics. Under the criteria, this meant a score of 150 – undoubtedly a submarine contact. On arrival at the scene, *Fraser* took over the pursuit of the contact from USS *Watts*. *Fraser* tried repeatedly to confirm the presence of a submarine, but her sonar, at best, indicated an object that had possible submarine characteristics. Under the criteria, this type of sighting was worth 25 points. Later, the sonar operator further downgraded the target to one with "doubtful submarine characteristics," worth no more than 5 points. Commander H.R. Tilley, the captain of *Saguenay*, concluded that the ships had in fact been pursuing a bed of kelp. Even so, the ships were ordered to pursue the contact because command continued to rely on the earlier assessment based on the aircraft sightings.[14]

Looking back at this incident in early 1963, ships' commanders were critical of the evaluation criteria. Commander R.C. Turber, captain of *Fraser*, suggested that the criteria were useful but that they required major alterations. Turber explained that points allocated for aircraft sightings were "unrealistically high"; MAD detection from an aircraft and any other indications automatically resulted in assessing a positive submarine contact. In October, all MAD sightings made by aircraft were later proven to be nonsubmarine. Turber believed that the aircraft were hampered by the poor weather conditions and that the criteria needed to assign fewer points when MAD sightings were made in adverse conditions.[15] Commander R.H. Leir of *Skeena* complained about the lack of opportunity to test the criteria in exercises, particularly aircraft/ship–coordinated operations. Thus, the defects in the criteria were only revealed during the operation in October. Like Turber, Leir argued that the criteria placed far too much emphasis on MAD and insufficient weight on sonar contacts, as assessed by captains and sonar operators.[16] Several months later, the commander of *Margaree*, who had not been present during the October incident, wrote that he agreed with the other officers. He believed the submarine contact evaluation could be useful:

> However, the numerical scale appears to be an arbitrary one based on the creditability of an individual and/or his equipment. In this regard, it cannot be stressed too strongly that the Force Commander in the contact area is the best person, regardless of the numbers available in any weighted scale, to assess, from all information available to him, the results of this action. In fact, his decision alone may be the only deciding factor and it will not be based on a numerical scale, but on experience.[17]

Tracking the Soviet Merchant Marine

While submarines remained the main military threat, the Soviet and Warsaw Pact merchant marine and fishing fleet was the principal ongoing security problem faced by the command. Soviet submarines may or may not have been lurking offshore, whereas fishing boats unquestionably operated off the west coast of Canada, and freighters regularly sailed through territorial waters on their way to Vancouver, Seattle, and other Pacific ports. These ships were not necessarily innocently pursuing trade or catching fish; many were involved, full- or part-time, in gathering useful intelligence on North America's defences. There was also an unsubstantiated belief that Soviet vessels were actively supporting clandestine operations within Canada and the United States. The Soviet merchant marine caused a multiplicity of issues for MARCOM. Keeping track of Soviet vessels operating in the command's area of responsibility was extremely difficult, and the problem was compounded by the dilemma of trying to sort out which vessels were engaged in legitimate commercial activities and which were involved in intelligence gathering. In peacetime, Canadian sovereignty extended only to the 3-mile limit; therefore, Canadian forces had to balance the need to monitor Soviet maritime activities, which often required the close observation of ships, with the risk of causing a diplomatic incident in international waters. Even within the 3-mile limit, Canadian authorities had to limit overly aggressive observations of Soviet ships. As early as the summer of 1956, Admiral Pullen, the FOPC, was forced to lodge strong protests with nearby American naval commanders after USN aircraft buzzed Soviet merchant ships travelling through Canadian waters.[18]

The first recorded direct incident involving the Soviet merchant marine occurred on October 1, 1957, when the presence of the Soviet merchant ship *Alexander Nevsky* near *Crescent, Fraser, and Athabaskan* forced the warships to curtail an air defence exercise. Pacific Command was concerned that the Soviet vessel might have electronic intelligence-gathering equipment that would allow it to gather important information on the radar and radio technology being used in the exercise.[19]

The number of encounters with Soviet vessels began to increase in the 1960s. On September 1, 1960, Admiral Finch-Noyes issued a command-wide surveillance policy to avoid giving the Soviet government "grounds for complaint." He began by citing a directive issued by the Chiefs of Staff Committee: "Care is to be exercised in surveillance measures involving Soviet vessels outside Canadian territorial waters. Very close surveillance by aircraft over Soviet vessels outside of Canadian territorial waters is to be avoided unless required by exceptional circumstances. Aircraft are not to fly directly over Soviet ships."[20]

Finch-Noyes stated that MARPAC ships and aircraft could conduct close observations of Soviet ships outside of territorial waters only when ordered to do so by command headquarters or if a commanding officer or an aircraft captain judged the ship to be acting in a suspicious manner. When a very close surveillance policy was not authorized, aircraft were not to pass directly overhead a vessel at below 1,000 feet; if operating below 1,000 feet, they were to stay at least half a nautical mile from the vessel. These figures were amended on October 20 so that aircraft could pass directly over a vessel, flying as low as 500 feet or, if flying below 500 feet, at least 700 feet from the vessel. Surface ships could exercise their right to verify the nationality of a vessel but were not to "interfere with or hamper the freedom of movement of ships encountered."[21]

Generally, MARPAC ships and aircraft operated within the parameters of these regulations; however, the amended figures allowing aircraft to pass directly overhead a ship when flying at an altitude of only 500 feet led to one incident and forced an amendment to the policy. On April 14, at New Westminster, the master of the Soviet merchant ship *Magnitogorsk* filed a formal complaint with Canadian authorities after two RCAF patrol aircraft "made four dangerous passes at 100 meters altitude over his vessel" on April 12 or 13. The Soviet captain informed Lieutenant-Commander A.A. Kalichack, an RCN intelligence officer, that he had been able to clearly read the aircraft identity numbers, that his crew had photographed the aircraft, and that he had recorded the incident in his deck log. The captain wanted to know why the safety of his ship had been jeopardized, when two passes at a reasonable altitude would have been sufficient to identify his ship by flag or funnel markings. The senior intelligence officer informed MARCOM that "this incident will undoubtedly be reported back to the USSR and used as propaganda in reporting harassment of peaceful merships [merchant ships]."[22]

A further investigation of the *Magnitogorsk* incident by MARPAC staff concluded that there was no evidence that the aircraft, two Neptunes from 407 Squadron, had violated procedures or endangered the Soviet ship. The investigation did reveal, however, that MARPAC guidelines not only might have caused a diplomatic incident but also violated the Chiefs of Staff directive. The Chiefs of Staff had specifically ordered aircraft not to fly directly over Soviet ships, whereas Finch-Noyes's surveillance order had allowed them to do so. On April 25, an amended surveillance policy was issued that specifically forbade aircraft from flying directly over Soviet vessels.[23]

In early 1962, in response to the growing numbers of Soviet vessels operating near the coasts of Canada, Naval Headquarters issued a number of orders intended to ensure effective intelligence gathering and analysis. On March 15, headquarters issued an order concerning the type of information that RCN and RCAF units were required to report. Close attention was to be paid to the Soviet merchant marine:

> Attention shall be paid to the activity, deployment and configuration of Soviet surface vessels, particularly those operating near detection arrays, in exercise areas or close to shore. Known Soviet research vessels, ELINT [electronic

FIGURE 20 A RCAF Neptune maritime patrol aircraft of 407 Squadron flying just off Victoria, circa 1960. Beacon Hill Park is in the foreground, downtown and the harbour in the background. The integration of RCAF and RCN forces in 1959 resulted in the creation of Maritime Command Pacific. (Courtesy DND)

> intelligence] trawlers and vessels whose operations appear suspicious should be kept under reasonable surveillance, as should large concentrations of Soviet vessels. When opportunity permits, reconnaissance of remote coastal areas for signs of Soviet activity is desirable.[24]

Although aircraft were now sanctioned by Ottawa to fly directly over Soviet vessels provided that they maintained a minimum altitude of 500 feet, captains were advised to avoid potentially "embarrassing situations." This change of policy was apparently the result of the passage by Parliament of the Canadian Aeronautics Act in December 1960; the act permitted flying over vessels at this altitude.[25] A few weeks after this directive, Naval Headquarters requested that all Canadian government ships, including those of the RCMP, the Fisheries Department, and the Coast Guard, assist the intelligence-gathering effort by reporting any sightings of Soviet Bloc vessels in waters adjacent to Canada.[26]

The seriousness of the situation on the West Coast is hard to measure because most Soviet activities continued to go undetected. Throughout 1962, despite

Naval Headquarters orders increasing surveillance and patrols by both ships and aircraft, only five Soviet trawlers were known to have operated in the MARPAC area in the Gulf of Alaska. All of these vessels were first detected by the USN.[27] In 1963, "Soviet fishing activities in MARPAC waters reached an all-time high with a maximum number of ships operating at any one time as high as 20." Some of these vessels operated as close as 18 nautical miles offshore. As well, during that year, thirty-five Soviet or Soviet Bloc merchant ships passed by Victoria for BC's Lower Mainland ports.[28]

In January 1964, MARCOM intelligence prepared a briefing on the Soviet trawler threat to the Pacific coast of Canada for the JSCP. According to MARCOM staff, Canada was "vulnerable" to Soviet peacetime intelligence gathering, and "no active measures" could be taken to prevent these activities in waters such as the Gulf of Alaska or off the BC coast. Soviet ships could visually observe Maritime operations and tactics as well as offshore defence installations. Electronic intelligence could provide even more information on such things as the movements, locations, and activities of naval and maritime air forces; the North American air defence system; the effectiveness of military forces; and the electronic characteristics of military radios and other electronic equipment. As well, the Soviet trawlers could monitor underwater cables, support long-range submarine patrols, and conduct research activities with military potential.

MARCOM intelligence officers assumed that if war broke out, the trawler fleet would become "a para-military force," since the fishing vessels operated too far from safe havens to escape destruction by Western forces. Although the actual plans for deploying the trawler fleet in wartime were unknown, it was "prudent" to assume that they would "undertake overt and covert operations" that would "cause the greatest possible damage" to Western war-making capacities. Activities might include the following: disrupting Allied communications by cutting submarine cables; jamming radio communications; laying mines; launching scuttling attacks to block ports; practising radio deception; raiding isolated shore targets; and supporting submarine and aircraft operations.[29]

These security concerns had a direct impact on plans for West Coast defence. Fears that trawlers would land agents – or, in wartime, launch raids on isolated installations – led to amphibious warfare exercises on the West Coast in 1964 and 1965 (see above). Security planning for the defence of British Columbia included arrangements to protect vital installations and to provide guards for Soviet seamen captured from trawlers and other merchant vessels. There was a very "loose estimate" that at least 3,000 seamen might be incarcerated, captured from as many as seventy vessels.[30]

So by 1962, a principal MARCOM mission was to keep track of the Soviet merchant marine and closely monitor any suspicious activities. That year,

Admiral Finch-Noyes arranged to receive all intelligence reports on Soviet trawler activities from the USN's Commander Alaska Sea Frontier.[31] Most of the information on the activities of the trawler fleet came from American naval intelligence; by the end of 1961, however, 407 Squadron was flying periodic patrols over the Gulf of Alaska. At least some of these flights involved refuelling at American naval air bases in Alaska. During one of these early patrols in mid-December, a Neptune sighted and photographed four trawlers in the MARPAC area. Later analysis by intelligence staff in Ottawa concluded that all of these vessels appeared to be equipped for normal civilian operations.[32] Beginning in 1962, however, there were several occasions when Soviet trawlers appeared to be doing something besides fishing in the MARPAC zone.

On June 8, USN maritime patrol aircraft were exercising with the submarine *Blackfin* 40 miles southwest of Cape Flattery. Late that afternoon, the aircraft spotted an East German–type trawler near the exercise area. The trawler was designated SRT 4454; she was 125 feet in length and weighed about 260 tons. USN aircraft periodically observed the trawler for the next two days before losing contact with it. Late in the afternoon of June 11, SRT 4454 was spotted again more than 40 miles off the west coast of Vancouver Island by a Neptune of 407 Squadron.

A little over three hours later, MARCOM ordered the frigate *Stettler* to come immediately to steam, and a recall of its crew was initiated. Within ninety minutes, the frigate had slipped and proceeded to sea at 17 knots. As soon as the ship cleared the strait, she turned north in pursuit of the Soviet vessel. Meanwhile, Neptunes continued to shadow the trawler. Just after 1500 on June 12, an aircraft detected "a disappearing radar contact" only half a mile astern of the trawler. This type of contact was indicative of a submarine, and the aircraft made a run close at the trawler to try to confirm the radar contact. All that could be observed out of the ordinary was an oil slick, "intense enough to calm a State Three sea," extending from several hundred yards to one-half mile astern of the trawler. Unable to pursue the contact due to the proximity of the Soviet vessel, the aircraft turned away to make contact with *Stettler*, which was some 13 miles away.[33] The aircraft signalled by lamp the location of the trawler to *Stettler*, which proceeded to close with the target. The warship switched off her radar and observed radio silence. Just after 4 p.m., the trawler was spotted some 5 miles away. Gradually *Stettler* passed the starboard side of the trawler, closing to within 1½ miles, before taking up a shadowing station, which varied from 4½ to 8 miles from the target. All this time the frigate used her radios and sonar to listen for any signals from the trawler. After shadowing the Soviet vessel for some eighteen hours, just before 1900 on June 13, *Stettler* closed to within 1,000 yards of the trawler to make a close observation. As the frigate approached, the trawler's crew was observed removing and covering various pieces of equipment. Since the frigate lacked her own camera, members of the crew were asked to use their own to snap photographs of the trawler. The poor quality of the resulting pictures made it impossible for intelligence analysts to identify the equipment the Soviet sailors were trying to hide. Shortly afterwards, the frigate made her way to Port Hardy to refuel. The frigate's captain concluded that the trawler's movements had been quite erratic and gave one the impression that it was "endeavouring to slip off unnoticed, or that he has a lot of time to wait in the general area, and may be deriving some amusement from the above tactics."[34]

After *Stettler's* departure, the trawler was not resighted by aircraft until late in the afternoon of the next day, by which time she had moved into the Task Force 31 area, which was the responsibility of the USN. American aircraft, however, failed to find the trawler, and she was not spotted again until she once again entered the MARCOM area on June 19. While aircraft from 407 Squadron maintained contact, the frigates *New Glasgaw* and *Jonquiere* were dispatched from Esquimalt to provide close surveillance of the Soviet vessel. The ships made visual contact with the trawler in the evening of June 22. For the next two days, one ship maintained a constant close watch on the Soviet vessel while the other carried out a search in surrounding area. The warships had a chance to closely observe the trawler's crew at work. They estimated "that the crew consisted of 12 to 16 persons, including at least two women, one of whom was young, slim, and lively, nicknamed 'Olga,' and the other of more massive and stolid bearing nicknamed 'powerful Katrina.'"[35]

The frigates observed the trawler crew at regular intervals streaming a plankton net and using a water sampling device consisting of four or five cylinders 4 inches in diameter and 3 to 4 feet in length. *New Glasgow*'s officers were suspicious of these activities, since "no seagulls were observed following the trawler." An intelligence analyst concluded that this fact tended "to support the suspicion that trawling operations were a hoax. Either nothing was caught, which seems unusual or else the trawl was deliberately left open to avoid catching anything." Later discussions between MARPAC intelligence officers and representatives of the Department of Fisheries and the Pacific Oceanographic Group in Nanaimo revealed that the Soviet vessel was trawling in waters too deep to catch many fish; also, there was little value in any fisheries research conducted so far off the coast. All of this tended to support the notion that the activities observed onboard the trawler were designed to hide its actual mission.

After assessing all of the information on the trawler's activities, MARPAC could only speculate as to its mission. The possible sighting of a submarine by the radar of a Neptune perhaps indicated it was operating in support of submarine activities. In the official report on the incident to Naval Headquarters, MARPAC staff conjectured that the trawler may have been planting underwater navigation fixing aides, which may have been fitted into a moored mine case. She may have doing this work in conjunction with a submarine, which could have found suitable places to moor the navigation devices on the sea floor. Other possible missions were discounted, since the trawler was too far from underwater SOSUS arrays to investigate them and did not carry sufficient electronic and signal intelligence gear to gather useful information. Whatever its mission, however, the mere presence of the trawler caused great concern at MARPAC headquarters. Admiral Finch-Noyes reported to Ottawa:

> It is realized this sortie by SRT 4454, on first consideration, seems rather unimportant when compared to the scale of Soviet Fishing Fleet activity on Canada's Eastern Coast; but in view of the known and suspected capability of such vessels to carry out ELINT or SIGINT collection and support Out of Area submarines, it is considered this incident may be a valuable indicator of future trends. At present, several Soviet Fishing vessels are operating freely in the Bering Sea and the Western Gulf of Alaska/Aleutian area. If these vessels were to move into the area east of Meridian 145° W in large numbers, Maritime Commander Pacific Forces would have difficulty keeping track of them.[36]

Finch-Noyes was correct that the appearance of SRT 4454 off the west coast of Canada was just the beginning of a large influx of Soviet "fishing" vessels into the MARPAC area. Less than two months later, the command's warships were again called upon to intercept a Soviet trawler operating in a suspicious manner off the Canadian coast. On August 14, a Neptune of 407 Squadron sighted the trawler *Vemchug* sailing in waters between Vancouver Island and the Queen Charlotte Islands. *Antigonish*, *Ste. Therese*, and *Beacon Hill* were already at sea on a ROTP cruise when they were ordered by MARPAC to form Task Force 38.1 and move to intercept the Soviet ship. Lieutenant-Commander E.M. Jones, captain of *Antigonish*, in command of the force, decided on novel tactics both to glean the maximum amount of intelligence information and to continue cadet training. To reach the trawler as soon as possible, *Antigonish* raced ahead of the other two vessels. Jones's plan called for his ship to keep the *Vemchug* under visual observation; meanwhile, *Ste. Therese* and *Beacon Hill* would assume station 10 to 15 miles away "in an effort to detect any consorts which may be attempting to affect rendez-vous [*sic*] with the trawler."

The frigates maintained radio silence as they approached the trawler and were guided to the target by a Neptune. *Antigonish* was ordered to closely observe the ship, and Jones sailed on a parallel course just 400 yards from the trawler for fifteen minutes. Nothing overtly suspicious was observed, although several large pieces of equipment were hidden under canvas. The efforts of the frigates' crews were hampered by the lack of a camera with a telephoto lens or a powerful pair of binoculars. The only activity onboard the trawler appeared to be the regular taking of bathythermographic readings using a series of cylinders attached to a long wire. There was no evidence the vessel was fishing. Attempts by *Antigonish* to contact the Soviet vessel only elicited the reply by light giving the ship's name and "an inaudible hail of about three words." After observing the trawler for twenty-four hours, the ships were ordered to break contact and continue with their training mission. As the task force departed, Jones allowed the crews of *Ste. Therese* and *Beacon Hill* to get a first-hand look at the trawler, "enabling them to form a basis on which comparisons may be made and have some idea of what to look for should these ships be required to take part in a similar activity at a later date."[37]

Despite a huge increase in Soviet fishing and merchant marine activities, there would be no further intercepts of suspicious vessels until May 1964. On May 25, two Soviet SIGINT (signals intelligence) trawlers, the *Barograph* and the *Ampermetr*, entered the MARPAC area 12 miles off Cape Flattery after working their way up the US Pacific coast. The ships spent two days near the Pacific Beach northern SOSUS array while being carefully monitored by RCAF and USN patrol aircraft. The destroyer escort HMCS *Qu'Appelle*, which had recently joined MARPAC, was ordered to divert from a coastal patrol to intercept the trawlers in order to obtain close-up photographs of the vessels. *Qu'Appelle* rendezvoused with the trawlers early on May 26 and followed them for the next eleven days as they moved northeast into the Gulf of Alaska. The DE observed "no overt" intelligence activities during this period.[38]

At the end of November, MARPAC decided to send the frigates *Antigonish* and *Stettler* "for an extended patrol into the Northern MARPAC Area." The ships were ordered "to investigate and report on all Soviet shipping encountered in MARPAC waters." MARPAC feared that the cruise would prove drearily routine, and in order to "maintain enthusiasm," the crews were encouraged to photograph every ship and tape every radio and radar transmission emanating from the Soviet vessels. Also, Rear Admiral M.G. Stirling, the commander of MARPAC, asked the Director of Naval Intelligence to send a letter of commendation to the ships' companies once the material was analyzed.[39]

FIGURE 21 HMCS *Stettler* and *Sussexvale* of the 4th Escort Squadron at sea, February 1962. (CFB Esquimalt Museum)

The frigates' encounters with the Soviet fishing fleet were uneventful but, as Lieutenant-Commander P.L.S. McCulloch, captain of *Antigonish*, explained, anything but routine to his crew:

> On the twenty-third of November *Antigonish*, in company with *Stettler*, sailed for a two week Maritime Patrol. Already the ship had 159 days at sea and 32 days in foreign ports, had not missed a single training cruise or squadron exercise and certainly had more seatime than any other ship in the Squadron if not the Command. By civilian standards the ports visited could be considered exotic – South America, Mexico, California and Hawaii. Yet, I was amazed at the number of men who informed me that our Maritime Patrol in the Gulf of Alaska had been the best "cruise" of the year. The reason is quite simple, in that we actually came face to face with the Russian trawler fleet. A more peaceful friendly confrontation with the "enemy" could not be imagined, however it was enough to stimulate a real sense of achievement amongst the ships [*sic*] company.[40]

McCulloch added that the entire crew enjoyed operating without the squadron commander, since his critical eye caused tremendous tension that was "felt right down to the lowest ordinary seaman." McCulloch concluded by urging MARPAC to consider more missions to investigate Soviet merchant marine activities, since until the trip his crew had lacked a sense of purpose. "Commanding officers and Squadron Commanders come and go, and the man is subjected to a never-ending series of training exercises, as if he's never going to be good enough to be trusted to do a real job of work." The army and the air force had operational opportunities, and so should the RCN. McCulloch was aware of the political implications this, and of the operational limitations placed on the fleet when carrying out such missions, but he believed that morale would be improved by giving the men a sense of real achievement, which visits to exotic ports did not provide.[41]

McCulloch's proposal was never acted upon. The following year, MARPAC ships had only one further encounter with the Soviet fishing fleet. In November 1965, *Stettler*, while on a routine MARPAC patrol, was ordered to rendezvous with the head of the Soviet fishing fleet and the Canadian fisheries patrol ship *Laurier.* The meeting was held to discuss the circumstances of the sinking of the Canadian fishing vessel *Aleutian Queen*, which had gone down after a collision with a Soviet trawler in Queen Charlotte Sound. The discussions with the Soviet officials were amicable and soon concluded. It seems that MARPAC was content to allow Soviet ships engaged in legitimate commercial operations to proceed without close oversight from the RCN.

The Cuban Missile Crisis

Of all the naval events of the Cold War, none has been more widely written about by historians than the Cuban Missile Crisis of October 1962. In the Atlantic, without clear direction from the Canadian government, Admiral Ken Dryer, the Flag Officer Atlantic Coast, integrated his squadrons with American naval operations keeping track of Soviet submarines operating off the coast of North America. In the Atlantic, the USN and the RCN were actively involved in the military operations carried out during the crisis; in the Pacific, things were much more serene. Admiral Jimmy Thach, the commander of the USN's ASW forces in the Pacific in 1962, later stated that he did not consider the Cuban Missile Crisis a "crisis."[42]

Peter Haydon, in his study of Canadian participation in the crisis, mentions MARPAC's involvement in a single inaccurate paragraph and fails to appreciate the situation the Pacific in the early 1960s. Haydon claims that Pacific Command went to a state of readiness at the same time as forces in the Atlantic, when in fact West Coast ships took no action until at least seventy-two hours after their East Coast cousins. Also, Haydon suggests that the 2nd Escort Group's assistance to the USN involved tracking what was possibly a real Soviet submarine. But as we have seen, Canadian officers involved in the hunt quickly concluded that the American ships had likely detected a bed of kelp. Moreover, Haydon states that 407 Squadron increased the pace of its ASW patrols during the crisis, when in fact they did not. However, the crisis did impact all operational RCN warships in the Pacific and represents the only time that the emergency defence plans were activated for an actual emergency.[43]

For MARPAC, the timing of the crisis could not have been better. At the beginning of October, after a major overhaul, MARPAC's operational headquarters was activated. For the first time since the Second World War, a twenty-four-hour watch was maintained at command headquarters. A new air/ground/sea communications system was introduced at the same time to allow direct communications between aircraft and ships and Maritime Command Headquarters. Previously, messages to aircraft had been passed via the air base at Comox. As well, an efficient intelligence centre and a mixed civil, RCAF, and RCN meteorological and oceanographic service were established and attached to command headquarters.[44] These reforms significantly improved MARPAC's ability to defend the west coast of Canada.

October was also the month when fleet training took place. From October 10 to 17, Operation Crab Pot was held off the west coast of Vancouver Island. Crab Pot consisted of a series of fleet ASW exercises that brought together elements of the 2nd and 4th Escort Squadrons, along with support ships. Opposition was provided by *Grilse* and the USS *Medregal*.[45] After Crab Pot ended, the ships of the 4th Escort Squadron, *Stettler*, *Sussexvale*, *New Glasgow*, *Jonquiere*, *Antigonish*, and *Beacon Hill*, remained in the area for another week to carry out their annual squadron ASW exercise with *Grilse*. Thus, a substantial number of the command's ships were already deployed in the area to which they were to be dispatched in the event of an emergency under the command's mobilization plans.

It remains unclear whether Admiral Finch-Noyes had any advance notice of the growing crisis before President John Fitzgerald Kennedy's announcement to the American people on Monday, October 22, that he had ordered a naval blockade of Cuba. Even then the command continued to follow its normal schedule of activities for several days. No effort was made to prepare *Margaree* and *Ottawa* for sea, even though both ships had just returned from Operation Crab Pot the previous Thursday. Instead, *Margaree* continued to prepare for her annual refit, which was due to commence on October 29; *Ottawa* remained tied alongside at Esquimalt while her crew began an extended leave. The day after Kennedy's announcement, *Fraser*, *Saguenay*, and *Skeena*, the only other ships of the 2nd Escort Squadron available, departed the base for a six-week training exercise in Hawaii with the USS *Yorktown*'s task group. The force was to sail to Hawaii via San Francisco.

There is little evidence that 407 Squadron's aircraft significantly increased the pace of their patrols as a result of the crisis. During Operation Crab Pot, the squadron flew thirty-three missions; over the rest of the month, it engaged in only nineteen further patrols.[46] Only on October 24 did MARPAC begin to take action to prepare the command for the possible outbreak of hostilities. On that day, the 4th Escort Squadron was ordered to select two ships to remain behind on the west coast of Vancouver Island after their squadron exercise terminated the following day. At almost the same time, MARPAC instructed *Fraser*, *Saguenay*, and *Skeena* to join the USS *Watts* and other USN units in hunting down a possible submarine contact off the coast of Oregon (see above). Once it was determined on October 25 that there was no submarine, the ships continued to San Francisco.

Therefore, it was only three days after Kennedy's speech that any action was taken, and this only because the 4th Escort Squadron's scheduled anti-aircraft exercise was cancelled due to bad weather. With their squadron training concluded, the frigates anchored in Mayne Bay. There the two frigates nominated to remain behind to act as a ready action force, *Stettler* and *Beacon Hill*, were resupplied, munitioned, and refuelled by the other four ships. Shortly after 1800, on completion of this transfer, the rest of the squadron sailed to Esquimalt. The two remaining ships formed TG 38.2 under the command of Lieutenant-Commander A.C. McMillin on *Beacon Hill*.[47]

On board *Stettler* and *Beacon Hill*, the crews prepared for war. Lieutenant-Commander A.F. Gladman, the captain of *Stettler*, reported that "all fighting equipment was now fully operational, and *Stettler* was for the most part completely replenished. An urgent but orderly period of exercises and drills was undertaken for the next four days to ensure the highest possible state of operational readiness."[48] Similarly, Commander McMillin observed that "the days at anchor at Mayne Bay were well spent, in cleaning ship after several days exercises, interspersed with action, damage control, and firefighting drills designed to increase our preparation for war." McMillin saw the effects that the sudden shift from peacetime routine to wartime preparation had on his crew:

> The effect of the current events on the ship's company was most noticeable and a general air of rather grave concern was most evident. News broadcast, reports from the United Nations, and radio commentary on international events, completely replaced all other programmes in popular radio listening onboard. Action drills were carried with greater frequency while at anchor and an increased enthusiasm in performance was noticeable.[49]

The frigates remained at anchor at Mayne Bay, ready for war or for relief. Meanwhile, at MARPAC headquarters, no one seemed to have immediately appreciated the fact that a force of two obsolete frigates provided little security for the West Coast. This delay may have been caused by lack of leadership at Esquimalt. Admiral Finch-Noyes was ill and was forced to take early retirement. His replacement, Rear Admiral W.M. Landymore, would not take over until November 1. Whatever the cause, it was only when information was received that, because of the crisis, the USN had cancelled the Hawaiian exercises, that the DEs of the 2nd Escort Squadron were ordered to return to Canadian waters. So it was late on October 25 that the DEs received orders to take over from *Stettler* and *Beacon Hill*. By this time the ships were approaching San Francisco, and they decided to refuel and resupply there before proceeding to Mayne Bay. The slow reaction by MARPAC did not go unnoticed among the squadron's officers; Commander H.R. Tilley, the captain of *Saguenay*, remarked that "while Canadian reactions appeared to be increasingly intense, the feeling of tension amongst United States officials seems to be easing."[50]

The DEs made a swift passage to Mayne Bay, hampered only by the heavy fog that was normal in northwest coastal waters at this time of year. The only

FIGURE 22 HMCS *Beacon Hill*, *Mackenzie*, and *Saskatchewan* at Hong Kong in 1965. The mixed group of a Prestonian-class frigate and two Mackenzie-class DEs is indicative of the downsizing of Pacific Command by the mid-1960s. (CFB Esquimalt Museum)

problem encountered was the wild rumours that spread rapidly among the sailors about the ships' mission. The rumours were hard to suppress because officers were forbidden to reveal any details of the mission to their crews. On arrival at Mayne Bay on October 28, the DEs found the frigates at anchor. The next day the naval auxiliary ships *Laymore* and *Dundurn* arrived from Esquimalt with munitions and fuel. Once the DEs were fully supplied, they relieved the frigates and assumed their duties as TG 38.2.

On the day the 2nd Escort Squadron arrived at Mayne Bay, Khrushchev announced the dismantling of Soviet missiles in Cuba, effectively ending the crisis. TG 38.2 continued to exist for another week, but the ships used the time not to stand ready for battle, but instead to engage in ASW exercises with *Grilse*.[51] Thus, during the greatest crisis of the Cold War, the West Coast was provided with no naval defence or, at best, a weak force of two frigates. MARPAC had been well aware that it would have little time to mobilize in the age of nuclear missile warfare, yet it had failed to take swift, decisive action. It remains unclear whether Naval Headquarters kept the command informed of events prior to October 22, but even after this date, crucial hours passed before the 2nd Escort Squadron was recalled.

The End of the Golden Age

Well before the Cuban Missile Crisis, the end of the golden age of the RCN's Pacific Fleet was in the cards. The massive growth of the navy during the 1950s (and of the army and the RCAF) could not be sustained. Economics and politics played equal roles in the navy's overall decline, although the nature of naval expansion and the rapid evolution of antisubmarine warfare were central factors as well. In the late 1950s, the new government of John Diefenbaker, faced with economic recession, took steps to bring defence spending under control. Over two years beginning in 1958, the government reduced the department's budget from $1.76 billion to just $1.4 billion. Major defence procurement programs – most notably the Avro Arrow jet interceptor – were cancelled due to their immense cost and doubtful utility in the looming age of the intercontinental ballistic missile (ICBM). The navy's share of funding, which had peaked in 1956 at $345 million, by 1961 stood at $245 million, this during a time of strong inflation.

The expansion of the navy during the early Cold War had focused on providing a large number of escort vessels to fulfill ill-considered commitments to SACLANT. The RCN had spent considerable money refitting Second World War destroyers as more modern ASW escorts. The conversion of wartime River-class frigates to Prestonian-class resulted in ASW vessels of dubious value except for basic training. While the design and building of the St. Laurent-class had been hailed as major achievement, the RCN was well aware that even before the ships entered service, they would have difficulty coping with streamlined high-underwater-speed submarines armed with missiles, let alone the atomic-powered boats that the Soviets would certainly be introducing into service in the 1960s. The hull-mounted sonar on the *St. Laurents* could not adequately track deep-diving submarines, which could use thermal layers to escape detection. It was doubtful that a ship, even if it did locate a submarine, would be able to bring the target within range of the limbo mortars and homing torpedoes that made up its antisubmarine armament. As well, tracking a submarine with active sonar or radar made an escort vessel vulnerable to counterattack by the submarine.

In the early Cold War, an extraordinary aspect of the RCN's history was the wide-ranging research projects that helped revolutionize antisubmarine warfare. The navy pioneered the development of variable depth sonar (VDS) – passive listening hydrophones attached to long cables, capable of penetrating thermal layers.[52] As well, the navy developed techniques to operate large helicopters from the deck of comparatively small warships, such as the St. Laurent-class destroyer escorts.[53] The VDS made possible the long-range passive detection of submarines. The helicopter had the speed to overtake the target, could use active dipping sonar or sonar buoys with impunity, and could easily get within range to deploy its own homing torpedoes.

The combination of declining budgets, aging escorts, and the need to spend vast sums to purchase Sea King helicopters and rebuild (or build from scratch) escorts that could incorporate VDS and helicopters, meant that the RCN would be substantially transformed during the 1960s. The most visible change was the reduction in size of the navy. Between 1961 and 1967, twenty-five warships were decommissioned, including all of the *Prestonians* and most of the destroyers. During the 1960s only nine new warships would enter service as replacements.[54]

In addition to the economic and technological challenges it faced, the navy had to do political battle with Paul Hellyer, who in 1963 was appointed defence minister in the new Liberal government of Lester Pearson. Hellyer's policy of forcing unification on the armed forces dominates the historical writings on the navy during this period. The undeniable turmoil caused by Hellyer's often heavy-handed and wrong-headed determination to enforce his policies on the navy, which in 1965 resulted the forced retirements and resignations of most senior RCN officers, was a key event in Canadian naval history. Unification had only a peripheral influence on the dramatic reduction of the Pacific Fleet's capabilities by 1965; it did, though, provide a crucial breakpoint in Canadian naval history, taking place as it did as the workable little fleet at Esquimalt ceased to exist.

In the early 1960s, MARPAC's main forces were organized into the 2nd Escort Squadron, consisting of seven St. Laurent-class destroyer escorts, and the 4th Escort Squadron, consisting of eight Prestonian-class frigates. The former provided the main operational punch of MARPAC; the latter focused on training. After 1962, all seven St. Laurents were gradually withdrawn from MARPAC and sent to be converted into helicopter-carrying destroyers or DDHs, each capable of carrying a single Sea King helicopter. The St. Laurents never returned to MARPAC; instead, they joined the Atlantic fleet. The RCN was determined to concentrate all of its most capable ASW vessels at Halifax to serve with NATO. Moreover, all of the navy's Sea King helicopters were based on the East Coast. Replacing the seven destroyer escorts in the Pacific were only the four destroyer escorts of the Mackenzie-class, slightly improved versions of the St.-Laurent class as originally completed.

By 1965, the organization of escort squadrons based on ship type, which had been implemented in 1957 as a result of difficulties the RCN had experienced operating mixed groups of destroyers and frigates, was replaced by a new system based on modern personnel management theory. The Cyclic System was designed to improve efficiency by bringing long-term predictability to a ship's crew. Ships were to operate in a sixteen-month cycle, divided into four equal phases – maintenance and coursing, working up, operational, and personnel assistance. This meant on the West Coast that only one of the *Mackenzies* was fully operational at any given time and that the DEs were matched with Prestonian-class frigates that were on the same cycle.[55] The decline in numbers of warships and the introduction the Cyclic System marked the end of the RCN having effective and cutting-edge operational capabilities in the Pacific for the next twenty-five years.

Conclusion

The Cold War was as real off Canada's West Coast as it was in the airspace over North America patrolled by NORAD or in the waters of the North Atlantic protected by RCN warships based at Halifax. A series of dubious reports of possible Soviet Navy submarines led Naval Headquarters to create "The Submarine Contact Evaluation Instructions" to enable ships to better distinguish between a false and a real sighting. While there were no confirmed submarine contacts in the MARPAC area of responsibility, the Soviet fishing fleet and merchant marine kept MARPAC busy keeping track of them. The officers and men of the command found their real encounters with Soviet vessels a more stimulating experience than any of their exercises.

The Cuban Missile Crisis was a rather anticlimactic event in the Pacific; even so, it marked the only occasion where the emergency plan was implemented to deal with an international crisis – one that in this case brought the world to the brink of nuclear war. The experience revealed the accuracy of the concerns of the commanders of MARPAC that they had insufficient numbers of modern warships to implement the emergency defensive plans *and* continue an active program of training and exercises. For several days at the height of the crisis, the maritime defence of the West Coast had relied on two obsolete Prestonian-class frigates.

Setting aside the inadequacies of MARPAC as revealed by the Cuban Missile Crisis, the so-called golden age of the Pacific Fleet would come to a sudden end by 1965. Remarkably, the dramatic reduction of MARPAC squadrons had nothing to do with the unification crisis; rather, it was the direct result of a general reduction in the overall defence budget and the growing obsolescence of many of the navy's warships. With even the nearly new *St. Laurent*-type destroyer escorts requiring costly upgrades, the RCN had little choice but to downgrade dramatically the Esquimalt-based squadrons in order to maintain some semblance of the service's commitment to NATO.

Conclusion

MARPAC HAD ALWAYS played second fiddle to its Atlantic cousin, but it was certainly not a "yacht club" in the twenty years after the Second World War. The 1964 White Paper on defence, written under Hellyer's leadership, explained the navy's focus:

> Since 1939, Canadian maritime programs have been heavily concentrated upon the defence of North Atlantic sea communications against submarine attack. The concentration has been based on the importance of these communications to the entire North Atlantic Community ... *At the same time an adequate anti-submarine warfare capacity is being maintained on the Pacific Coast.*[1]

A definition of "an adequate anti-submarine warfare capacity" was not provided. As we have seen, by 1964 the erosion of ASW capacity in the Pacific was already accelerating.

The story of the Royal Canadian Navy in the Pacific during the early Cold War is an important correction to the Eurocentric focus of almost everything that has been written about the history of the service since 1945. While it is true that the RCN remained focused on its commitments to NATO, it also gave considerable attention to West Coast continental defence and provided a significant proportion of the fleet to the Pacific when resources were available. How those resources were allocated by Naval Headquarters must await a history of naval policy based on records that remain "classified." This fundamental work will eventually be used to write a new history of Canadian naval and defence policy in the early Cold War. It is only one of several such detailed studies that need to be written. After the publication of this present work, however, it will no longer be possible to ignore the Pacific dimension of Canadian defence policy during the Cold War.

The activities of navies in peacetime are all too often ignored. Accounts of exercises, manning policy, and planning show how navies maintain a state of readiness when not at war. The naval facility at Esquimalt and the squadrons based there played a vital role in defending the west coast of Canada and in training new generations of personnel for the entire service.

The account of American and Canadian defence cooperation for Pacific maritime security has never before been told. West Coast defence planning had little to do with both countries' commitments to NATO. The US Pacific Fleet, and other American services' West Coast commands, operated outside the NATO environment, as did MARPAC. The bilateral ALCANUS plans are more akin to the far better-known NORAD agreement for continental air defence. MARPAC was very well integrated into the US Pacific Fleet, and that relationship was at least as close as the RCN's forces in the Atlantic enjoyed with their NATO allies. Cooperation with the Americans, however, had its limits. Admiral Rayner's refusal to accede to Admiral Hopwood's demands that Canada adopt American rules of engagement in prewar situations is an outstanding example of a Canadian who defended our sovereignty from the demands of our most important and powerful ally.

Exercises and defence plans show the rapidly evolving technological environment of naval warfare in the two decades after the Second World War. The RCN's first postwar schemes for West Coast defence proved unworkable even before they could be implemented. Passive defences, including coastal artillery and minefields, with limited support from a few old minesweepers, could not safeguard British Columbia. Given the desperate state of the navy until after the Korean War and the priority conceded to NATO, there was, in effect, no defence for the Pacific, despite commitments made under the ALCANUS accords.

As the navy's Cold War expansion began to show results, Canada's overall readiness dramatically improved just in time to meet a whole new generation of weapons systems that made safeguarding the coastal approaches even more problematic. Fast conventional submarines, equipped with surface-launched nuclear-armed cruise missiles, required a forward defence hundreds of kilometres out into the Pacific. In 1958, Admiral Rayner's "Operational Emergency Defence Plan Pacific" provided the first realistic defence plan for the MARPAC area, one that used existing resources to provide an outer defensive barrier more than 300 miles from the coast. Rayner envisioned stopping Soviet submarines before they could reach their firing positions, using the RCAF's maritime patrol aircraft, which had recently been integrated into his command, and the new St. Laurent-class destroyer escorts. MARPAC determined that in times of crisis, warships would respond to the reality of the nuclear threat by abandoning their vulnerable base at Esquimalt and deploying to an isolated anchorage on the west coast of Vancouver Island.

Fortunately, the effectiveness of Rayner's plans was never tested; only during the Cuban Missile Crisis was even part of the scheme activated for a potential war situation. MARPAC's experience during that crisis showed the difficulty of providing adequate defences while engaging in an active program of international exercises and fleet maintenance.

Setting aside the almost comical experience of MARPAC during the Cuban crisis, there were real security threats in the Pacific. The growth in numbers and effectiveness of the Soviet Pacific Fleet was of particular concern to MARPAC. While none of the many sightings of submarines in the coastal waters of British Columbia were confirmed – in fact, most were dismissed as false by the navy – the appearance of Soviet spy ships in the region was of great concern to the RCN.

Exercises with US Pacific Fleet and other allied navies made it clear that while the St. Laurent-class ships were the best ASW vessels in the Pacific, they lacked passive variable depth sonar and long-range antisubmarine weapons systems to defeat the most modern conventional-powered submarines, let alone the much more potent threat posed by nuclear-powered vessels. The need to rebuild the almost new destroyer escorts, the obsolescence of older ASW warships, and large budget cuts to defence that began in the late 1950s resulted in a major reduction in the size of the navy in the 1960s. This led to the downsizing of MARPAC, which brought an end to the brief happy time enjoyed by Canada's Pacific Fleet. How the armed forces determined the allocation of the much reduced number of warships available between the two coasts must also await a history of Canadian naval policy in the early Cold War.

In the years immediately after unification, MARPAC's situation would only get worse. Marc Milner dubbed the period between 1968 and 1980 the RCN's "Locust Years." If the Atlantic Fleet suffered famine and pestilence during the dark days of Pierre Trudeau's government, then the Pacific Fleet was rendered almost extinct. MARPAC did not quite cease to exist during these years, although the number of ships dropped significantly after the *Prestonians* were retired at the end of the 1960s.

Perhaps the most significant addition to MARPAC after unification was the arrival of the supply ship HMCS *Provider* on the West Coast in 1969. For the first time, Canadian warships could operate throughout the vast expanse of the Pacific Ocean without relying on other navies or foreign ports. In the early 1970s, the four *Mackenzies* were grouped into Training Force Pacific. To replace them in the 2nd Destroyer Escort Squadron, four improved Restigouche-class DEs, *Restigouche*, *Gatineau*, *Kootenay*, and *Terra Nova*, were transferred from Halifax to Esquimalt. These ships had been refitted to mount improved electronics, VDS, and ASROC ASW missile launchers. The ASROC missile could carry a homing torpedo up to 9 kilometres from the ship. These missiles were a big improvement over the limbo mortar originally fitted to the ships, but they were neither as flexible nor as long-ranged as a Sea King helicopter.

In December 1974, HMCS *Rainbow*, which had replaced *Grilse* as the West Coast–based submarine six years earlier, was retired, leaving MARPAC without a submarine for the rest of the century. At Comox, 407 Squadron's maritime patrol aircraft continued to operate and were likely the most capable asset in maintaining control of the MARPAC area throughout the 1970s and 1980s.

The very existence of the Pacific Ocean was all but ignored by Maritime Command, as the RCN and Maritime squadrons of the RCAF were renamed after unification. Once again, those serving on the West Coast were referred to by their East Coast counterparts as members of a yacht club. Very limited forces were available to the navy during the Trudeau years; all helicopter-carrying DEs, as well as the three O-class submarines acquired by the RCN in the late 1960s, operated with Maritime Command Atlantic.

Despite the paltry resources available to MARPAC after 1965, the Pacific Fleet operated along the pattern set in the early Cold War. Training, of course, took up most of the command's resources. The few ships based at Esquimalt continued to participate in exercises with the USN's Pacific Fleet and more broadly with other allies in the Asia–Pacific region. Canadian responsibilities under the ALCANUS accords remained. Soviet ships seem to have been even more active in the Pacific during the rest of the Cold War. For instance, in October 1981, *Kootenay*, along with *Provider*, tracked a Soviet force of a Kara-class guided-missile cruiser, two Krivak-class guided missile frigates, and an oiler operating in the Gulf of Alaska. The Canadian ships were later joined by the American Spruance-class destroyer *Fife*. In 1973, Esquimalt-based ships, including *Kootenay* and *Terra Nova*, patrolled the coast of Vietnam in support of Canadian forces, serving with the International Commission of Control and Supervision. A full account of MARPAC in the later Cold War remains to be written.

In the late 1980s, the emergence of the Asia–Pacific region as an economic and military powerhouse led to a major transformation in Canadian strategic thinking. That Canada was a Pacific nation suddenly re-entered the consciousness of the Ottawa defence and diplomatic establishment. A 1987 White Paper showed that the DND accepted the need to better balance Canada's limited naval and maritime air forces between Halifax and Esquimalt. However, the White Paper contained much more about the need to improve the defence of the Arctic Ocean than the Pacific. This focus on the northern waters was directly related to Maritime Command's unsuccessful efforts to justify acquiring atomic-powered submarines.[2]

Still, in 1987 HMCS *Huron*, a Tribal-class DDH, arrived at Esquimalt. Accompanying the ship were the lead elements of 443 Anti-Submarine Helicopter Squadron, based at Patricia Bay (Victoria International Airport). For the first time, a helicopter- and VDS-carrying warship was based in the Pacific, a mere twenty years after the first such warship entered service. In 1989, the DDH HMCS *Annapolis* was also transferred from Halifax to Esquimalt.

The end of the Cold War allowed for a further concentration of the navy in the Pacific. The 1994 Defence White Paper gave the rationale for this renaissance of interest in the region:

> As our interest in Asia has grown over the past few years, Canada has become more active in a variety of regional security initiatives – particularly through the encouragement of regional security dialogues such as the Asia Regional Forum, the Council for Security Cooperation in Asia Pacific, and the Canadian Consortium on Asia Pacific Security. All of these activities will continue, and, as our economic stake in the region grows, Canada will play a more active role in its security.

The White Paper presented a remarkably inaccurate survey of Canada's military involvement in the Asia–Pacific region since 1945:

> Aside from its role in the Korean War, Canada's participation in Asia-Pacific security affairs since the end of the Second World War has been largely limited to the commitment of forces to various peacekeeping and observer missions (including the International Commission for Supervision and Control in Vietnam, and the United Nations Transitional Authority in Cambodia), along with participation in the "RIMPAC" air and naval exercises with the United States, Japan, Australia, and, on occasion, other Asia-Pacific countries.[3]

Although the White Paper mentioned the close relationship between MARPAC and the US Pacific Fleet, the history of the broad Canadian naval involvement in the Asia–Pacific region during the early Cold War was all but forgotten.

In the next decade, the entire navy would go through a rebirth. All of the ships based on the St. Laurent design, including the Mackenzie and Restigouche classes, as well as the *Annapolis*, were decommissioned and replaced with twelve new, cutting-edge City-class patrol frigates. Joining the City-class were four extensively modernized Tribal-class destroyers, which had entered service in the early 1970s and had served exclusively in the Atlantic until 1987. Of these sixteen surface combatants, five frigates and two destroyers were assigned to MARPAC. All of these ships were capable of carrying helicopters and had enhanced sonar, radar, electronic counter-measure, missile, and antimissile capabilities. By the end of the 1990s, for the first time since the early 1960s, there was a small but effective Canadian naval presence in the Pacific.

Into the twenty-first century, the RCN (as Maritime Command was renamed in 2011) has maintained about 40 percent of its forces in the Pacific. In 2003, HMCS *Victoria* became the first Canadian submarine attached to MARPAC since 1974. Long-term plans call for two of the four Victoria-class submarines to be based at Esquimalt. As a result of the decision to increase its naval presence in the Pacific, the Canadian government has committed nearly $1 billion to rebuilding and expanding Canadian Forces bases at Esquimalt, Patricia Bay, and Comox. This is the most significant investment in Pacific Coast defences since the Second World War.

Since the 9/11 terrorist attacks, MARPAC has been more operationally active than at any time since the Korean War. Ships have served in UN peacekeeping operations such as in East Timor, in antiterrorism operations off Southeast Asia, and in antipiracy patrols in the Indian Ocean. The navy has secured the coastal waters of British Columbia, intercepting drug smugglers and ships carrying illegal immigrants. As of 2012, the RCN in the Pacific consisted of the frigates *Ottawa*, *Calgary*, *Regina*, *Vancouver*, and *Winnipeg*, the destroyer HMCS *Algonquin*, the supply ship *Protecteur*, the submarine *Victoria*, and five Kingston-class coastal defence vessels.

Not all is well in the Pacific Fleet. The pace of operations since the mid-1990s strained the resources of the navy more than at any time since Korea. In 2000, personnel shortages in the navy resulted in the mothballing of the destroyer *Huron*. The ship was scrapped in 2005. Some problems, such as shortages of trained personnel, never seem to go away. The *Huron's* withdrawal from service left MARPAC with only one destroyer, which has better command and control arrangements and anti-aircraft armament than the frigates. In August 2013, an accidental collision between *Protecteur* and *Algonquin* resulted in heavy damage to the destroyer. On February 28, 2014, a fire onboard *Protecteur* while on passage from Pearl Harbor to Esquimalt caused extensive damage to the ship's machinery. On September 22, 2014, DND announced that a number of warships, including *Protecteur* and *Algonquin*, would be retired. The loss of the only Esquimalt-based supply ship and destroyer, years before replacements are contemplated, will significantly reduce the RCN's capabilities in the Pacific.

Today, serving on the West Coast is no longer viewed as being a member of a yacht club. But as we have seen, during the Cold War, the Pacific "yacht club" had always been a fantasy of Halifax-based sailors. As *The Crowsnest* explained in 1948, the truth was that "the West Coast is a great place, it is no more placid than the East Coast and activities here can be just as lively as anywhere else." The role of the RCN's Pacific Fleet in the Cold War was a vital one, integral to maintaining the nation's security. After the publication of this book, it will be necessary to rewrite the history of Canada in the early Cold War, since it will no longer be possible to ignore the Pacific dimension of the defence of North America.

Notes on Sources

Primary Documents

Since this book breaks new ground, it has primarily been shaped by Pacific Command's operational records at the National Archives of Canada (now inexplicably renamed Library and Archives Canada). Other naval records, particularly Naval Service Headquarters central registry files, have also been used extensively. These records were found in Record Group (RG) 24. Since completion of the research, the National Archives has begun a renumbering of many of these files into R112. The original volume and file numbers have been retained in the notes. Many of these documents were declassified for this publication. Other primary documents, including certain Reports of Proceedings, are from the collection of the Directorate of History and Heritage, Department of National Defence, Ottawa. Ships' files and the magazine *Crowsnest* found at the CFB Esquimalt museum have also been used.

Efforts to incorporate US naval sources were thwarted by the fact that the American documents were either still classified or uncatalogued at the time that research for this project was undertaken.

Secondary Literature

Until the publication of the third volume of the official history of the RCN, *The Restless Wave: The Official History of the RCN, 1945–68,* Marc Milner's *Canada's Navy: The First Century* (Toronto: University of Toronto Press, 1999) remains the most useful study of the postwar navy. Understandably, Milner's work makes almost no mention of the RCN in the Pacific during the Cold War. Less useful is Tony German's *The Sea Is at Our Gates: A History of the Canadian Navy* (Toronto: McClelland and Stewart, 1990). W.A.B. Douglas, Roger Sarty, and Michael Whitby's *A Blue Water Navy* (St. Catharines: Vanwell, 2007), a new official operational history of the navy in the later part of the Second World War, provides an excellent account of the RCN in the Pacific during the Second World War and on planning for the postwar fleet.

Although three proceedings of conferences on the history of the Royal Canadian Navy have been published, they contain little on the navy in Pacific in the Cold War. In 1997 at Esquimalt, a small conference titled *Canada's Pacific*

Naval Presence: Purposeful or Peripheral (Halifax: Centre for Foreign Policy Studies, Dalhousie University, 1999), ignored MARPAC's role in the Cold War.

Peter Haydon's *The 1962 Cuban Missile Crisis: Canadian Involvement Reconsidered* (Toronto: Canadian Institute of Strategic Studies, 1993) does not examine the Pacific dimension of the crisis. Steve Ewing's *Thach Weave: The Life of Jimmie Thach* (Annapolis: Naval Institute Press, 2004) does not mention the RCN but provided valuable information on the US Pacific Fleet in the early 1960s and on the Cuban Missile Crisis. *The Admiral: Canada's Senior Naval Leadership in the Twentieth Century* (Toronto: Dundurn Press, 2006) provides useful biographical background on some of MARPAC's commanding officers and on certain aspects of naval policy. However, the Pacific is once again almost completely ignored. A number of MA theses and PhD dissertations have proved useful, particularly for the period up to the Korean War. These include Tyrone Pile's "Behind the Workable Little Fleet: Post-War Planning and Policy in the RCN 1945–48" (MA thesis, University of Victoria, 1998), Richard Gimblett's "Gunboat Diplomacy: Mutiny and National Identity in the Postwar Royal Canadian Navy: The Cruise of HMCS *Crescent* to China" (PhD diss., Laval University, 2000), and Peter Archambault's "Mutiny and the Imperial Tradition: The Canadian Naval Mutinies of 1949 and Experience of Mutiny in the Royal Navy" (MA thesis, University of New Brunswick, 1992), which examine the work stoppages on board Canadian warships in the late 1940s. Gimblett has published several articles on *Crescent's* trip to China, the most important of which is "'Too Many Chiefs and Not Enough Seamen': The Lower Deck Complement of a Postwar Canadian Navy Destroyer – The Case of HMCS *Crescent*, March 1949" (*Northern Mariner* 9, 3 [July 1999]: 1–22).William March's "The Evolution of a College: HMCS Royal Roads, 1940–48" (MA thesis, University of Victoria) helps trace the development of Esquimalt as a major naval training centre.

Michael Hennessy's "The Rise and Fall of Canadian Maritime Policy, 1939–65: A Study of Industry, Navalism, and the State" (PhD diss., University of New Brunswick, 1995) provides information on the expansion and contraction of the navy. Wilfred Lund's "The Rise and Fall of the Royal Canadian Navy, 1945–64: A Critical Study of the Senior Leadership, Policy, and Manpower Management" (PhD diss., University of Victoria, 1999) is the only available examination of naval policy during the early Cold War. Lund's bleak analysis of the navy's management of manpower is not completely supported by this examination of Pacific Command.

Notes

Introduction

1 *The Crowsnest* 1, 1 (October 1948): 8.
2 Ibid.
3 The only work to focus on the RCN in the Pacific is *Canada's Pacific Naval Presence: Purposeful or Peripheral*, proceeding of the 1997 Maritime Command Historical Conference. The essays in this book did not examine the navy in the Cold War. No publication data were provided in this publication.
4 Tyrone Pile, "Behind the Workable Little Fleet: Post-War Planning and Policy in the RCN 1945–48," MA thesis, University of Victoria, 1998.
5 Wilfred Lund, *The Rise and Fall of the Royal Canadian Navy, 1945–1964: A Critical Study of the Senior Leadership, Policy and Manpower Management*, PhD diss., University of Victoria, 1999, 3.
6 Richard Gimblett, "Gunboat Diplomacy: Mutiny and National Identity in the Postwar Canadian Navy: The Cruise of HMCS *Crescent* to China," PhD diss., Laval University, 2000.
7 See, for instance, Joseph T. Jockel, *Canada in NORAD, 1957–2007: A History* (Montreal and Kingston: McGill–Queen's University Press, 2007); Joseph T. Jockel, *Canada and International Peacekeeping* (Toronto: Canadian Institute of Strategic Studies, 1994); Sean M. Maloney, *Canada and UN Peacekeeping: Cold War by Other Means, 1945–1970* (St. Catharines: Vanwell, 2002).
8 James Fergusson, *Beneath the Radar: Change and Transformation in the Canada–US North American Defence Relationship* (Ottawa: Canadian Defence and Foreign Affairs Institute, 2009), 5.
9 Timothy Wilford, *Canada's Road to the Pacific War: Intelligence, Strategy, and the Far East Crisis* (Vancouver: UBC Press, 2011); John Price, *Orienting Canada: Race, Empire, and the Transpacific* (Vancouver: UBC Press, 2011).

Chapter 1: The Legacy of War and Demobilization

1 Chapter 6, "The Pacific Coast and Alaska, December 1941 to July 1943" (draft chapter), in *Official History of the RCN*, vol. 2, 12.
2 Ibid., 28–29.
3 William March, "The Evolution of a College: HMCS Royal Roads, 1940–48," MA thesis, University of Victoria, 1993.
4 See, for example, Memorandum from D.A. Collins, Secretary to the Chief of Naval Staff, Extracts from the Minutes of a Meeting of the Cabinet held 15th November, 1946, November 27, 1946, NAC RG 24 accession 83–84/169, vol. 610, file 11818–1 v.1.
5 Marc Milner, *Canada's Navy: The First Century* (Toronto: University of Toronto Press: 1999), 158.
6 G.F. Todd, Post-War Strategic Security of Canada, April 15, 1944, NAC RG 24 accession 83–84/169, box 610, file 11818–1 v.1.
7 Commodore H.G. Wolf to Naval Minister, Naval Requirements During Phase II – Post-War Proposals, July 31, 1945, NAC RG 24 accession 83–84/169, box 610, file 11818–1 v.1. Emphasis added.

8 The Continuing Royal Canadian Navy, no date but likely the first half of 1945, NAC RG 24 accession 83–84/169, box 610, file 11818–1 v.1.
9 Ibid.
10 Lieutenant-Commander E.E.G. Boak, acting Assistant Director of Plans (Strategy), "A Naval Appreciation on Canada's Role in the Defence of North America," February 28, 1946, NAC RG 24 accession 83–84/169, box 610, file 11818–1 v.1.
11 Directorate of Naval Plans and Intelligence, Royal Canadian Navy Future Planning – to 1956, November 4, 1946, NAC RG 24 accession 83–84/169, box 610, file 11818–1 v.1.
12 Wilfred Lund, *The Rise and Fall of the Royal Canadian Navy, 1945–1964: A Critical Study of the Senior Leadership, Policy and Manpower Management*, PhD diss., University of Victoria, 1999, 68.
13 Lieutenant-Colonel E.W.T. Gill, Secretary of the Chiefs of Staff Committee, to the Ministers, "West Coast Defences – Transfer of Naval Headquarters from Vancouver to Esquimalt," September 12, 1945, NAC RG 24 accession 83–84/167, box 515, 1700–102/2 v.1.
14 A/Captain F.A. Price, Director of Plans to CNS, Transfer of COPC to Esquimalt, August 4, 1945, NAC RG 24 accession 83–84/167, box 5151, NSS 1700–102/2 v.1.
15 Lieutenant Commander J.R. Kidston, SO (P) to Director of Plans, August 9, 1945, NAC RG 24 accession 83–84/167, box 5151, NSS 1700–102/2 v.1.
16 Lieutenant-Colonel E.W.T. Gill, Secretary of the Chiefs of Staff Committee, to the Ministers, "West Coast Defences – Transfer of Naval Headquarters from Vancouver to Esquimalt," September 12, 1945, NAC RG 24 accession 83–84/167, box 515, 1700–102/ 2 v.1.
17 Commanding Officer Pacific Coast, Report of Proceedings [COPC ROP], October 1945, NAC RG 24 series D11, box 11925, NIE 18–6-21.
18 COPC ROP, October 1945 to February 1946.
19 A/Captain (E) T.H. Evans, Engineer Superintendent, Ship Repairs West Coast to COPC, Dismantling A/S Fixed Defences – Ridley Island, Prince Rupert, September 12, 1945; November 9, 1945, NAC RG 24 series D-11, box 11781, COPC 9020–102/2; COPC ROP, October–December 1945, December 1946.
20 COPC ROP, December 1946. Note: This ROP is misdated and reads December 1947.
21 COPC ROP, October 1945.
22 Ibid.; and March 1946.
23 A/Commander P.E. Haddon, Senior Officer Ships in Reserve to COPC, December 31, 1945, NAC RG 24, series D-11, box 11783, COPC 1926–281.
24 A/Captain C.D Donald, Senior Officer Ships in Reserve to COPC, Report on Proceedings in Reserve Fleet, May 30, 1946, NAC RG 24m series D-11, box 11783, COPC 1926–281.
25 COPC ROP, October and December 1945.
26 COPC ROP, March 1947.
27 Naval Secretary to COPC, January 4, 1946, NAC RG 24, v. 11775, accession 83–84/167, v. COPC S.1700–102/2 v.1.
28 Naval Secretary to COPC, March 22, 1946; also see COPC to Naval Secretary, February 1, 1946, NAC RG 24, v. 11775, accession 83–84/167, v. COPC s.1700–102/2 v.1.
29 COPC ROP, March 1947.
30 COPC ROP, May 1946 and January 1947.
31 COPC ROP, October–November 1945.
32 John P. Tully to Rear Admiral E.R. Mainguy, November 10, 1947, NAC RG 24 accession 83–84/167, v. 11920, SI 13–2-2.
33 Flag Officer Pacific Coast Report of Proceedings (FOPC ROP), June 1949, NAC RG 24, series D11, box 11925, NIE 18–6-21.
34 Harold Escott to the Director of Naval Intelligence, Royal Roads, May 13, 1948, NAC RG 24 accession 83–84/167, v. 11920, SI 13–2-2.

35 R. Roberts, A/Staff Officer (Intelligence and Trade) West Coast to H. Escott, May 17, 1948, NAC RG 24 accession 83–84/167, v. 11920, SI 13–2-2.
36 ROP FOPC, April 1948.
37 Lieutenant-Commander R. Roberts, Staff Officer (Intelligence and Trade) to the General Manager, Union Steamships Limited, Vancouver, April 10, 1947; COPC to Messs. Bogle, Bogle, and Gates, Seattle, May 30, 1947, NAC RG 24 accession 83–84/167, v. 11920, SI 13–2-2.
38 ROP FOPC, April 1948.
39 *The Crowsnest* 1, 1 (October 1948): 8.
40 COPC ROP, March 1947.
41 COPC ROP, January and March 1946.
42 W. Redford, master, FPC *Howay*, to the Chief Supervisor of Fisheries, Vancouver, April 7, 1948, NAC RG 24 accession 83–84/167,v. 11920, SI 13–2-2.
43 ROP FOPC, June 1952.

Chapter 2: From Peace to Cold War, 1945–50

1 Wilfred Lund, *The Rise and Fall of the Royal Canadian Navy, 1945–1964: A Critical Study of the Senior Leadership, Policy and Manpower Management*, PhD diss., University of Victoria, 1999, 88.
2 Ibid, 124.
3 Ibid, 192.
4 *The Crowsnest* 1, 1 (September 1949): 16.
5 See organizational chart accompanying Naval Secretary to COPC, Re-organization – Pacific Coast Command, April 7, 1946, NAC RG 24, V. 11775, Accession 83–84/167, V. COPC S.1700–102/2 Vol. 1.
6 Lund, *The Rise and Fall*, 128.
7 Memo by Naval Secretary, "Employment of the Canadian Naval Forces during 1946–47," July 18, 1946, DHH Naval Historians Files, NSS 1650–26 v.1.
8 ROP FOPC, 1945–50; for upgrading of destroyers, see Memo DNPO to ACNS, VNCS, December 30, 1945, DHH Naval Historians Files, 1650–26 v.2 and 257th Naval Board Meeting Minutes (NB), August 23, 1948; Richard Gimblett," Gunboat Diplomacy: Mutiny and National Identity in the Postwar Royal Canadian Navy: The Cruise of HMCS *Crescent* to China," PhD diss., Laval University, 2000, 13–14.
9 The accounts of these incidents are summarized from Marc Milner, *Canada's Navy: The First Century* (Toronto: University of Toronto Press, 1999), 188–91.
10 Peter Archambault, "Mutiny and the Imperial Tradition: The Canadian Naval Mutinies of 1949 and Experience of Mutiny in the Royal Navy," MA thesis, University of New Brunswick, 1992.
11 Milner, *Canada's Navy*, 195.
12 Report of Proceedings HMCS *Crescent*, October 1 to November 7, 1945, NAC RG 24, series D-11, vol. 11776, file COPC S 1926–358/36.
13 ROP *Crescent*, January 1946, NAC RG 24-D-1, vol. 11776, file COPC S 1926–358/36.
14 Richard Gimblett, "'Too Many Chiefs and Not Enough Seamen': The Lower Deck Complement of a Postwar Canadian Navy Destroyer – the Case of HMCS *Crescent*, March 1949," *Northern Mariner* 9, 3 (July 1999): 1–22.
15 ROP *Crescent*, April 1947.
16 Report of Proceedings HMCS *Uganda*, February 5 to May 11, NAC RG 24, National Defence, series D-11, vol. 11786, file COPC C 1926–347/5.
17 ROP *Crescent*, November 1946.

18 Memo Dwt (Raymond) to ACNS, DNPI, May 15, 1947, DHH Naval Historians, files NSS 1650–26 vol. II.
19 COPC ROP, August 1947.
20 ROP *Crescent*, October–November 1947; COPC ROP, October 1947.
21 ROP *Cayuga*, May 1950, NAC RG 24, series D-11, vol. 11786, file COPC C 1926–355/30.
22 C. Anthony Law, Operation Nootka, August 19, 1948, Reports of Proceedings HMCS *Cayuga*, August 1948, NAC RG 24, series D-11, vol. 11776, COPC S 1926–355/30.
23 T.W. Creery, Operation Sink the Fleet, Reports of Proceedings HMCS *Cayuga*, August 1948, NAC RG 24, series D-11, vol. 11776, COPC S 1926–355/30.
24 Law, Operation Nootka.
25 Ibid. Also see John A. Charles, Commanding Officer HMCS *Crescent*, to Commander Canadian Destroyer Division Pacific, Proceedings of Exercises of August 17, 1948; Lieutenant H.E.T. Lawrence for Commander *Cayuga*, to Commander Canadian Destroyer Division West Coast, Exercise – August 17, 1948, all in Reports of Proceedings HMCS *Cayuga*, August 1948, NAC RG 24, series D-11, vol. 11776, COPC S 1926–355/30.
26 O.C.S. Robertson, Appendix I to ROP *Cayuga*, August 1948.
27 Lieutenant J.S. Gill to the Commander, Canadian Destroyer Division, August 27, 1948; also see the report of Lieutenant J.M. Paul, the Battalion Commander, Operation Soldier, to Commander, Canadian Destroyer Division, August 26, 1948; and Appendix I, Operation Soldier, n.d. but August 1948, all in Reports of Proceedings HMCS *Cayuga*, August 1948, NAC RG 24, series D-11, vol. 11776, COPC S 1926–355/30.
28 ROP *Crescent*, March 1949.
29 ROP *Crescent*, April 1949.
30 Ibid.
31 Gimblett, "Gunboat Diplomacy," 133.
32 As quoted in ibid., 138.
33 ROP *Athabaskan*, June and July 1949, NAC RG 24-D-11, vol. 11786, file COPC C 1926–355/31; ROP *Cayuga*, December 1949.
34 *Report on Certain "Incidents" Which Occurred on Board HMC Ships Athabaskan, Crescent, and Magnificent* (Ottawa: October 1949), 22; ROP *Cayuga*, July 1950.
35 COPC ROP, October 1945.
36 COPC ROP, November 1945.
37 COPC ROP, September 1945 to November 1947.
38 COPC ROP, September 1946; ROP *Crescent*, September 1946.
39 Jamie Glazov, *Canadian Policy toward Khrushchev's Soviet Union* (Montreal and Kingston: McGill–Queen's University Press, 2002), 10.
40 Charles H. Deerwester, Colonel, AC, US Air Member for General Clay to S.F. Rae, Secretary, Canadian Section, PJBD, Department of External Affairs, Ottawa, June 27, 1947, NAC RG 24, series D-1-c, v.8183, NSC 1660–17.
41 Vice Admiral H.E. Reid, acting Chief of Staff to Claxton, July 30, 1947; 397th Meeting of the Chiefs of Staff Committee, July 30, 1947, NAC RG 24, series D-1-c, v.8183, NSC 1660–17.
42 35th Meeting of the Cabinet Defence Committee, August 18, 1947, NAC RG 24, series D-1-c, v.8183, NSC 1660–17.
43 The Canadian Ambassador to the United States to the Secretary of State for External Affairs, August 21, 1947, NAC RG 24, Series D-1-c, v.8183, NSC 1660–17.
44 Excerpts from the Minutes of the Meeting of the PJBD, September 11–12, 1947, NAC RG 24, series D-1-c, v.8183, NSC 1660–17.

45 NSHQ to COPC, October 30, 1947, NAC RG 24, National Defence, series D-1-c, vol. 8153, file 1660–17.

Chapter 3: Defending the West Coast in the Nuclear Age

1 Marc Milner, *Canada's Navy: The First Century* (Toronto: University of Toronto Press, 1999), 205–8.

2 Procedures regarding Minutes and Submissions from Joint Service Committees, Pacific, Atlantic, and Newfoundland, May 14, 1946, NAC RG 24, National Defence, series B-1, vol. 21368, CSC 1789:1, Title: Joint Services Committee – Pacific – General.

3 JSCP, Minutes of Meeting 69, December 8, 1948, NAC RG 24, National Defence, series B-1, vol. 21368, CSC 1789:1, Title: Joint Services Committee – Pacific – General.

4 JSCP, Minutes of Meeting 71, February 15, 1949, NAC RG 24, National Defence, series B-1, vol. 21368, CSC 1789:1, Title: Joint Services Committee – Pacific – General.

5 JSCP, Minutes of Meeting 72, April 28, 1949, NAC RG 24, National Defence, series B-1, vol. 21368, CSC 1789:1, Title: Joint Services Committee – Pacific – General.

6 Canada–United States Military Cooperation Committee: History and Organization, no date but circa 1965, NAC RG 24, National Defence, series G-9–1, vol. 21854, file FMC 3121–2, Plans, Operations & Readiness – Joint United States–Canada Emergency Defence Plans – ALCANUS.

7 "Soviet Capabilities and Probable Courses of Action Against Canada, the United States and the Areas Adjacent Thereto," October 21, 1948, NAC RG 24, National Defence, series D-1-c, vol. 8145, file 1480–29, Agreed Canada–United States Estimate.

8 JSCP, Minutes of Meetings 75, September 7, 1949, and 76, January 16, 1950, NAC RG 24, National Defence, series B-1, vol. 21368, CSC 1789:1, Title: Joint Services Committee – Pacific – General.

9 Directorate of Naval Plans Aide Memoire for CNS, ALCANUS EDP-W-49, January 10, 1950, NAC RG 24 accession 83–4/167, vol. 232, 1400–48 n.1, Canada–US Emergency Plan for Alaska–Western Canada–Western US Defence (ALCANUS).

10 JSCP, Appendix to 77th Meeting, March 7, 1950, NAC RG 24, National Defence, series B-1, vol. 21368, CSC 1789:1, Title: Joint Services Committee – Pacific – General. It remains unclear which vessel was referred to as HMC PTC 724.

11 JSCP, Minutes of 78th Meeting, (Date?), NAC RG 24, National Defence, series B-1, vol. 21368, CSC 1789:1, Title: Joint Services Committee – Pacific – General.

12 Minutes of 79th Meeting, July 7, 1950, NAC RG 24, National Defence, series B-1, vol. 21368, CSC 1789:1, Title: Joint Services Committee – Pacific – General.

13 Annex no. VII to Canada–United States Emergency Defence Plan for Alaska–Western Canada–Western United States, August 15, 1950, NAC RG 24, National Defence, series B-1, vol. 21368, CSC 1789:1, Title: Joint Services Committee – Pacific – General.

14 Ibid.

15 EDP-51 has not been found. Details provided here are contained in Memorandum to DNPO from Lt. H.G.J. Walls, Staff Officer Policy, December 8, 1951; Report by Joint Planning Committee on ALCANUS EDP/51, January 10, 1952, NAC RG 24 accession 83–4/167, vol. 232, 1400–48 n.1 Canada–US Emergency Plan for Alaska–Western Canada–Western US Defence (ALCANUS).

16 AC Wedemeyer Lt Gen, HQ Sixth Army Presidio, Canada–US Emergency Defence Plan for ALCANUS ALCANUS-EDP-51, March 14, 1951, NAC RG 24 accession 83–4/167, vol. 232, 1400–48 n.1 Canada–US Emergency Plan for Alaska–Western Canada–Western US Defence (ALCANUS).

17 Memorandum to DNPO from Lt. H.G.J. Walls, Staff Officer Policy, December 8, 1951.

18 A.H.G. Storrs Captain, Member Joint Planning Committee, to Sec. Joint Planning Committee, ALCANUS 51, December 13, 1951, NAC RG 24 accession 83–4/167, vol. 232, 1400–48 n.1 Canada–US Emergency Plan for Alaska–Western Canada–Western US Defence (ALCANUS).

19 Report by Joint Planning Committee on ALCANUS EDP/51, January 10, 1951, NAC RG 24 Acc 83–4/167 vol. 232, 1400–48 n.1 Canada US Emergency Plan for Alaska-Western Canada-Western US Defence (ALCANUS).

20 R.L. Raymont ESO to CCO to Stores, Sec. JPC March 22, 1952, NAC RG 24 accession 83–4/167, vol. 232, 1400–48 n.1 Canada–US Emergency Plan for Alaska–Western Canada–Western US Defence (ALCANUS).

21 An examination of the Requirements for Seaward Defences at Yorke Island, December 2, 1954, NAC RG 24 accession 83–4/167, vol. 239, 1404–166 vol. 3.

22 Naval Secretary to FOPC, Provision of Suitable A/S Patrol Vessels for the Defence of Johnstone Strait at Yorke Island and the Defence of the Strait of Juan de Fuca, May 29, 1951, NAC RG 24 accession 83–4/167, vol. 239, 1404–166 vol. 2.

23 An Appreciation of the Situation Regarding the Provision of Adequate Defences Against Attack by Sea for Ports in the Georgia Strait–Puget Sound–Strait of Juan de Fuca Area, November 9, 1950, NAC RG 24 accession 83–4/167, vol. 239, 1404–166 vol. 2.

24 An Appreciation of the Situation Regarding the Provision of Adequate Defences Against Attack by Sea for Ports in the Georgia Strait–Puget Sound–Strait of Juan De Fuca Area, Esquimalt, December 15, 1950, NAC RG 24 accession 83–4/167, vol. 239, 1404–166 vol. 2.

25 Minutes of the First Staff Meeting of the Coastal Defence Commander, Pacific Coast, January 23, 1951, NAC RG 24 accession 83–84/167, vol. 176, 1282–110.

26 An Appreciation of the Situation Regarding the Provision of Adequate Defences Against Attack by Sea for Ports in the Georgia Strait–Puget Sound–Strait of Juan De Fuca Area, Esquimalt.

27 Creery to Naval Secretary, The Provision of Adequate Defences Against Attack by Sea for Ports in Georgia Strait, Puget Sound and Straits of Juan de Fuca Areas, December 22, 1950, NAC RG 24 accession 83–4/167, vol. 239, 1404–166 vol. 2.

28 J.P. Singleton, Technical Report on FOPC Letter TS 11400–28, January 2, 1951; E.P. Tisdall, The Provision of Defences in the Straits of Juan de Fuca and Johnstone Strait, January 8, 1951, NAC RG 24 accession 83–4/167, vol. 239, 1404–166 vol. 2.

29 Minutes of the First Staff Meeting of the Coastal Defence Commander, Pacific Coast, January 23, 1951, NAC RG 24 accession 83–4/167, vol. 239, 1404–166 vol. 2.

30 Naval Secretary to Flag Officer Pacific Coast, Provision of Suitable A/S Patrol Vessels for the Defence of Johnstone Strait at Yorke Island and the Defence of the Strait of Juan de Fuca, May 29, 1951, NAC RG 24 accession 83–4/167, vol. 239, 1404–166 vol. 2.

31 Creery to Naval Secretary, Seaward Defence West Coast, August 9, 1951, NAC RG 24 accession 83–4/167, vol. 239, 1404–166 vol. 2.

32 Singleton, Memorandum to the Director Naval Plans & Operations, August 10, 1951, NAC RG 24 accession 83–4/167, vol. 239, 1404–166 vol. 2. Emphasis added.

33 Simonds to Chairman, Chiefs of Staff, Seaward Defences – Yorke Island, March 31, 1954, NAC RG 24 accession 83–4/167, vol. 239, 1404–166 vol. 3.

34 King to CNS, Seaward Defences – West Coast – Provision of a Gun at Yorke Island, June 22, 1954; King to VCNS, CNS, Seaward Defences – Yorke Island, September 2, 1954, NAC RG 24 accession 83–4/167, vol. 239, 1404–166 vol. 3.

35 An Examination of the Requirements for Seaward Defences at Yorke Island, December 2, 1954, NAC RG 24 accession 83–4/167, vol. 239, 1404–166 vol. 3. Emphasis added.

36 CANAVHED to CANFLAGANT and PAC, found with telegram, CANAVHED to CONFLAGLANT and CANFLAGPAC info CNO Admiralty, C in C LANT C in C Pac

COMWESTSEAFRON and COMEASTSEAFRON, August 19, 1950, NAC RG 24, series D-11, vol. 11922, SI 19–7-3 [Staff Officer Intelligence, West Coast] – Submarines – Sightings and attacks.

37 From COMWESTSECTOR Western Sea Frontier to COMFORWESTSEAFRON copy to CANFLAGPAC, December 17, 1950, NAC RG 24, series D-11, vol. 11922, SI 19–7-3 [Staff Officer Intelligence, West Coast] – Submarines – Sightings and attacks.

38 CANFLAGPAC to COMWESTSECTOR Western Sea Frontier, December 17, 1950, NAC RG 24, series D-11, vol. 11922, SI 19–7-3 [Staff Officer Intelligence, West Coast] – Submarines – Sightings and attacks.

39 COMWESTSECTOR Western Sea Frontier to CANFLAGPAC, December 17, 1950, NAC RG 24, series D-11, vol. 11922, SI 19–7-3 [Staff Officer Intelligence, West Coast] – Submarines – Sightings and attacks.

40 COMWESTSECTOR Western Sea Frontier to CANFLAGPAC, December 18, 1950, NAC RG 24, series D-11, vol. 11922, SI 19–7-3 [Staff Officer Intelligence, West Coast] – Submarines – Sightings and attacks.

41 F. Corneille Lt RCN (r), Chief Officer MV Imperial Nanaimo to FOPC, May 5, 1950, NAC RG 24, accession 1983–84/167, box 4034, NSS-8910–1, Parts: 1, Enemy Submarine Activities – General Outside Dates: 1944–1950.

42 Crusader to CANFLAGPAC, May 24, 1951, NAC RG 24, series D-11, vol. 11922, SI 19–7-3 [Staff Officer Intelligence, West Coast] – Submarines – Sightings and attacks.

43 Terms of Reference – Merchant Navy Liaison Officers, November 1, 1950, NAC RG 24, National Defence, series D-11, vol. 11774, file COPC S 1550–1.

44 A.D.P. Heeney, Under-Secretary of State for External Affairs, to the Deputy Minister, Department of Transport, January 10, 1951, ibid.

45 RDB, SO (T), Danger of "unconventional" weapons in Russian or satellite merchant ships, March 13, 1951, ibid.

46 Staff Officer (Intelligence) Esquimalt, Report on Canadian Trade Unions, June 29, 1951, NAC RG 24, National Defence, series D-11, vol. 11925, NIE 12–1-1.

47 SUPYARD ESQ TO CANAVHED, September 26, 1951; CANFLAGPAC to CANAVHED, September 27, 1951; SUPYARD ESQ to CANAVHED, September 27, 1951, NAC RG 24, National Defence, series D-11, vol. 11925, file NIE 12–1-1.

48 CANAVHED to SUPYARDESQ, September 29, 1951, ibid.

49 SUPYARD ESQ to CANAVHED, September 29, 1951, ibid.

50 SUPYARD ESQ to CANAVHED, September 29, 1951, SUPYARD ESQ to CANAVHED, October 2, 1951, ibid; ROP FOPC, September 1951.

51 ROP FOPC, October 1951.

Chapter 4: Cold War Expansion

1 FOPC ROP, July 1950.

2 Naval Staff Minute 496–3. The arrangement for the fleet was confirmed by the Naval Board on September 13, 1950, Meeting of the Naval Board, 331–32.

3 ROP FOPC, June 1950 to December 1953; ROP HMCS *Antigonish*, NAC RG 24, National Defence, series D-11, vol. 11835, file PC 1926–381/2, June 1950 to December 1953; ROP HMCS *Crusader*, NAC RG 24, National Defence, series D-11, vol. 11835, file PC 1926–358/38, May 1951–January 1952.

4 ROP FOPC, February 1951.

5 ROP HMCS *Antigonish*, February 1952.

6 Naval Staff Minute 496–3.

7 ROP Superindendent, HMC Dockyard, Esquimalt, February–April 1951, DHist.

8 ROP *Crusader*, April 1951.
9 Wilfred Lund, "The Rise and Fall of the Royal Canadian Navy, 1945–1964: A Critical Study of the Senior Leadership, Policy and Manpower Management," PhD diss., University of Victoria, 1999, 15.
10 ROP *Crusader*, April 1951. Emphasis added.
11 ROP *Crusader*, May 1951.
12 NAC RG 24, National Defence, series D-11, vol. 11853, file C 1270–102/2, file title: [HMCS NADEN, Esquimalt] – Committees and conferences, Flag Officer Pacific Coast weekly meetings. The first weekly meeting was held in mid-April 1953.
13 The two directives were Seamen non-substantive training – NSS 4300–1, vol. 4 (Staff), January 26, 1953, which was forwarded to COMBRAX Esquimalt on February 16, 1953; and Manning Problems – NS 4300–1 Pers (N) B, January 3, 1953, forwarded to COMBRAX Esquimalt, January 20, 1953. These documents are cited in Flag Officer Pacific Coast weekly meetings, 2nd Meeting, April 28, 1953.
14 Flag Officer Pacific Coast weekly meetings, 2nd Meeting, April 28, 1953.
15 Flag Officer Pacific Coast weekly meetings, 4th Meeting, May 19, 1953; 5th Meeting, May 26, 1953. Also See FOPC ROP, May 1953.
16 Flag Officer Pacific Coast weekly meetings, 7th Meeting, June 16, 1953.
17 Flag Officer Pacific Coast weekly meetings, 18th Meeting, August 25, 1953.
18 Flag Officer Pacific Coast weekly meetings, 19th Meeting, September 1, 1953.
19 Flag Officer Pacific Coast weekly meetings, 26th Meeting, November 24, 1953.
20 Reports of proceedings – HMCS *Jonquiere*, March 1955, NAC RG 24, National Defence, series D-11, vol. 11834, file PC 1926-FFE 318; Report on Operation Jackpine and other supporting documents in NAC RG 24, National Defence, series D-11, vol. 11774, file COPC S 1650–1, file title [Flag Officer Pacific Coast] – Operations, general.
21 ROP *Athabaskan*, October 1955.
22 ROP *Cayuga*, October 1955.
23 Taylor, Memo to FOPC, November 9, 1955; memo by Pullen, November 30, 1955, both attached to Report of Proceedings, HMCS *Jonquiere*.
24 FOPC Weekly Meeting, 66th Meeting, February 22, 1955. Also see 68th Meeting, March 6, 1955.
25 ROP FOPC, August 1955.
26 See the Briefing Notes on PACTRAEX 56L in NAC RG 24, series D-11, vol. 11774, file COPC S 1650–1, [Flag Officer Pacific Coast] – Operations, general.
27 ROP *Ste. Therese*, November 1955, NAC RG 24-D-11, vol. 11834, file PC 1926-FFE 309.
28 FOPC ROP, November 1955.
29 ROP 2nd Escort Squadron, February 1957, D.Hist.
30 Reports on WESTPAC CONVEX REX 58J, March 1958, NAC RG 24, National Defence, series D-1-c, vol. 8157, file 1660–58, Tactical Operations and Projects – Exercise Convex.
31 ROP 2nd Canadian Escort Squadron, July 1956, D.Hist.
32 ROP *Cayuga*, November 1955.
33 ROP 2nd Canadian Escort Squadron, ROP *Athabaskan*, March 1957.
34 ROP *Athabaskan*, July 1956.
35 ROP *Sioux*, July 1956.
36 ROP 2nd Canadian Escort Squadron, July 1956.
37 ROP 2nd Canadian Escort Squadron, March 1957.
38 ROP 2nd Canadian Escort Squadron, July and September 1957.
39 Good examples of these technological shortcomings can be found in the Reports on WESTPAC CONVEX REX 58J, March 1958.

40 ROP 2nd Canadian Escort Squadron, April 1956.
41 Staff Minute Sheet on Report of Proceedings, July 1956, Note of August 14, 1956, found in ROP *Sioux*, July 1956.
42 On the formation and role of the 4th Escort Squadron, see ROP *Sussexvale*, January 1957, NAC RG 24, series D-1-c, vol. 34014, file 1926-DE 313 pt 2.
43 ROP 2nd Canadian Escort Squadron, January 1957.
44 See Taylor, Endurance – Tribal Class Destroyers, April 23, 1956; and Staff Minute on Endurance – Tribal Class Destroyers, n.d., in ROP *Cayuga*, March 1956. The Briefing Notes on PACTRAEX 56L contain information on the endurance of Canadian warships; ROP *Sioux*, February 1956.
45 Marc Milner, *Canada's Navy: The First Century* (Toronto: University of Toronto Press, 1999), 180–83, 213–15.
46 ROP 2nd Canadian Escort Squadron, May 1957.
47 ROP 2nd Canadian Escort Squadron, August 1956.
48 FOPC, Note to Naval Headquarters, September 18, 1956, found with ibid.
49 ROP *Skeena*, April and May 1957, NAC RG 24, series D-22, vol. 11402, file DSA-1926-DDE 207.

Chapter 5: Reorganization of Pacific Command and West Coast Defence Planning, 1958–61

1 Minutes of the 583rd Meeting of the Chiefs of Staff, October 26, 1955.
2 Lieutenant-Commander A.H. McDonald, Staff Officer Strategy, to DNPO, Joint Service Headquarters, January 6, 1954, NAC RG 24, National Defence, series D-10, vol. 11174, file ACS 1700–151, [Flag Officer Atlantic Coast] – Organization and administration – Permanent Maritime Headquarters, Atlantic.
3 93rd meeting, Joint Services Committee – Pacific July 7, 1953, NAC RG 24, National Defence, series B-1, vol. 21368, file CSC 1789:1, pts. 1, File Title: Joint Services Committee – Pacific – General.
4 Selection of Maritime Headquarters, n.d. but 1956, NAC RG 24, National Defence, series D-10, vol. 11174, file ACS 1700–151.
5 Commodore D.L. Raymond, Assistant Chief of Naval Staff (Plans), Maritime Headquarters – West Coast, February 28, 1958, NAC RG 24, National Defence, series D-10, vol. 11174, file ACS 1700–151; ROP FOPC, October 1959.
6 H.S. Rayner, Organization Maritime Commander Pacific, December 1, 1958, NAC RG 24, National Defence, series D-10, vol. 11174, file ACS 1700–151.
7 Hugh Campbell, Maritime Organization – West Coast, February 11, 1959, NAC RG 24, National Defence, series D-10, vol. 11174, file ACS 1700–151.
8 J.A. Charles, Memorandum to the CNS, Maritime Organization – West Coast, February 23, 1959, NAC RG 24, National Defence, series D-10, vol. 11174, file ACS 1700–151.
9 Minutes of the 129th Meeting of the Policy and Projects Committee, February 3, 1958, NAC RG 24, accession 83–84/167, vol. 147, RCN Committees. Meeting & Conferences Policy and Project Coordination Committee. 1279–145 v.3.
10 The actual numbers of cadets were: ROTP, 67 first year, 48 second year; Venture, 67 first year, 50 second year; and UNTD, 260 first year, 210 second year, and 170 third year. Only some of third-year UNTD and 27 third-year ROTP cadets that did not require sea billets. Minutes of the 118th Meeting of the Policy and Projects Committee, October 27, 1957, NAC RG 24, accession 83–84/167, vol. 147, RCN Committees. Meeting & Conferences Policy and Project Coordination Committee. 1279–145 v.3.
11 Composition of the Fleet – 1959, NAC RG 24, National Defence, series D-10, vol. 11158, file ACS 1650–26 Sub.4, [Flag Officer Atlantic Coast] – Operations and plans – Employment of the fleet, 1959.

12 The RCN's appreciation of the growing Soviet submarine threat, although not specifically how it relates to Pacific security, can be found in Minutes of the Special Meeting, Chiefs of Staff Committee, October 26, 1957.
13 ROP FOPC, March 1958.
14 This plan was found in the papers of the RCAF. RCN files of various ALCANUS plans were purged of older planning documents when newer versions superseded them. NAC RG 24, National Defence, series E-1-c, accession 1983–84/049, box 131, file 098–110, Maritime Planning – Maritime Commander Pacific Emergency Defence Plan.
15 The most recent RCN Emergency Plan was titled CBCN 6904 (57); the latest ALCANUS plan was ALCANUS-57(c).
16 Ibid.
17 Emergency ASW Search and Patrol Order 1/58, Appendix (A) to MAROPEDPAC-58, ibid.
18 Emergency Minesweeping Order 1/58, Appendix (B) to MAROPEDPAC-58, ibid.
19 Employment of the Fleet – 1959, Enclosure B to NSS 1650–26, December 12, 1958. Reference: NAC RG 24, National Defence, series D-10, vol. 11158, file ACS 1650–26 Sub.4, v.2, [Flag Officer Atlantic Coast] – Operations and plans – Employment of the fleet.
20 Rayner to Naval Secretary, Proposed Composition and Employment of the Fleet 1959, 25 September 1958, NAC RG 24, National Defence, series D-10, vol. 11158, file: ACS 1650–26 Sub.4, vol. 2 [Flag Officer Atlantic Coast] – Operations and plans – Employment of the fleet.
21 Ibid.
22 See, for example, Commodore H.V.W. Groos to the FOPC, Conditions of Service Esquimalt Port Division, Men on Loan to Halifax, December 11, 1958; Naval Secretary to FOPC, FOAC, Manning – Composition of the Fleet – 1959, September 26, 1958, NAC RG 24, National Defence, series D-10, vol. 11158, file ACS 1650–26 Sub.4, vol. 2 [Flag Officer Atlantic Coast] – Operations and plans – Employment of the fleet.
23 Rayner to the Naval Secretary, Employment of the Fleet, June 8, 1959, NAC RG 24, National Defence, series D-10, vol. 11158, file ACS 1650–26 Sub.5, vol. 2 [Flag Officer Atlantic Coast] – Operations and plans – Employment of the fleet.
24 Naval Secretary to Rayner, June 26, 1959, ibid.
25 ROP FOPC, ROP *St. Laurent*, October 1959, NAC RG 24-D-1-c, vol. 35402, file 1926-DDH 205 pt. 2.
26 Instructions for the Coordination of Canada–United States ASW Operations in the Defence of North America, August 7, 1958, NAC RG 24, National Defence, series E-1-c, accession 1983–84/049, box 113, file 096–107–13, pts. 1, Planning – Defence Planning – Alcanus West Coast
27 H.G. DeWolf, Concept and Plan of Operations for the Co-ordinated Canada–United States Defence of North America Against Attack by Submarine, August 7, 1958, ibid.
28 Report of ALCANUS Planners' and Commanders' Conference, December 2–11, 1958, NAC RG 24, National Defence, series D-11, vol. 20028, file MCP S 1281–166/11, Alcanus Defence Committee.
29 Ibid.
30 All of these documents are cited in Aide Memoire re Naval Annex to ALCANUS-59 and Combined CAN/US ASW OPORDER, August 21, 1958, NAC RG 24, National Defence, series D-11, vol. 20028, file MCP S 1281–166/11, Alcanus Defence Committee.
31 Proposed Canada–US A/S Operational Orders, August 17, 1959, NAC RG 24, accession 83–84/049, box 556, file 096–107–5.
32 Rayner to Chairman, Chiefs of Staff, ALCANUS EDP-59, September 11, 1959, NAC RG 24, National Defence, series D-11, vol. 20028, file MCP S 1281–166/11, Alcanus Defence Committee.

33 ROP *Skeena*, March 1959.
34 Rayner to Chairman, Chiefs of Staff, ALCANUS EDP-59, September 11, 1959, NAC RG 24, National Defence, series D-11, vol. 20028, file MCP S 1281–166/11, Alcanus Defence Committee.
35 Coordinated Canadian–United States Peacetime ASW Emergency Defence OPORDER (Note: Canadian editors changed the word coordinated to Combined and gave it the short title CANUSPACOP), n.d., but spring 1961. Also see Acting Commodore G.G. Truscott, Office of the Maritime Commander Pacific to Naval Secretary, April 5, 1961. Attached to this letter is "The Procedures for Canadian Maritime Units Upon Contacting Unidentified or Hostile Submarines," and a map titled Canada/United States Areas of Responsibility for Peacetime Operations. NAC RG 24, National Defence, series E-1-c, accession 1983–84/049, box 113, file 096–107–13, pts.: 1, Planning – Defence Planning – Alcanus West Coast.
36 ROP *Skeena*, March 1959.
37 Soviet SSG Appreciation Pacific Coast, May 31, 1960. Included with this report are two enclosures: An Appreciation of the Threat from Submarine-Launched Guided Missiles in the Pacific Area; and The Selection of the Aim. The authorship of the report is provided in Office of the Maritime Commander Pacific to the Naval Secretary, Chief of Air Staff and Air Officer Commanding, Maritime Air Command, Halifax, Maritime Operations on the Pacific Area, May 31, 1960. NAC RG 24, box 235, accession[?], file 1400.166/11 v.2.

Chapter 6: The Golden Age

1 ROP *Antigonish*, January 1959.
2 ROP *Skeena*, March 1958.
3 ROP *Antigonish*, September 1959.
4 Brief History HMCS *Cape Breton*, Second of Her Name, Directorate of History Files, 8000.
5 ROP FOPC, July 1960; September 1960; October 1961; October 1962.
6 ROP *Cape Breton*, October–November 1963, NAC RG 24, series D-1-c, vol. 34002, file 1926-ARE 100 pt. 1; ROP *Skeena*, November 1963.
7 ROP *Grilse*, January 1962, NAC RG 24, series D-1-c, vol. 34062, file 1926-SS 71.
8 Minutes of the 68th Meeting of the Policy and Projects Co-ordination Committee, June 29, 1956, Report on the Ad Hoc Committee on RCN Submarine Requirements, NAC RG 24 accession [?], box 146, file 1279–145, v.2.
9 ROP FOPC, July 1959.
10 Ibid., October 1959.
11 ROP *Saguenay*, February 1960.
12 ROP *Saguenay*, November 1960.
13 ROP *Margaree*, February 1959, NAC RG 24, series D-1-c, vol. 34588, file 1926-DDE 230 pt. 1.
14 FOPC to Naval Secretary, May 26, 1961, found in ROP *Saguenay*, March 1961.
15 The section on the acquisition of *Grilse* is taken from documents assembled by Captain A.B.F. Fraser-Harris, Director of Naval Ship Requirements, found with *Grilse*'s ROP file at the Directorate of History. Also see Captain R.W. Timbrell, Director of Undersea Warfare to VCNS, Loan of USN Submarine, November 17, 1959; Draft Agreement Between the United States and Canada on the Loan of USS *Burrfish* SSR 112, n.d.; Financial Arrangements for the Loan of USS *Burrfish*, n.d.; Naval Secretary, Arrival Conference – USS *Burrfish (Grilse)*, December 9, 1960; Acquisition of *Burrfish/Grilse*, n.d., all in NAC RG 24, series D-11, vol. 20024, file CSP S 8000-SS 71 File [Commodore Superintendent Pacific Coast] – General information – Submarines; Telegram, September 15, 1960, NAC RG 24, series D-11, vol. 20031, CSP 8000–55/71, [Maritime Command Pacific] – General

information – Submarine. An account of the commissioning of *Grilse* can be found in *The Crowsnest*, May 1961.

16 ROP *Grilse,* May and June 1961.

17 A detailed account of preparations needed to accommodate *Grilse* at Esquimalt is contained in Sub-Lt. A.P.D. Smith to Chief of Staff, Preparation for the Operation of USS *Burfish* from Esquimalt, August 5, 1960, NAC RG 24, National Defence, series D-11, vol. 20031, file CSP 8000–55/71.

18 For an example of the hopes of senior command for the *Grilse*, see FOPC to Naval Secretary May 26, 1961, found in ROP *Saguenay*, March 1961.

19 ROP FOPC, March 1959.

20 ROP *Skeena,* November 1963.

21 For instance, see the ROP *Margaree*, March 1959, for a report on USN attitudes towards RCN warships.

22 ROPs *Crescent*, *Cayuga*, *Fraser*, *Margaree*, and *Skeena*, January–April 1958.

23 ROP *Saguenay*, April 1960.

24 ROP *St. Laurent*, April 1960.

25 ROP *St. Laurent, Ottawa,* NAC RG 24, series D-1-c, vol. 35402, file 1926-DDH 229, and ROP *Saguenay*, March–April 1960.

26 ROPs *St.Laurent, Ottawa,* and *Saguenay*, March 1961. Quotes from *Saguenay*.

27 ROP *St. Laurent,* March 1961.

28 ROP *Antigonish*, October 1959.

29 ROP FOPC, October 1961.

30 ROP *Saguenay,* July 1960.

31 ROP FOPC, October 1961.

32 ROP *Ottawa*, February–March 1962; ROP FOPC, April 1962.

33 Ibid.

34 ROP *St. Laurent*, March 1964.

35 Joint Services Committee/Pacific, Minutes of the 104th Meeting, October 1, 1963, NAC RG 24, National Defence, series D-11, vol. 20031, CSP 801–108, [Maritime Command Pacific] – Joint Services Committee – Pacific.

36 ROP *Antigonish*, November 1964.

37 ROP FOPC, November 1965.

38 See the documents in NAC RG 24, National Defence, series D-11, vol. 20025, file MCP S 1640–13, Maritime Command Pacific – Regional shipping control. Documents in this file include An Appreciation of the Objectives of the Control of Shipping Organization (Pacific Coast of Canada), August 22, 1961; Analysis – Control of Shipping (Pacific) Exercise-61, November 9, 1961; W.L. Hurford, Regional Shipping Director West Coast of Canada to Commander Antisubmarine Warfare Force, Report on Exercise Prairie Wolf National Shipping Administration, March 26, 1962. There are sample copies of the instruction envelopes for merchant captains. Also see ROP FOPC, March 1963 and June 1965.

Chapter 7: The Cold War on the Pacific Coast, 1958–65

1 NAC RG 24, National Defence, series D-11, vol. 20025, file MCP S 1640–13, From the Office MARCOMPAC, Emergency Instructions Merchant Ships Dispersal Envelopes, February 20, 1963. Note: Samples of envelopes and their contents are included with this document.

2 ROP *Saguenay*, July 1960.

3 ROP *Grilse*, April 1962.

4 Office of Canadian Maritime Commander Pacific, CANCOMARPAC Operation Order 3/59 For CHARPAT, September 16,1959, NAC RG 24, series D-11, vol. 20025, MCP S 1650–1

Sub.8, [Maritime Command Pacific] – Operations – Anti-submarine search and reconnaissance.

5 Ibid.

6 In Shore/Off Shore Patrol, November 28–December 5, 1960, NAC RG 24, National Defence, series D-11, vol. 20025, file MCP S 1650–1 Sub.8.

7 Procedures for Operating Surface Units and Aircraft in Conjunction with SOSUS, May 31, 1960, NAC RG 24, box 235, accession [?], file 1400.166/11 v.2.

8 Commander I.B.B. Morrow to MARCOMPAC, Inshore Patrol – September 4–8, 1960, September 22, 1960; Commander E.M. Chadwick to MARCOMPAC, HMCS *Saguenay* – Support of SOSUS Patrol – September 12–16, September 19, 1960, NAC RG 24, National Defence, series D-11, vol. 20025, file MCP S 1650–1 Sub.8.

9 ROP *Skeena*, May 1958; ROP FOPC, May 1958.

10 Interrogation Report – Whiskey 5, Turn Point, Stuart Island, Washington, USA, December 13, 1961, NAC RG 24, National Defence, accession 1983–84/167, box 4035, S-8910–24–1, Reports of Unidentified Submarines from Joint RCN/USN Stations, 1958–1964.

11 Unfortunately, detailed reports of this operation have not been located. See ROP FOPC, October 1960.

12 Naval Secretary to Maritime Commander Pacific, Submarine Classification Criteria, June 10, 1960, NAC RG 24, National Defence, series D-11, vol. 20025, MCP S 1485–1 pt. 2, [Maritime Command Pacific] – Foreign activities.

13 Submarine Contact Evaluation Instructions – 1962, NAC RG 24, National Defence, series D-11, vol. 20025, MCP S 1485–1 pt. 2.

14 Commander R.C. Thurber, Captain HMCS *Fraser*, to the Commander Second Canadian Escort Squadron, Submarine Classification Criteria, January 4, 1963, NAC RG 24, National Defence, series D-11, vol. 20025, MCP S 1485–1 pt. 2; ROP *Saguenay*, October 1962.

15 Ibid.

16 Commander R.H. Leir, Captain of the *Skeena*, to the Commander 2nd Escort Squadron, January 5, 1963, NAC RG 24, National Defence, series D-11, vol. 20025, MCP S 1485–1 pt. 2.

17 Commander *Margaree* to Commander 2nd Escort Squadron, March 11, 1963, NAC RG 24, National Defence, series D-11, vol. 20025, MCP S 1485–1 pt. 2.

18 ROP FOPC, April and May 1956.

19 ROP 2nd Escort Squadron, October 1957.

20 Finch-Noyes to the Commanding Officers of all Escort Squadron, 407th Squadron, all DE and frigate Captains, September 1, 1960, NAC RG 24, National Defence, series D-11, vol. 20025, MCP S 1485–1, [Maritime Command Pacific] – Foreign activities. Note: See marginal note giving amended height and distances on page 2 of the document.

21 Ibid.

22 SO(I) to MCSO (O), Flights Over *Magnitogorsk*, April 18, 1961, NAC RG 24, National Defence, series D-11, vol. 20025, MCP S 1485–1, [Maritime Command Pacific] – Foreign activities.

23 Commander J.E. Korning MCSO (O), Surveillance Policy – Soviet Vessels, April 18, 1961; G.G. Truscott for Rear Admiral to all Escort Squadron Commander, Commander 407th Squadron, all DE and frigate Captains, Surveillance Policy – Soviet Vessels, April 25, 1961, NAC RG 24, National Defence, series D-11, vol. 20025, MCP S 1485–1, [Maritime Command Pacific] – Foreign activities.

24 Soviet Activity in Waters Adjacent to Canada, March 15, 1962, NAC RG 24, National Defence, series D-11, vol. 20025, MCP S 1485–1, [Maritime Command Pacific] – Foreign activities.

25 Ibid.

26 Merchant Vessels Situation Report (MERSITREP), May 23, 1962, NAC RG 24, National Defence, series D-11, vol. 20025, MCP S 1485–1, [Maritime Command Pacific] – Foreign activities.

27 S/L K.L.D. Sam, MSO (I), Surveillance of Soviet Trawler Activity in the Gulf of Alaska, December 12, 1962, NAC RG 24, National Defence, series D-11, vol. 20025, MCP S 1485–1, [Maritime Command Pacific] – Foreign activities.
28 Intelligence Briefing for JSC/P: Soviet Trawler Threat to the Pacific Coast of Canada, January 27, 1964, NAC RG 24, National Defence, series D-11, vol. 20031, CSP 801–108, [Maritime Command Pacific] – Joint Services Committee – Pacific.
29 Ibid.
30 Joint Services Committee/Pacific minutes of the 104th Meeting, October 1, 1963, NAC RG 24, National Defence, series D-11, vol. 20031, CSP 801–108, [Maritime Command Pacific] – Joint Services Committee – Pacific.
31 E.W. Finch-Noyes, Rear Adm, Maritime Commander Pacific to Commander Alaskan Sea Frontier, January 24, 1962, NAC RG 24, National Defence, series D-11, vol. 20025, MCP S 1485–1, [Maritime Command Pacific] – Foreign activities; G.G. Truscott, for Rear ADM MARCOMPAC, to Naval Secretary, August 14, 1962, NAC RG 24, National Defence, series D-11, vol. 20025, MCP S 1485–1, no. 2, file title [Maritime Command Pacific] – Foreign activities.
32 Russian Trawler Activity Gulf of Alaska, December 15, 1961; Naval Secretary to Maritime Commander Pacific, January 4, 1962, NAC RG 24, National Defence, series D-11, vol. 20025, MCP S 1480–1, [Maritime Command Pacific] – Intelligence – Situation reports.
33 MARCOMPAC, Letter Report on Activities of SRT 4454 and Associated Unidentified Contact Designated W-3, August 10, 1962, NAC RG 24, National Defence, series D-11, vol. 20025, MCP S 1485–1 pt. 2.
34 Report on Trawler Surveillance – June 12–13, 1962, June 13, 1962, NAC RG 24, National Defence, series D-11, vol. 20025, MCP S 1485–1, [Maritime Command Pacific] – Foreign activities.
35 MARCOMPAC, Letter Report on Activities of SRT 4454 and Associated Unidentified Contact Designated W-3, August 10, 1962, NAC RG 24, National Defence, series D-11, vol. 20025, MCP S 1485–1 pt. 2. Quote from Intelligence Notes, June 28, 1962, attached to this report.
36 Ibid.
37 Lieutenant-Commander E.M. Jones, Captain *Antigonish*, to MARCOMPAC, Report of Operations August 14–15, 1962, September 4, 1962, NAC RG 24, National Defence, series D-11, vol. 20025, MCP S 1485–1 pt. 2.
38 SIGINT Trawlers MARPAC Area, May 25–June 6, 1964, June 24, 1964, NAC RG 24, National Defence, series D-11, vol. 20025, file MCP S 1480–1, Maritime Command Pacific] – Intelligence – Situation reports.
39 Rear Admiral M.G. Stirling to Director of Naval Intelligence, MARPAC Patrol, November 23–December 4, 1964, NAC RG 24, National Defence, series D-11, vol. 20025, file MCP S 1480–1, [Maritime Command Pacific] – Intelligence – Situation reports.
40 ROP *Antigonish,* January 1965.
41 Ibid.
42 Steve Ewing, *Thach Weave: The Life of Jimmie Thach* (Annapolis: Naval Institute Press, 2004), 266.
43 Peter T. Haydon, *The 1962 Cuban Missile Crisis: Canadian Involvement Reconsidered* (Toronto: Canadian Institute of Strategic Studies, 1993).
44 ROP FOPC, October 1962.
45 The warships involved were *Ottawa, Saguenay, Margaree, Sussexvale, Beacon Hill, Stettler, Jonquiere, and New Glasgow*. *Cape Breton* and the naval auxiliary *Dundurn* provided support. ROP FOPC, October 1962.
46 Ibid. Of these nineteen patrols, two were flown over a Soviet research ship, the *Zarya*, and four over the Soviet fishing fleet in the Gulf of Alaska. This source does not provide the specific dates of any of these missions.

47 Ibid.; ROPs *Stettler,* NAC RG 24, series D-1-c, vol. 34013, file 1926-DE 311 pt. 3; *Beacon Hill,* NAC RG 24, series D-1-c, vol. 34002, file 1926-ARE 100 pt. 2; and *Saguenay,* October 1962.
48 ROP *Stettler,* October 1962.
49 ROP *Beacon Hill,* October 1962.
50 ROP *Saguenay,* October 1962.
51 Ibid., ROP FOPC, October 1962.
52 Marc Milner, *Canada's Navy: The First Century* (Toronto: University of Toronto Press, 1999), 207, 224–25.
53 Shawn Cafferky, *Uncharted Waters: A History of the Canadian Helicopter-Carrying Destroyer* (Halifax: Centre for Foreign Policy Studies, Dalhousie University, 2006).
54 Milner, *Canada's Navy,* 256.
55 "The Cyclic System," *The Crowsnest,* August 1964.

Conclusion

1 *White Paper on Defence* (Ottawa: Queen's Printer, 1964), 14. Emphasis added.
2 DND, *Challenge and Commitment: A Defence Policy for Canada* (Ottawa: 1987), 49–55.
3 DND, *1994 Defence White Paper* (Ottawa: 1994), 37.

Index

Studies In Canadian Military History

John Griffith Armstrong, *The Halifax Explosion and the Royal Canadian Navy: Inquiry and Intrigue*

Andrew Richter, *Avoiding Armageddon: Canadian Military Strategy and Nuclear Weapons, 1950–63*

William Johnston, *A War of Patrols: Canadian Army Operations in Korea*

Julian Gwyn, *Frigates and Foremasts: The North American Squadron in Nova Scotia Waters, 1745–1815*

Jeffrey A. Keshen, *Saints, Sinners, and Soldiers: Canada's Second World War*

Desmond Morton, *Fight or Pay: Soldiers' Families in the Great War*

Douglas E. Delaney, *The Soldiers' General: Bert Hoffmeister at War*

Michael Whitby, ed., *Commanding Canadians: The Second World War Diaries of A.F.C. Layard*

Martin Auger, *Prisoners of the Home Front: German POWs and "Enemy Aliens" in Southern Quebec, 1940–46*

Tim Cook, *Clio's Warriors: Canadian Historians and the Writing of the World Wars*

Serge Marc Durflinger, *Fighting from Home: The Second World War in Verdun, Quebec*

Richard O. Mayne, *Betrayed: Scandal, Politics, and Canadian Naval Leadership*

P. Whitney Lackenbauer, *Battle Grounds: The Canadian Military and Aboriginal Lands*

Cynthia Toman, *An Officer and a Lady: Canadian Military Nursing and the Second World War*

Michael Petrou, *Renegades: Canadians in the Spanish Civil War*

Amy J. Shaw, *Crisis of Conscience: Conscientious Objection in Canada during the First World War*

Serge Marc Durflinger, *Veterans with a Vision: Canada's War Blinded in Peace and War*

James G. Fergusson, *Canada and Ballistic Missile Defence, 1954–2009: Déjà Vu All Over Again*

Benjamin Isitt, *From Victoria to Vladivostok: Canada's Siberian Expedition, 1917–19*

James Wood, *Militia Myths: Ideas of the Canadian Citizen Soldier, 1896–1921*

Timothy Balzer, *The Information Front: The Canadian Army and News Management during the Second World War*

Andrew B. Godefroy, *Defence and Discovery: Canada's Military Space Program, 1945–74*

Douglas E. Delaney, *Corps Commanders: Five British and Canadian Generals at War, 1939–45*

Timothy Wilford, *Canada's Road to the Pacific War: Intelligence, Strategy, and the Far East Crisis*

Randall Wakelam, *Cold War Fighters: Canadian Aircraft Procurement, 1945–54*

Andrew Burtch, *Give Me Shelter: The Failure of Canada's Cold War Civil Defence*

Wendy Cuthbertson, *Labour Goes to War: The CIO and the Construction of a New Social Order, 1939–45*

P. Whitney Lackenbauer, *The Canadian Rangers: A Living History*

Teresa Iacobelli, *Death or Deliverance: Canadian Courts Martial in the Great War*

Graham Broad, *A Small Price to Pay: Consumer Culture on the Canadian Home Front, 1939–45*

Peter Kasurak, *A National Force: The Evolution of Canada's Army, 1950–2000*

Isabel Campbell, *Unlikely Diplomats: The Canadian Brigade in Germany, 1951–64*

Richard M. Reid, *African Canadians in Union Blue: Volunteering for the Cause in the Civil War*

Andrew B. Godefroy, *In Peace Prepared: Innovation and Adaptation in Canada's Cold War Army*

Nic Clarke, *Unwanted Warriors: The Rejected Volunteers of the Canadian Expeditionary Force*

Studies in Canadian Military History
is published by UBC Press in association with the Canadian War Museum.

Printed and bound in Canada by Friesens
Set in Minion and Helvetica by Apex CoVantage, LLC
Copy editor: Matthew Kudelka
Proofreader: Frank Chow
Cartographer: Eric Leinberger